MW00324201

Children into Swans

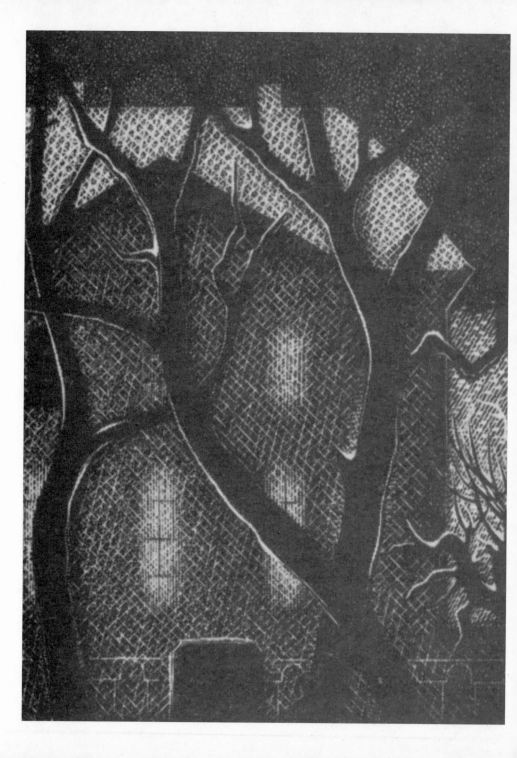

CHILDREN INTO SWANS

Fairy Tales and the Pagan Imagination

Jan Beveridge

McGill-Queen's University Press

Montreal & Kingston | London | Ithaca

ISBN 978-0-7735-4394-2 (cloth)
ISBN 978-0-7735-9616-0 (ePDF)
ISBN 978-0-7735-9617-7 (ePUB)

Legal deposit fourth quarter 2014
Bibliothèque nationale du Québec

Printed in Canada on acid-free paper that is 100% ancient forest free
(100% post-consumer recycled), processed chlorine free

McGill-Queen's University Press acknowledges the support of the
Canada Council for the Arts for our publishing program. We also
acknowledge the financial support of the Government of Canada
through the Canada Book Fund for our publishing activities.

Library and Archives Canada Cataloguing in Publication

Beveridge, Jan, 1945–, author
Children into swans : fairy tales and the pagan imagination /
Jan Beveridge.

Includes bibliographical references and index.
Issued in print and electronic formats.
ISBN 978-0-7735-4394-2 (bound).–
ISBN 978-0-7735-9616-0 (ePDF).–
ISBN 978-0-7735-9617-7 (ePUB)

1. Fairy tales–Europe–History and criticism.
2. Fairy tales–Europe–Themes, motives. I. Title.

GR135.B49 2014   398.2094   C2014-903646-9
                                          C2014-903647-7

For Terry

Contents

Contents

Acknowledgments

With pleasure I acknowledge my gratitude to those who read the manuscript or parts of it and offered advice: Nancy Fischer, Gwen Swick, Anna Barnett, my daughter Bree Walpole, and Donna McCaw who enthusiastically read it twice. I owe a deep debt of gratitude to Dana Rodgers, whose careful reading of the manuscript and thoughtful suggestions resulted in many improvements. I am also indebted to Mary Anne Neville for her helpful corrections to the text. The book benefited greatly from recommendations of the anonymous reviewers who read and commented on the manuscript for the publisher. While I was researching for this project, library staff in Toronto, Galway, Dublin, and Copenhagen were helpful in making resources available, and Robin Bergart at the University of Guelph's McLaughlin Library went over and above the usual to bring in material for me. I cannot adequately express what I owe to Mark Abley, editor at McGill-Queen's University Press, who saw something interesting in the early pages that arrived on his desk about stories from the depths of a distant past, and from that time on was supportive of this project and made the book real. I am grateful to Ryan Van Huijstee and everyone else at McGill-Queen's who was involved with the book, with special thanks to Kate Baltais for editing and to David Leblanc who designed the cover; it fits the book perfectly. My thanks go as well to JoAnn Hayter and Jan Feduck who encouraged and inspired me to see this project through, to Braden Beveridge for book arrangement and design suggestions, and to my husband Terry who taught me, by example, to never stop learning.

Preface

This book has been with me for a long time. The topic has been in my mind one way or another beginning with a high school German class. I was slowly translating a poem by Goethe, "Erlkönig," about an elf king who beckons to a dying child held tight in his father's arms, as father and son ride home on horseback through the night. As the words became clear the poem gave me shivers, and I wanted to know more about this haunting elf figure in folklore.

At the University of Toronto, Northrop Frye inspired my academic interest in the fairy tale genre. By then, I had been reading fairy tales for several years and was curious to know why certain themes, such as swan-maidens and shape-changing enchantments with magic wands, appeared in stories from very different regions of Europe and, in fact, from many countries around the world. I was granted an appointment to talk to Dr Frye about this. Northrop Frye was very famous, almost godlike in the field of literary scholarship at that time, and I was nervous as I knocked on his office door and then sat in the chair across the desk from him. But he was kind and interested. He encouraged me to continue studying these recurring themes in European fairy tales and to look for the mythic principles of this literary tradition. I was beginning to suspect, though, that this was not simply a literary question I was dealing with.

A few years later, I was working at the University of Western Ontario library as a research assistant in the rare book room. This is where I came upon Lady Gregory's books of Irish myths and sagas, *Gods and Fighting*

Men and *Cuchulain of Muirthemne*. With just a brief glance at these stories, some of them originally written over ten centuries ago, I found many of the very same fairy tale concepts that had puzzled me. I was convinced, then, that these were old concepts, so old that they faded away into prehistory. I searched out other stories from the oldest narrative material following the Classical Era and was amazed that this early European literature was so rich and imaginative. Tolkien had certainly read some of these ancient tales; his elves and dwarfs have stepped right out of the stories of Norse mythology. I was inspired to pursue literary detective work. Having discovered familiar fairy tale elements that were deeply rooted in something very old in European culture, I wanted to know how old they were, how far into the past they could be traced in the ancient literature of Europe.

The project remained an interest for many years. Piles of folk and fairy tale books grew high on a shelf. I sought out books by folklore scholars, beginning with *Teutonic Mythology*, Jacob Grimm's vast treatise on folklore and mythology. Notes from spare hours in libraries filled cartons. The more I read the earliest stories, however, the more these became my passion.

One winter day, when I was closed in at home with a blizzard outside, I read again my old notes of first discovery. The excitement came flooding back and I decided to write this book. I love these stories, and because most of them are lost to anyone who is not a scholar in the area, I wanted to share my enthusiasm for them and my admiration for the early scribes, who, so very long ago, prepared the inks and calf- and sheepskins they needed to write the tales down, to preserve what they valued and loved, and for the sheer joy of them.

A Note on Spelling

I would like the reader to be aware that standardized spellings do not exist for names of the ancient Irish and Norse characters, places, and story titles. For example, the goddess known as the Mórrígan appears in the literature as Morrigan, Morrigu, Mór-Ríogain, and other variants. For Irish words and proper names, I referred to the spelling in James MacKillop's *Dictionary of Celtic Mythology*, 2004 edition. For Norse words and names, I used John Lindow's *Norse Mythology: A Guide to the Gods, Heroes, Rituals, and Beliefs* (2002). Accents have been removed from the names "Odin" and "Thor" since this is the way their names usually appear, and I used "Finn" rather than "Fionn" for the same reason. There are inconsistencies in the text, however, since spellings within quotations are occasionally different. When stories are first introduced, the English translation is given with the Irish or Norse title in italics, for example, "The Lay of Skírnir" (*Skírnismál*), but afterwards only the English title is used.

The Pronunciation of Some Names and Words

Áine	*An*-yuh
Beltaine	Bal-*tinna*
Conchubar	*Kon*-cho-var
Conaire	*Kon*-ur-uh
Creiddylad	Kray-*thil*-ad
Cuchulain	Koo-*hool*-n
Emer	*Ay*-ver
Étain	*Ey*-deen
Finn mac Cumhaill	*Fin* mak *Coo*-il
Geis	gyesh
Gessa	*gyass*-uh
Imram	*Im*-ruv
Lug	Loo
Máel Dúin	*Meyl Doon*
Medb	*Mayv*
Myrddin	*Merth*-in
Naoise	*Nee*-sha
Niamh	*Nee*-av
Niall	*Nee*-ul
Oisín	Oh-*sheen*
Sadb	Sive
Samain	*Sow*-n

Sidhe	Shee
Taliesin	Tally-*es*-in
Tuatha Dé Danann	Too-*a*-*ha*-dae-donnan
Uisliu	*Ish*-loo

PART ONE

History

1

Early Storytellers

airy tales are certainly strange. A girl wanders alone on a moor and comes upon a plum tree. No sooner have her lips touched a plum than she is in a different world, surrounded by hundreds of little people who are pleased that she has arrived to look after their children and brew their beer. In another tale, a girl watches her twelve brothers suddenly change into ravens and fly away over the trees. The cottage where they had just been eating their meal vanishes, and she is left standing alone in the wild forest. In another, an evil stepmother casts a magic spell on her stepsons turning them into swans, and they remain in this feathered form until their sister breaks the enchantment.[1] Thousands of such stories exist, from every country of Europe and throughout the world. There is nothing at all ordinary about these stories. Yet, many of us are ingrained in a tradition of these fairy tales, and we might ask the question: where did the ideas in these wild tales of the imagination come from?

This is a challenging question. There have been magical creatures of all kinds and miraculous transformations in stories and folklore since ancient times. In the earliest stories of northern Europe, there is ample evidence of just how long-established many familiar "fairy tale" elements have been in the culture and traditions of European storytelling. Magic wands, spells, enchantments, and a variety of supernatural beings such as fairies, elves, dwarfs, and giants were intrinsic to stories of Celtic and Norse mythology. These fairy tale themes reflect an ancient imagination.

The following well-loved Irish legend, *Oidheadh Chlainne Lir*,[2] is another "children into swans" story. It has a recurring fairy tale theme – royal children have a spell put on them by their stepmother.

The Fate of the Children of Lir

Lir was a great Irish king. His wife died in childbirth, and his grief for her loss was lightened only by his four lovely children who were his joy and delight. After some time, Lir married the children's aunt; unknown to him, however, this beautiful woman was a sorceress. The new queen was kind to the children at first, but then became so fiercely jealous of Lir's love for them that hatred and evil thoughts consumed her. Her life would be better if the stepchildren disappeared!

One morning, on the pretence of a long journey to visit their grandfather, the queen took them in a chariot far from the castle. They stopped on the way at a lake where the children bathed and played. The stepmother drew out her sword intending to slay them when they stepped onto the shore, but at the last moment used her witchcraft instead. She struck each one with her wand, putting a spell on the children that changed them into four beautiful, perfect white swans. The oldest child, Finnguala, asked her how long their punishment would last. For nine hundred years, the cruel queen told them. They would inhabit lakes and the sea until a nobleman from the north married a noblewoman from the south, and until they heard the sound of a bell ringing for prayers.

The enchantment did not change the swans' human voices however, and it broke Lir's heart to hear his children singing near his castle. Yet, no one could undo the curse of the evil queen, who was transformed for her crime into a demon of the air. For the spell's first three hundred years, the children's exquisite songs brought joy and wonder to those who heard them on the lakes of Ireland. For the next three hundred years, the spell banished the swans to the far north where they could barely endure the cold, stormy waters, and their feathers sometimes froze in ice. The swans were isolated for the final three hundred years on a small island off Ireland's west coast. Here it was not as cold, but there was no one except themselves to hear their voices, and they were lonely. They dreamed of returning home to their own people.

One day, the swans were drawn to land and the sound of a chapel bell, since the end of their enchantment coincided with the beginning of Christianity in Ireland. At first they hid in the long reeds, but then came closer. A Christian hermit found the four swans gathered near his little church and was amazed that they could speak. They told the young man of their long, strange life, and he recorded what they said so the people of Ireland would always know their story.

Unknown to the swans, their stepmother's prophecy of a nobleman from the north marrying a noblewoman from the south had come to pass. When the swans began to sing for the monk the beautiful ballads of their people from long ago, he blessed them, and finally the enchantment was over. The swans' feathers fell to the ground. They became human again, but lived only briefly, just long enough to be baptized. By this time, they were over nine hundred years old, and they simply turned to dust.

In Dublin, in a garden in Parnell Square, this little story is depicted by a bronze statue of four swans rising into the air, while the children fall beneath them. The garden in the heart of Dublin is dedicated to the memory of those who lost their lives fighting for Irish independence. In the nineteenth century, the story of the swan-children was taken up by those who were struggling for the cause of Irish freedom, and for them the story represented the centuries of repression of the Irish under British rule. The legend is also commemorated with a stone cross on a little island off the Donegal coast.

The tale is part of the Mythological Cycle of stories, which take place in the time of the gods. In these tales, the divine race known as Tuatha Dé Danann had retreated into the world of stories and legend, where they seem to be almost human. Lir was one of the earliest of the mythic god-kings of pre-Christian Ireland, and his story is set some time in the first centuries AD. Stories such as these have been told in cottages all along the Irish coast for many centuries, some of them for well over a thousand years.

Ireland has a long history and tradition of storytelling. The ancient texts allude to a highly regarded caste of poet-seers who were masters of all traditional knowledge. They were also storytellers. These *filid* belonged to the households of clan chieftains in early Ireland, where one of their important roles was relating the stories of the great narrative sagas, and this being an entirely oral tradition, they were required to memorize a great repertoire of all the primary tales of Ireland as well as local lore and legends.[3] One of these storytellers, in an ancient narrative, assumed the task of telling a tale to an Ulster king every night from Samain (Hallowe'en) to Beltaine (the first of May).

As early as the seventh century the first stories were written down.[4] The oral tradition then coexisted with a literary one that was based in the monastic culture of Christian Ireland. We have no way of knowing if the early secular stories changed over the years to reflect Christian teachings, or to what extent the stories as they were written down ever reflected a pagan oral tradition, but undoubtedly, the early writers drew heavily from their pagan past. Of the vast number of Irish stories that have survived, some attributed to the eighth and ninth centuries, almost all are tales of a mythic pre-Christian world.[5]

A long, unbroken Celtic heritage was likely a factor in Ireland's lasting tradition of these vivid and imaginative narratives. From before the time when the Romans invaded England, elements of Celtic culture were evident in Ireland, and for a thousand years this was the culture that prevailed there. The culture would have changed with Christianity. Ireland became Christianized early, in the fifth century, but the new faith did not completely assimilate the popular indigenous heritage; it adapted to it, fused with it. The new faith became Irish. For one thing, the widespread Irish devotion to saints and their cults, often focused at localized places like holy wells, reflected a connection of religion and the landscape of Ireland that was distinctly Celtic. Within this Christian culture, the tales of Ireland's mythological past were often presented as stories so worthy that they should be told to a monk, as in "The Children of Lir," or to Saint Patrick. For the Christian scribes writing the stories in monasteries, this heritage of secular storytelling remained rich and alive as an important and valued part of the fabric of society.

The early Welsh people also treasured their own heritage of tales, heard in poems and prose narratives related by storytellers entertaining at gatherings and feasts.[6] Welsh bards, known as *cyfarwyddiaid*, were accomplished narrators and performers who knew a large repertoire of story material, including saga-cycles set in a remote past.[7] Some of the old Welsh stories include the earliest mention of Merlin and King Arthur. Although this narrative tradition was entirely separate from the Irish, the Irish and Welsh stories have much in common. They are remarkably similar in their concept of an otherworld, and together they reflect the oldest Celtic literary ideas.

Parallel with the Celtic stories, tales of Norse mythology are among the oldest narratives of Europe after the Classical Age, again, so old that their origins have long disappeared into prehistory. Along with the many tales of gods and giants, much of this early northern literature is focused on one famous, long legend, the story of a family of warriors called Völsungs and their hero, Sigurd, slayer of dragons.[8] This is a story with supernatural elements: a magic apple, a valkyrie, dwarfs, dreams of prophecy, a dragon, and golden treasure, including one small ring with a curse on it that brings destruction to everyone who possesses it. Similar in its corrupting power, the ring in Tolkien's *Lord of the Rings* was likely an idea borrowed from the Norse legend. The stories of this northern narrative tradition were written mainly in one remote corner of the Nordic world – in Iceland.

Is it surprising that two of the richest cultures of European literature to emerge from what used to be known as the "Dark Ages," the centuries following the collapse of the Roman Empire, flourished on these two islands on the west coast of the continent – Ireland and Iceland? The reasons for the survival of literature from these remote settings were more than simply the islanders' inclination to tell and write stories. Language would have been one reason the Irish and Icelandic stories endured. Unlike France, for example, which was a country of micro-civilizations each with its own language, Irish was the primary language spoken in Ireland throughout its history. Ireland's was an early vernacular literature; in other words, narratives were written in the native language of the people. In Iceland, the Old West Norse language of the first settlers was the basis of Old Icelandic. This was a vernacular that could be understood throughout Norway and Iceland and was used in manuscripts until the fourteenth century. There is a more fundamental reason, however, for the survival of these narratives. Stories that have been passed down to us as belonging to a mythology were those that had a distinctive importance within a culture in defining that culture's heritage. Whereas, in the other countries of Europe, tales and legends faded away before they were written down, the Irish and the Icelanders were determined that their unique stories would endure in written form.

Stories from their Norse heritage had a special meaning for the early Icelanders. Iceland was first settled in the late ninth century, mainly by farming families who had left Norway and its tyrannical king in order to preserve their accustomed ways of life in a new country, where there happened to be free land available for the taking. A few Icelandic farmer-chieftains from time to time outfitted ships and set out on summer raiding expeditions, like other Vikings, plundering and terrorizing along the coasts of Europe and beyond. These Vikings presented to the world a society that was not particularly civilized. However, despite that reputation of fierceness, poetry flourished in the settlements of Viking Age Iceland and became a less remembered but important part of that culture.

The early Icelandic poetry had a unique form that had been developed in Norway by court poets (called skalds) and became popular in the north in Viking times. There is nothing quite like this kind of poetry today. "Skaldic poetry" was cryptic and difficult to understand, resembling a series of riddles.[9] The poets repeatedly used metaphors of two or three words, called kennings, and their listeners had to be familiar with a great many of the traditional old stories in order to decipher the meaning. A god would not be named simply "Thor," for example, but might be "Hrungnir's bane," alluding to a tale of Thor killing this giant. In this way, through kennings, stories were retained within this early poetry.

In *Myths of the Pagan North*, Christopher Abram reviews the poetry of the skalds who continued this poetic tradition in Iceland. Although there was no need for court poetry in Iceland, "the settlers took the skaldic form with them to their new home, and Icelanders soon gained a reputation as the finest poets in the Viking world, whose skills were much in demand overseas."[10] One of the important medieval Icelandic poets was Egil Skallagrímsson (c. 900–983), who is portrayed as a farmer and a warrior-poet in *Egil's Saga*. The notion of a farmer-warrior-poet was not an unlikely one in early Icelandic culture.

The Nordic countries were removed from cultural changes wrought through many centuries in the rest of Europe. Scandinavia had remained beyond Roman influences, and, like Ireland, for the most part was spared the turmoils and migrations that affected so many tribes of central Europeans in the Early Middle Ages. Unlike in other parts of Europe, the pagan religion held on in the north for a long time. At the end of the tenth century Norwegian kings began promoting the new Christianity, and then both pagan and Christian belief systems existed together, although parts of the interior of Norway reverted back to full paganism for some time. It was not until well into the eleventh century that Christianity became the dominant religion throughout Scandinavia and Iceland. Still, in parts of Sweden and Finland, in remote areas and in the far north, paganism retained a quiet but firm hold. And so, when some Icelandic poems were composed in the tenth and eleventh centuries, the pagan lore alluded to in the poems was not from a distant past.

In the thirteenth century, this heritage experienced a revival as Icelanders took a renewed interest in their pagan roots. They began to write poetry and prose of the old mythic lore and to compose sagas that were set in the days of pre-Christian settlement. Abram points out that what had been forbidden in the north under the new Christian belief system was pagan ritual, not pagan myth. The old stories never disappeared from people's consciousness, and "the fact that Norse mythology sprang up in new and vibrant forms in thirteenth-century Iceland suggests that the flame of pagan myth, as a cultural rather than religious phenomenon, was never entirely extinguished. People soon learned that it was best not to believe in Odin, Thor, or Freyr, and they were certainly not free to worship them as they had previously done. But the *stories* of the old gods were resilient, as myths tend to be, and merely awaited a new generation of poets and authors who could bring them to life again in a Christian context. This revival would be a distinctively Icelandic movement."[11]

Producing manuscripts represents a remarkable achievement of these

Icelanders. A single manuscript could require skins from twenty-five to a hundred cows or a greater number of sheep, pastureland was scarce, and there was little light to work by in the long winter months. Still, the small population, living in harsh and often isolated conditions on this windswept island, produced a great many manuscripts. There is consensus that most have been lost, a significant number of these in the great 1728 Copenhagen fire, which destroyed the library. But those that have survived, including fragments, number in the hundreds. Some of the poems and stories in two of them, the *Poetic Edda*[12] and the *Prose Edda*,[13] preserve lore and legends from the pagan Viking Age.

Undoubtedly, other European cultures had their own ancient stories, but few traces of them remain. Folk poems of the Finnish *Kalevala* contain mythic elements, such as the figure Ilmarinen who may belong to their pre-Christian culture. Siegfried, the dragon slayer in the German *Nibelungenlied*,[14] composed around 1200, had likely for centuries been the subject of legends on the banks of the Rhine and the Danube. This old Germanic tale is based on fifth-century Burgundians and Huns. Very early, the same epic narrative was developed in Scandinavia as the legend of the Völsungs with their champion Sigurd. References in several Latin and Anglo-Saxon poems indicate that the legend had at one time been widespread throughout the continent. The longest of these is *Beowulf*. It is altogether likely that besides *Beowulf* at one time in England there were other long Anglo-Saxon poems of heroic legend in oral or written form, but none survive.

From the literature that exists, it appears that early medieval writers, well into the Christian era, preferred to write stories that were set in a pre-Christian past. The Irish tales portray a time before the fourth century. Tales from the pagan world had an undeniable hold on people's imaginations all through the Middle Ages and even became popular again in the nineteenth century. That something so ephemeral as stories could survive for over a thousand years is an extraordinary phenomenon. It is hard to imagine any story written today lasting as long. Yet, these stories not only survived, but they have influenced folk and fairy tales, as well as works such as Wagner's epic operas *Der Ring des Nibelungen*, Tolkien's *Lord of the Rings*, countless fantasy novels, many movies, and even video games. There are elements from them in the popular Harry Potter novels. It bears asking, then, what these early stories were about that they were celebrated and preserved by early cultures and continued to strike such a chord over the years.

These are unlike stories set in a Christian world. Most of them are dark and tragically sad, and they portray more hostility, violence, and vengeance than we can imagine. Yet, they are filled with energy, are vibrant, sometimes beautiful, and the rewards for any reader are great. Their antiquity leads us, as through a door, into a primitive world, but one with a mythic dimension. It is a Tolkien-ish world, with vast spaces and deep, wild forests, and altogether a world constantly touched by the dangers and wonders of a supernatural realm. There are fair maidens, and noble warriors with fierce courage, tall spears, and shining swords, who often find themselves in strange lands where they meet unpredictable and unknowable dangers and contend with ogres and giants. In this world, fairies, elves, and dwarfs exist. Other supernatural beings, such as ghosts, appear and vanish. Sorcerers with magic wands cast spells. There are witches and troll women, magical objects, and animals that fly. Humans shape-shift into animals. There is a sense of transitoriness; nothing is permanent. All of this is the basic material of fairy tales.

The ancient stories introduce us to one predominant idea, a fairy tale idea, that was central to Celtic and Norse pre-Christian tradition – there is an unseen otherworld existing alongside the visible realm we know. This is a world of spirits, dreams, and visions, yet is just as clear and bright as our own. This remarkable and beautiful concept is presented in the next chapter's story.

2

The Oldest "Fairy" Tale

The ancient narratives of northern Europe were spoken and recorded over many centuries across the Middle Ages. I wanted to discover the oldest tales of all, so began the project with a search through the earliest manuscripts for any stories with fairy tale subject matter. I assumed that this would be a daunting task, but I was wrong. There was no need to look further than the very first manuscripts with narrative material, since these most ancient texts were filled with fairies and giants living in imaginary worlds.

I was intrigued by the very oldest of the manuscripts, the *Book of the Dun Cow*, which was written around 1100 and is therefore half a century older than similar Irish texts. My husband Terry was teaching a summer course at the University of Galway, and so this time in Ireland was the perfect opportunity to visit Dublin and the Royal Irish Academy on Dawson Street where the manuscript is kept. After showing me a facsimile (the original is too fragile to be exhibited), a helpful librarian provided me with a typewritten, working description of the manuscript's one hundred and thirty-four pages, the fragment of the original that still exists. Poring over this material, much of it in Irish, I was excited to find what I was looking for – "Ectra Condla" – the adventure of Connla.

This is the oldest story with a fairy in it.[1] We have evidence that Connla's adventure had been written down even two or three centuries earlier than the *Dun Cow* manuscript, in a long-lost monastic book, the *Cín Dromma Snechta*. Although this small manuscript has been lost for centuries, it did not disappear without a trace. A contents list has been pieced together from annotations referring to it in other early manuscripts, and the inclusion of Connla's adventure in the list indicates that this story had been written down possibly in the eighth century.[2] The tale still appears from time to time in collections of early Irish stories with few changes from the oldest existing version.

The ancient tales are different from the stories we are accustomed to reading today, most of which tend to draw together at the end with an uplifting or satisfying conclusion. In the very early stories, there is rarely a happy ending. In some ways, these are more like the harrowing stories we might tell around a campfire. The following text, which is taken from Joseph Jacobs' *Celtic Fairy Tales*, a shortened version, is otherwise true to the story in the *Dun Cow* manuscript.[3]

Connla and the Fairy Maiden

Connla of the Fiery Hair was son of Conn of the Hundred Fights. One day as he stood by the side of his father on the height of Usna, he saw a maiden clad in strange attire coming towards him.

"Where did you come from, maiden?" said Connla.

"I come from the Plains of the Ever Living," she said, "where there is neither death nor sin. There we have holiday always, nor do we need help from any others in our joy. And in all our pleasure we have no strife. And because we have our homes in the round green hills, men call us the Hill Folk."

The king and all with him wondered much to hear a voice when they saw no one. For save Connla alone, none saw the Fairy Maiden.

"Who are you talking to, my son?" said Conn the king.

Then the maiden answered, "Connla speaks to a young, fair maid, whom neither death nor old age awaits. I love Connla, and now I call him away to the Plain of Pleasure, Moy Mell, where

Boadag is king, and there has been no complaint or sorrow in that land since he has held the kingship. Come with me, Connla of the Fiery Hair, ruddy as the dawn with your tawny skin. A fairy crown awaits you to grace your handsome face and royal form. Come, and never shall your handsomeness fade, nor your youth, till the last awful day of judgment."

The king in fear at what the maiden said, which he heard though he could not see her, called aloud to his Druid, Coran.

"Oh, Coran of many spells," he said, "and of cunning magic, I call upon your aid. A task is upon me too great for all my skill and wit, greater than any laid upon me since I seized the kingship. An unseen maiden has met us, and by her power would take from me my dear, my comely son. If you do not help, he will be taken from your king by woman's wiles and witchery."

Then Coran the Druid stood forth and chanted his spells towards the spot where the maiden's voice had been heard. And none heard her voice again, nor could Connla see her any longer. Only as she vanished before the Druid's mighty spell, she threw an apple to Connla.

For a whole month from that day Connla would take nothing, either to eat or to drink, save only from that apple. But as he ate, it grew again and always kept whole. And all the while there grew within him a mighty yearning and longing after the maiden he had seen.

But when the last day of the month of waiting came, Connla stood by the side of the king his father on the Plain of Arcomin, and again he saw the maiden come towards him, and again she spoke to him.

"It is indeed a glorious place that Connla holds here among short-lived mortals awaiting the day of death. But now the folk of life, the ever-living ones, beg and bid you come to Moy Mell, the

Plain of Pleasure, for they have learned to know you, seeing you in your home among your dear ones."

When Conn the king heard the maiden's voice he called aloud to his men and said:

"Summon swiftly my Druid Coran, for I see she has again today the power of speech."

Then the maiden said: "Oh, mighty Conn, fighter of a hundred fights, the Druid's power is little loved; it has little honour in the mighty land, peopled with so many of the upright. When the Law will come, it will do away with the Druid's magic spells that come from the lips of the false black demon."

Then Conn the king observed that since the maiden came Connla his son spoke to no one that spoke to him. So Conn of the Hundred Fights said to him, "Is it to your mind what the woman says, my son?"

"It is hard on me," then said Connla; "I love my own folk more than all things; but yet, a longing seizes me for the maiden."

When the maiden heard this, she answered and said: "The ocean is not so strong as the waves of your longing. Come with me in my curragh, the gleaming, straight-gliding crystal canoe. Soon can we reach Boadag's realm. I see the bright sun sink, yet far as it is, we can reach it before dark. There is, too, another land worthy of your journey, a land joyous to all that seek it. Only wives and maidens dwell there. If you are willing, we can seek it and live there alone together in joy."

When the maiden ceased to speak, Connla of the Fiery Hair rushed away from them and sprang into the curragh, the gleaming, straight-gliding crystal canoe. And then they all, king and court, saw it glide away over the bright sea towards the setting sun. Away and away, till eyes could see it no longer, and Connla and the Fairy

Maiden went their way on the sea, and were seen no more, nor did anyone know where they had gone.

The mystical starkness of this story is representative of the ancient tales. Similar to Irish ballads that softly draw the listener in, it is sad and beautiful at the same time. Who was this woman who appeared to Connla? Was she sent as an emissary from the king of the otherworld, who had chosen Connla to join their realm? Or was she acting alone? Had the fairy strayed into the world of humans and become intoxicated with desire for the young prince? And, did Connla feel joy or terror as he stepped into her boat?

The story is part of a group of narratives that describe adventures and exploits in the days of early Irish kings, and in these Connla's father, Conn, is portrayed as a powerful king who ruled Ireland in the early second century. *The Annals of Clonmancoise* record that Conn had three sons, Conly, Crienna, and Artemar, but the oldest, Conly, did not succeed his father as king.[4] Connla's story, then, is a legend set in an ancient world.

It is a type of Irish narrative called an *echtra*, which is an adventure, and specifically an adventure involving a visit to the otherworld. The same manuscript contains a fragment of another story, "The Voyage of Bran" (*Imram Brain*), which is similar to Connla's tale in that a young man leaves the world of humans to join a fairy woman's realm. This theme of young men drawn away to the otherworld, and also the story motifs of apple branches and fairy apples, appear again and again in the early Irish tales. The supernatural women in the stories are "folk from the fairy mounds," *áes sídhe*, a name that refers to the Irish fairies and to the Tuatha Dé Danann, the divine race from old Irish tradition that dwelt underground and on islands. The druid appears here in a way that druids often do in the early narratives, as someone capable of communicating with the supernatural world, and, for a time, he drives the fairy woman away with his spells. The fairy's words, "When the Law will come, it will do away with the Druid's magic spells that come from the lips of the false black demon," seem out of place in the fairy's voice, and these may have been the added touch of a Christian scribe who wanted to draw attention to the new faith and to emphasize the declining power of druids.[5] Above all, the story portrays the most lovely of Celtic beliefs, that of an other-world of everlasting youth and peace, an island inhabited by fairies that is beautiful beyond any imagining.

While I was searching in libraries in Toronto, Dublin, and Galway piecing together bits of information about the history of this strange tale, how it came to be written down, and then why the vellum pages on which it was written outlasted other books, I came to realize how remarkable it is that any manuscript could have survived for over nine hundred years. This one – the *Book of the Dun Cow* – has a particularly compelling story to tell.

3

The Manuscript

The year is 1100 AD. In the scriptorium of a quiet Irish monastery on the banks of the Shannon River, a scribe, Mael Muiri, is working at a long table with other scribes, copying words onto pages of vellum. These are young men and boys, since this task is difficult for old hands and eyes. The scribes work for long hours every day, beginning at sunrise and finally stopping for supper and prayers only when the daylight has faded and it is too dark in the chilled monastery room to continue. Mael Muiri's fingers ache with cold and cramp. Yet, there will still be months of writing before his manuscript is finished and then hung, finally, in its own leather satchel from a peg on the scriptorium wall, alongside the other books.

The scribe has noted on one page that he is taking his stories from older books, and to his left on the table is the manuscript he is copying. Some of his stories will be copied from manuscripts kept in monasteries throughout Connacht, Leinster, and Ulster, and for these he will travel with his writing materials long distances to other monasteries to work. Mael Muiri's project is an important one. He is compiling a collection of the great stories of early Ireland. Scholars of Irish philology have determined from the subject matter, syntax, and vocabulary, for example, old forms of nouns and their use of gender, that the original texts of Mael Muiri's stories had first been written down many centuries earlier. Possibly, some were originally written as early as the seventh century. These are extremely old stories!

To Mael Muiri's right on the table are fresh, clean pieces of vellum. In front of him are a pumice stone to smooth flaws in the pages, a ruler and stylus to mark the margins and fine lines that his script will follow, and a small sharp knife. This is painstaking work. He writes slowly and carefully, creating two neat columns on each page with a clear, round, small-letter style of writing, the graceful and legible "Irish minuscule."[1] The historian Thomas Cahill describes this pleasing Irish script as "more readable, more fluid, and, well, happier than anything devised by the Romans."[2] The scribe leaves spaces at the beginning of sections for large, decorative initial letters to be drawn in afterwards, with the spiral and knot designs of early Irish art and with animal forms. He will colour these with yellow, purple, and red dyes. On three pages, Mael Muiri has written his name in the margin.

Periodically, he stops, sets his inkhorn into a hole cut in the table for this purpose, and trims his quill pen. He has a supply of fresh quills formed from goose and swan feathers and a few from crow feathers that he will use for fine detail work. All of these are precisely shaped and notched to control the flow of the inks, which have been prepared from iron salts and oak tree galls.[3]

The vellum pages on the table are calfskins, which have been saved for this special book, since they provide whiter pages than the more plentiful parchment made from skins of the sheep easily farmed on the Irish hills. Still, the pages are thick and rough. Cahill notes of these pages, "It is interesting to consider that the shape of the modern book, taller than wide, was determined by the dimensions of a sheepskin, which could most economically be cut into double pages that yield our modern book shape when folded."[4] The process of preparing the pages involved soaking and treating the skins to loosen the hair, scraping, stretching and drying them, cutting them into uniformly sized pieces, and rubbing them with pumice and then with chalk so they could take the ink. This was work undertaken in the autumn, when many of the animals were butchered to conserve fodder for the herd over the winter, and was a chore rewarded with a feast for the monks from the available meat.

Mael Muiri is not writing in Latin, the language of the scriptural books and psalters usually written in the monasteries. His stories are in the Irish Gaelic language, which was not unusual for the saga material, or for manuscripts from this monastery of Clonmacnoise according to Michael Slavin's *Ancient Books of Ireland*: "In contrast to other scholastic centres such as Bangor or Armagh, which concentrated on Latin learning, Clonmacnoise was for the first 600 years of its existence marked as the headquarters of Gaelic learning."[5]

The manuscript begins with ecclesiastical material in the hand of another scribe whom we know only as "A." It then includes at least thirty-seven of the old Irish tales. Mael Muiri has included the famous love story of Midir, a king of the fairies, and his wife Étaín who existed through several incarnations. When these lovers were finally reunited, they both turned into swans and flew away. Other stories are the abduction of Connla, the fantastic adventures of Máel Dúin, and the strange voyage of Bran,[6] which today may be the most familiar of them. Some are tales of kings and heroes from the oldest Ulster Cycle. Others are adventure stories involving the supernatural. There are stories of voyages, not to far-off lands, but to places beyond the real world. All of them demonstrate the richness of the Celtic imagination with its sense of the marvellous and magical.

What must this devout scribe be thinking of these tales he is copying? Most of them are quite wild and strange. In two places, he has broken convention and written scribal glosses, or notes, that indicate his feelings about the text. After one story, Mael Muiri had to comment. "The Wasting Sickness of Cúchulainn" (*Serglige Con Culainn*) is a tale of the seductive Fand, one of the ever-living ones from the otherworld, who brings an illness on the hero with a dream vision. To Mael Muiri, this supernatural woman is a demon: "That is the story of the disastrous vision shown to Cú Chulainn by the fairies [folk of the *síd*]. For the diabolical power was great before the faith, and it was so great that devils used to fight with men in bodily form, and used to show delights and mysteries to them. And people believed that they were immortal."[7]

Another story, "Bricriu's Feast" (*Fled Bricrenn*), has hideous, terrifying giants. One is ready to cut heads off with his enormous axe, and another is so huge that he picks up a young champion in one hand, grinds him between his palms like a millstone, and throws him over the stronghold wall and into a ditch. In notes to his translation of this text, George Henderson comments, "The scribe seems to have had an eerie feeling when he came to copy the description of the giants, and above page 105[a] he wrote in Latin (no doubt piously crossing himself) *in dei nomine*; and again, *in dei nomine, Amen*, above page 112[b]. Nothing could more clearly illustrate the difference in feeling between the good Culdee of Clonmacnoise and the original author of the Feast of Bricriu."[8]

The word "Culdee" used here refers to a fundamentalist religious sect of some monastic communities such as Clonmacnoise at this time. Mael Muiri has grown up in this religious community, where his father is a confessor and his grandfather held a high position and was known as "Conn of the Poor" for his generosity to the unfortunate. His is an important ecclesiastical family of abbots and scholars that has had roots at Clonmacnoise going back to the eighth century.

When Mael Muiri's book is complete, it will be given a name associated with the lore of this religious settlement; it will be *Lebor na hUidre* or *Book of the Dun Cow*, named after the hide of a dun-coloured cow, a sacred relic of the community. The monastery's founder and first abbot, Saint Ciarán, had brought this favourite cow with him when he first came to Clonmacnoise, probably on foot, in the early sixth century. The significance of the cowskin comes from a legend about Saint Ciarán that illustrates an aspect of Irish saintliness – the ability to communicate with people who had long been dead.[9] One night, Saint Ciarán summoned the old warrior-king Fergus mac Róich from his grave to tell a story, and as the dead warrior related events of an ancient battle, Saint Ciarán copied the ghost's words onto the cowhide.[10] In his manuscript, Mael Muiri has copied the same story, "The Cattle Raid of Cooley" (*Táin Bó Cuailnge*), about a proud queen and the conflict between the Irish provinces of Ulster and Connacht. It is the oldest existing version.

Saint Ciarán's monastery became renowned as a centre for religion. Here was such sacred land that kings of dynasties from afar sought rights of burial at Clonmacnoise. It was also renowned as a centre for learning, writing, and art. This was a monastic community of the type that was a precursor of universities, and distinguished scholars of Europe came great distances to be educated there. Creating a fine library in each monastery was important work throughout Europe, but the preservation of litera-ture by collecting and copying books was undertaken in Ireland much earlier, at a time when literacy was all but forgotten on the continent. By Mael Muiri's time, Ireland already had a history of copying texts that had extended for many hundreds of years. This was unique in Europe. As early as the seventh century, or even earlier, monks and scribes worked in iso-lated Irish monasteries, often out of doors for better light, carefully copy-ing texts onto pages that they had made out of these dried animal skins. Most often these were Christian books, but from time to time there were also classic Greek and Roman texts. Living in the most primitive condi-tions on the rugged Irish coast at the edge of the world, over hundreds of years these scribes played an important role in keeping European literary culture alive through the "Dark Ages."

The monks undertook this work as an act of faith for the glory of God. Each completed manuscript, even a manuscript of stories from pre-Christian times, was an accomplishment of spiritual devotion. Many of the manuscripts, such as the famous *Book of Kells*, were also masterpieces of calligraphy and illumination. Through all of the unsettled centuries of the Early Middle Ages, the Irish monks remained devoted in their endeavour to preserve all known literature. Their role was critical in preventing the texts of the Greek and Roman writers, as well as their own stories, from being lost forever.

Sadly, almost all of these manuscripts were eventually destroyed. The monastic centres of Ireland, including the community of Clonmacnoise, were raided and pillaged repeatedly over the centuries. The large monasteries came under especially heavy attack in the early ninth century by Norse Vikings, who had discovered that these religious centres were being provided with wealth from patron kings and were rich in valuable objects such as gold and silver artifacts, chalices, crucifixes, candlesticks, and reliquaries. Viking raids continued for two hundred years, and all of the most important religious centres, Lindisfarne in England, Iona in Scotland, and the Irish monasteries of Inis Murray, Skellig Michael, Armagh, and others were ravaged. Buildings were set on fire, items of value stolen, books burned, and the abbots and monks tortured, taken as slaves, or murdered. Most religious centres were raided and burned over and over, and many of the great monasteries fell, never to be inhabited again.

Although Clonmacnoise was many miles from the coast and was surrounded by swampy meadows, making an approach to it by either water or land difficult, still this monastery was attacked, looted, and burned on at least ten different occasions. The Vikings were not only pagan but were ferociously anti-Christian. A particularly violent raid was led by a famous Norse tyrant, Turgesius, who had established a Viking fort at Dublin. After capturing Clonmacnoise, Turgesius established his pagan wife Ota as high priestess there.

Clonmacnoise was rebuilt and repaired after each of these raids, and by the year 1100 the Viking attacks had finally ended. The recent years had been relatively free of looting and violence, the work of the monastery had revived, and the library was once more being restored. Clonmacnoise was now a large religious settlement with streets and houses surrounding the churches. It was a monastic town, where scholars and craftsmen were producing some of the finest Celtic works of art, including crosses, chalices, and other items of gold, silver, and bronze.

Still, even these were unstable times. Now it was the Irish themselves, sometimes banding together with ruthless Northmen, who were moved to barbarous acts as Irish chieftains and kings engaged in deadly struggles for wealth and power. Monasteries had both wealth and political alliances, and so periodically attacks were still mounted against them in which buildings were sacked and monks were killed.

We do not know how large a group raided the monastery in 1106. In fact, we know little about that raid except the year. Mael Muiri may have run into the sanctuary to save the chalices and holy items, or he may have been taken completely by surprise, but even in this sacred place the robbers did not stop their vicious attack. Mael Muiri was murdered. His death is reported in the *Annals of the Four Masters* under the year 1106 AD. Mael Muiri, grandson of Conn of the Poor, was killed on the floor of the cathedral of Clonmacnoise by plunderers.[11]

The scribe would never have imagined that his manuscript would last so long, but now, very many centuries later, we can continue the tale of the *Book of the Dun Cow*. The book survived, and likely its name associated with the saintly relic of the monastery helped to ensure its safety. The lives of the saints were a cherished subject in medieval Ireland; Christ was a remote figure, but the saints were local and seemed much more real. In popular Christianity, the cult of saints was expressed as a belief in the sacredness of saintly relics and their power to appeal directly to God. Although it is unlikely that the vellum used for this manuscript was actually the hide of Saint Ciarán's cow, the book was revered by some as such a holy relic.

Some years after the raid, the manuscript came into the possession of a powerful family in Donegal with the name O'Donnell, and it is reasonable to think that it was removed from Clonmacnoise for safekeeping. When Normans began invading Ireland the residents of monasteries had new fears of attacks against them. Durrow and Kells were both seized. In 1178, forces under the English knight Hugh de Lacy plundered the town of Clonmacnoise, and although the churches were spared this time, the scriptorium suffered the full force of aggression.[12] The monastery had endured centuries of attacks, but in 1552 the English finally destroyed it. Its broken buildings were then abandoned and left to ruin. It would be nearly three hundred years before there would be any monasteries in Ireland again. Today, Clonmacnoise, which at one time had been a large settlement with eight churches, is only haunting ruins by a peaceful bend in the Shannon River.

The manuscript was kept safe in the Donegal castle and was protected there for over a century and a half – until 1359. That year, several members of the O'Donnell family, as well as a boy who was closely connected with the family, were taken hostage by another powerful clan, the O'Connor family. This was not unusual in those times. It was a practice between warring clans to take hostages, and then agreements or items of value were negotiated as settlement for their release. The *Book of the Dun Cow* and a smaller manuscript, the *Lebor Gearr*, were seized from the O'Donnells as a ransom to free the boy, and the two books were taken by the O'Connors to their castle at Sligo. It is hard, now, for us to think that there was a time when books had such value that they could be used as a ransom payment!

The two clans, the O'Connors and O'Donnells, had been rivals for a long time, and the O'Connor castle at Sligo was a contentious property. The castle and its lands were considered part of Connacht, although it was on a piece of land that had at one time been held by the chieftains of the old kingdom of Ulster. It was territory that the O'Donnells laid claim to as well as all of Donegal. The O'Connors had been given rights to this land by the English, yet the O'Donnells maintained they had paid a yearly tithe on the land for a thousand years, since the time of Saint Patrick. From time to time they made a claim for the castle.[13] In 1470, after a long siege, the O'Donnells captured the Sligo castle. Over a hundred years after the two books had been taken from them, the family recovered them and took them back to Donegal.

The second book of the ransom payment, *Lebor Gearr*, is documented as later having been stolen from a monastery by a student who took it with him to sea. It was never heard of again. The *Book of the Dun Cow* was protected during the long period that it remained in the great castles of Donegal and Connacht and was not badly damaged. In fact, at some time in the fourteenth century, lettering that had been fading was carefully restored. The manuscript was still in Donegal in 1631 when it was men-tioned by scholars at a Franciscan convent there. After that time it re-mained in several private collections, its location unknown for centuries, until 1844 when it appeared in a collection of 227 manuscripts that was sold to the Royal Irish Academy in Dublin. This is where the surviving pages, about half of the original book, have since been kept.

From the story of this one manuscript, we understand how tenuously the oldest literature held on, and how very much was destroyed and lost. In the chapters that follow, we will come upon one after another of Mael Muiri's stories and will see what a remarkable book this is. This is Ireland's oldest book of narratives, and it is invaluable; yet, other manuscripts, including the important *Book of Leinster*, also preserve the tales of Irish mythology. These tales, created by the earliest medieval imaginations and developed over centuries, depict imaginary worlds full of wonders.

In the early narratives of Europe we discover elements of mythic lore deeply held in ancient storytelling tradition. Traces of lore of these an-cient stories endured in a tradition of folk tales handed down by story-tellers over the years, to become further expanded upon in fairy tales – the tales of fantasy that would become so popular in the nineteenth century.

4

Folk Tales and Fairy Tales

lthough Ireland is unique in Europe for its long tradition of
oral and written stories, most countries of the world have a
heritage of tales that have been passed down generation by
generation as an oral tradition, and thousands of fairy tales
have drawn upon these for inspiration. Until the nineteenth century, folk
stories were not regarded seriously by academics. They seemed simply a
part of rural peasant life, with little intrinsic worth. Yet, they were an integral part of rural life. Storytellers entertained at weddings and chris-
tenings, at community celebrations, and at simple gatherings of families
and friends when the outdoor work was done. Grandmothers told stories
to children, and in this way folk tales were passed on as a spoken legacy,
preserving the memory of a common heritage. In his book on oral storytelling, *Homo Narrans*, John Niles stresses the important roles in certain
early and rural cultures of both accomplished individual storytellers and
cohesive, like-minded communities in perpetuating oral narrative traditions and keeping stories alive.

At the turn of the nineteenth century, the Romantic Movement swept
through Western Europe. Caught up in this new movement's values of
nostalgia for the past, and the idealization of rustic simplicity and all aspects of rural life, scholars began to collect these folk tales, documenting
them exactly as they were told. In the beginning, folklorists studied the
stories for nationalistic reasons, with the intention of learning through
them something of the origins and true soul of their national cultures,

and they published the tales as records of their narrative folkloric traditions. But they soon discovered that these tales of imagination also, simply, had an appeal, and readers were fascinated. Collections of folk and fairy tales were eagerly received as literary works on their own.

The first of these folklorists were the Grimm brothers, Jacob and Wilhelm, who published in two volumes in 1812 and 1815 a collection of one hundred and fifty-six stories as *Children's and Household Tales* (*Kinder und Hausmärchen*). At first, the sale of these books was not remarkable. But, in 1823, an English edition with illustrations was published, and in 1825, a new illustrated German edition came out just in time for Christmas. The great popularity of Grimms' fairy tale collections, which in Germany have since rivalled the Bible as bestsellers, had begun. The term "folk tales" came into usage from the Grimms' "*Volksmärchen*," "tales of the folk," which referred to these popular and traditional stories of the countryside. Although we know now that the sources of the Grimms' tales were not always peasant storytellers, but were often other books and the Grimms' own friends, the stories were accepted as being the authentic thing, tales from a rural world. They have roots in a folk tradition, and the brothers' seminal scholarship on this tradition laid a foundation for future folklorists.

In the nineteenth century, all over Europe, there were others similar to the Grimm brothers. Peter Christen Asbjørnsen and Jørgen Moe collected the folk tales of Norway. Asbjørnsen was a zoologist whose field studies took him to all parts of his country, and when he travelled to remote coastal villages he asked to hear the traditional stories. He took frequent walking tours with his good friend Jørgen Moe, a poet and a pastor, who was also interested in the stories of the people he met, other travellers, boatmen on the fjords, and storytellers at community gatherings. Together and singly Asbjørnsen and Moe published books of folk and fairy tales, and theirs are the classic Norwegian stories. Similarly, Herman Hofberg collected traditional Swedish folk tales, and there were several important Danish collectors. Jón Árnason, the Grimm of Iceland, gathered stories of trolls, elves, ghosts, and goblins from every part of his country, where a century and a half ago storytelling was the predominant entertainment, and he published six volumes of these tales. In Finland, Elias Lönnrot took trips from Helsinki to the Karelian provinces on the Russian border where old folk poetry was still remembered. He collected traditional Finnish ballads and songs that had never before been written down, and using these as a basis created his strange, long epic poem, *Kalevala*.

Crofton Croker, Patrick Kennedy, Joseph Jacobs, and many others re-told the Irish stories. Lady Jane Francesca Wilde, the mother of Oscar, published a large collection of Irish folklore. The Irish had a particular reason for collecting stories from their own heritage. At the end of the nineteenth century in Ireland, the Celtic Revival grew out of the Irish passion to reclaim a cultural nationalism. The desire for political inde-pendence certainly fuelled this revival. Literature was a cornerstone of the movement, and the important writers connected with it often gathered at Coole Park, the country home of the author Lady Augusta Gregory, to discuss their plays, poems, and the books of Irish stories they were writing. Her good friend William Butler Yeats spent his summers there, listening to the old people in the area tell their tales.

An important aspect of the work of these folklorists, who spent years travelling about the countryside, seeking out talented storytellers with a mastery of traditional material, listening to their tales, and writing them down, was that they preserved many stories that otherwise would have been lost. When Asbjørnsen and Moe collected their stories in Norway, few people still remembered them. In Ireland, at the end of the nineteenth century, grandparents told the stories in Irish, but their English-speaking grandchildren did not know the old language well enough to carry on the tradition. Certainly, the custom of storytellers providing entertain-ment through the long winter evenings when there was little light in-

doors was disappearing. It is fortunate, then, that these folklorists published the stories before many of them were forgotten.

Throughout Europe, readers were enthralled with these collections of
folk tales. For many, it was a discovery of their country's rich and beautiful folk tradition. In Norway, academics and intellectuals in Christiania,
now called Oslo, were amazed at national folk tales that they had not
known existed in remote parts of their country. The Finnish *Kalevala*
astounded the literary world of Europe in the 1840s, when it revealed a
tradition of Finnish epic poetry and song that few Finnish people were
aware of. The great popularity of the books kindled new interest in this
cultural history and brought folk and fairy tales into the world of
literature.

How did folk tales become fairy tales? Since "pure" folk tales were the
oral stories, which would have been re-created, varying slightly, each time
they were told, with written tales it is often difficult to distinguish between the two. In *The Irresistible Fairy Tale*, Jack Zipes conveys how complex it has been for scholars to pin down the fairy tale as a genre: "the
intricate relationship and evolution of folk and fairy tales are difficult to
comprehend and define ... they are inextricably dependent on one another."[1] In essence, folk tales were simple stories closely based on an oral
narrative tradition, while fairy tales, sometimes with roots in an oral culture, were imaginative tales with a more intentional literary treatment.[2]
Grimm scholar Maria Tatar comments, "The Grimms' *Nursery and
Household Tales* can be said to embrace both folk tales and fairy tales and
to run the gamut from folklore to literature."[3] In the Grimms' collection,
"The Peasant's Clever Daughter" is closer to a folk tale, while the story
called "Sleeping Beauty" or "Brier Rose" would be a fairy tale.

Fairy tales as a literary genre did not begin with the Grimm brothers.
In Italy, Straparola's *Le Piacevoli Notti* (published 1550–53) includes some
fairy tales in a collection of jokes and stories arranged as tales told during
thirteen nights of a carnival in Venice. Among fairy tales in Giambattista

Basile's *Il Pentamerone* (published 1634–36) were early versions of "Sleeping Beauty," "Cinderella," Snow White," and "Puss in Boots." These Italian tales would influence French fairy tale authors fifty years later. The first to be actually called "fairy tales" or *"contes de fées,"* were the French tales of Charles Perrault and Madame d'Aulnoy, who are credited with first popularizing the fairy tale. Reciting tales of fairies, princesses, and enchantments came into fashion in the salons of Paris. Among ladies of the French aristocracy and also within circles of intellectual women of a cultured French society, this brief but compelling taste for fairy tales reached its height in the last years of the seventeenth century. While the French vogue for fairy tales faded, Perrault's stories remained popular in a wider European culture, some of them becoming tales that the Grimms would include in their collection.

With the outpouring of new tales in the nineteenth century, the genre found a receptive audience: "These literary fairy tales that experimented and expanded upon folk materials, using folk motifs, figures, and plots for their own esthetic and philosophical purposes, were to be enormously influential," Carole Silver comments in her book on fairy tales and the Victorian consciousness. They "would have a major impact on the Victorians."[4]

The impact was not at first as children's literature. Fairy tales were not originally written for a juvenile audience; they had inappropriate, sometimes brutal, subject matter. In England, the French fairy tales had been driven underground on Puritan moral grounds, and there was even greater opposition to fairy tales by Victorian educators and parents. There is no simple piety in these stories. In the first edition of the Grimms' tale, for example, Rapunzel becomes pregnant when the prince visits her in her tower. And, indeed, there is no denying the cruelty and bloodthirstiness in many of the stories. In "The Juniper Tree," an evil stepmother cuts off her stepson's head, hacks him into little pieces, and makes him into soup. The wicked queen in "Snow White" is made to put on a pair of red-hot iron shoes and dance in them until she dies, and the cruel sisters in "Cinderella" have their eyes picked out by pigeons.

In Victorian England, it was felt that literature for children should have a moral purpose, and all tales of the supernatural, with fairies, witches, and giants, were unacceptable reading material. But many Victorian poets and painters loved these tales of wild fairy lore. The respected philosopher John Ruskin declared in his preface to an edition of Grimms' *German Fairy Tales* that children have a natural goodness, and they do not need "moral tales." When beautifully illustrated books with softened versions of the fairy tales were finally published for a juvenile audience, something quite remarkable happened. "From the 1840s–1890s, Victorian England witnessed undoubtedly the greatest flowering of writing for children in the history of literature,"[5] writes Jonathan Cott in his introduction to *Beyond the Looking Glass*; "No one reason can fully explain this munificent productiveness. Writing fairy tales for children had become an acceptable literary activity."[6]

Academics became interested in fairy tale scholarship. They first arranged these tales by subject matter, by their motifs and story types, and listed variants of the types. Some were humorous tales of tricks and cunning; others were moral tales; many included the supernatural. Scholars have since studied the stories for their origins and history, their underlying structures, their psychological implications, their ideological aspects, and particularly, recently, their social and historical contexts. These different approaches have allowed us to more fully understand the nature and significance of these stories, and have taught us that we can appreciate them from a wide range of different viewpoints.

Very early, scholars found similarities in fairy tale theme and content. Although each tale was unique, these stories were not isolated, but were part of a fairy tale tradition, with familiar elements. The reader could come to them with the expectation that the tales would stay on the rails of a fairy tale form. The stories were timeless, set in some undefined time in the past. Some seemed medieval. Most of them had human heroes and heroines. Unlikely heroes showed inner strength and worth, and a kind heart was always rewarded. Many were wonder tales of magic and the supernatural, with fairy promises, magic wishes – always three of them – young men and women who had been transformed into animals, magic wands, spells, and disguises, wicked stepmothers, supernatural helpers appearing as old men and women, journeys to other worlds across the sea or under the waves, monsters, and of course, fairies, elves, dwarfs, and giants. Just how old and mythic in European literature these supernatural elements of fairy tales are we are about to discover in the following chapters.

In a paper on language and the creation of stories, the Italian writer Italo Calvino depicts the continuing connection between fairy tales and myth. An early storyteller of a tribe is putting together his tale – "the younger son gets lost in the forest, he sees a light in the distance, he walks and walks; the fable unwinds from sentence to sentence, and where is it leading? To the point at which something not yet said, something as yet only darkly felt by presentiment, suddenly appears and seizes us and tears us to pieces, like the fangs of a man-eating witch. Through the forest of fairy tale the vibrancy of myth passes like a shudder of wind."[7]

PART TWO

Characters

5

Fairies

"Hidden people" have inhabited the folklore of many countries, perhaps most countries of the world, but fairies came alive in the Celtic imagination. Fairy lore forms a huge part of folk tradition in Ireland, while the Cornish piskies, the Scottish good people, the Welsh fair family or Tylwyth Teg, and the French fées are all closely akin to their Irish counterparts. The word "fairy" is derived from the Old French "faerie," a word that for the French referred either to a fairyland or to those who lived there. In his paper "On Fairy-Stories,"[1] Tolkien remarks on how relatively rare fairies are in fairy tales, but he adds, all the same, that there are many stories about "faerie," as a place where all hidden folk exist, including fairies, elves, dwarfs, witches, trolls, giants, dragons, and humans, too, when they are enchanted.

It is difficult to pin down what these non-human, half-spirit beings called fairies are exactly, but certain ideas in the earliest stories and in folk and fairy tales stick to them. One recurring fairy theme is their abduction of either children or attractive, healthy young adults away from their homes and families to live with them. Similar to "Connla and the Fairy Maiden," which has come to us across more than ten centuries, are many folk tales, poems, and bits of folklore that tell the same story. The little Welsh tale below was recorded in the late nineteenth century by Wirt Sikes, and I have included it here as it was told to him by a peasant in Cardiganshire. The Tylwyth Teg in the story have the small size that we often associate with fairies. Although usually benevolent, these fairy folk, like the others, were known to attract and take young people.

Shuï Rhys and the Fairies[2]

Shuï was a beautiful girl of seventeen, tall and fair, with a skin like ivory, hair black and curling, and eyes of dark velvet. She was but a poor farmer's daughter, notwithstanding her beauty, and among her duties was that of driving up the cows for the milking. Over this work she used to loiter sadly, to pick flowers by the way, or chase the butterflies, or amuse herself in any agreeable manner that fortune offered. For her loitering she was often chided; indeed, people said that Shuï's mother was far too sharp with the girl, and that it was for no good the mother had so bitter a tongue. After all, the girl meant no harm, they said. But when one night Shuï never came home till bedtime, leaving the cows to care for themselves, dame Rhys took the girl to task as she never had done before.

"Ysgwaetheroedd, mami," said Shuï, "I couldn't help it, it was the Tylwyth Teg." The dame was aghast at this, but she could not answer it – for well she knew the Tylwyth Teg were often seen in the woods of Cardigan. Shuï was at first shy about talking of the fairies, but finally confessed they were little folk in green coats, who danced around her and made music on their tiny harps; and they talked to her in language too beautiful to be repeated; indeed, she couldn't understand the words, though she knew well enough what the fairies meant. Many a time after that Shuï was late; but now nobody chided her, for fear of offending the fairies. At last one night Shuï did not come home at all. In alarm, the woods were searched; there was no sign of her; and never was she seen in Cardigan again. Her mother watched in the fields on the Teir-nos Ysprydion or three nights of the year when goblins are sure to be abroad; but Shuï never returned, and it was the sad belief that the fairies had carried her off.

Fairies are frequently depicted today as miniature, fragile creatures with dragonfly wings, hardly taller than toadstools, and certainly not frightening. This is an entirely modern idea that was first popularized by the Victorians. In the nineteenth century, the usually female fairies were more often the size of three-year-old children or as tall as humans and looked like them. The early Irish tales, however, portray fairies that are entirely different from the modern depiction of these creatures. The early fairies are neither little nor fragile, and most of them are dangerous, "but what strikes one chiefly is the great beauty of most of the Irish fairies," Katharine Briggs observes in *The Fairies in Tradition and Literature*: "Again and again we hear of their magnificence, their love of music and poetry, their feasts and rides, the beauty of the fairy women and the fairy horses. There is a close connection between them and the dead, but their splendour seems to derive from their god-like qualities – in Ireland more than anywhere else one feels the fairies to be shadows of the departed gods of the country."[3]

In popular beliefs and among folklorists there were varying theories about the origin of fairies in European folk tradition. Some believed they were nature spirits, but more often they were believed to be souls of people who had died, spirits of ancient ancestors or of the brave men and women of legends who had lived long ago. Most beliefs expressed some relationship between the fairies and the dead. It makes sense to consider that the Italian and French fairies could have derived from the "fates" of Roman mythology, whereas in Ireland and Wales we find such a wealth of fairy tradition that would seem to have sprung from its own roots. I feel it unwise to attempt to determine a source of fairy beliefs.

However, it is widely held by scholars that one origin of the Irish fairies, with their distinctly divine quality, was the ancient race called the Tuatha Dé Danann.

Early Irish texts are filled with stories about this divine race. No written records exist regarding the beliefs or worship of the gods that populated the pagan Irish world; everything that we know about the Tuatha Dé Danann is from their stories, which may, in fact, have little to do with actual pagan beliefs. We simply don't know. What does exist is an extensive literature that was developed in ancient times about these immortal folk who seem to be almost human as well as divine. Chief among them was the Dagda, who knew all things and could make prophecies. His son Angus Óg was a god of youth and love; Dian Cécht was a god of healing; Lug knew arts and crafts; Ogma understood language and invented the ogham form of writing; the Mórrígan was a goddess of battle; Manannán was god of the sea, and there were many, many others. Every one of them was skilled in magic. In her book *Gods and Heroes of the Celts*, Marie-Louise Sjoestedt explains that in the Celtic world there were two pervasive forces, religion and magic: "And if one of the two should be emphasized, it is the second. We have seen that the Irish regarded the gods as master magicians, so that the sacred and the magical are not distinct notions."[4]

A story accounting for the arrival of this divine race in Ireland is related in a text called the *Book of Invasions* (*Lebor Gabála Érenn*),[5] which presents the mythological prehistory of the first tribes, both human and divine, that inhabited Ireland. The first Irish settlers are represented as coming ashore in a series of mythic invasions. A small band of Tuatha Dé Danann came in one of these invasions, arriving, not by ship, but in a dark cloud that landed on the lonely west coast where they stayed and settled. They fought with and defeated a group of earlier settlers called Fir Bolg, and then conquered the Fomorians, who were a race of demonic sea-raiders. Using their magic, the Tuatha Dé Danann won fierce battles against these adversaries. The gods then held power over Ireland for almost three hundred years, but eventually their supremacy came to an end.

The next mythic invaders in the story of Ireland's history were the Milesians. With magical spells, the Tuatha Dé Danann raised a raging storm to prevent the invaders' ships from landing, but eventually the Milesians came ashore and took possession of territory from the gods, pushing them back into remote areas and to islands. Finally, there was a peace agreement between the two races, and the gods were given all of the underground hill-dwellings of Ireland. These new settlers were the first of the Celts who dominated Ireland for the next thousand years, and their arrival marked the end of the supernatural aspect of Ireland's history. From this time on, the stories are of human kings and heroes.

With the arrival of the Milesians, the Tuatha Dé Danann became invisible. The old gods settled on islands and on remote heaths and moors where there was a little pastureland for their horses and cattle. They lived in forts underground, which men came upon sometimes when they were walking or riding on hills and green mounds or near barrows and cairns. In the early stories, a mist could appear around these dwelling places, surrounding men unexpectedly, and it frightened them. Then their horses stopped, not wanting to go into it, but by that time the mist was all around them and there was no other way to go. When the men passed through it, they emerged into a supernatural world full of dangers.

The retreated gods became known as the *áes sídhe* (people of the mound). Eventually, in folklore, they were simply "the Sidhe" (pron. "shee"), a supernatural race that never died or faded away but lived forever on islands and in mounds, in a realm separate from the world of humans – the Celtic otherworld. Very early, these shadows of the old race, the áes sídhe, and later the Sidhe, were referred to as fairies, and so in many versions and translations of ancient Irish stories, as in the Connla story, the word fairy is used when referring to one of them.

Several of the old gods became kings and queens in popular fairy lore. The Dagda's daughter Áine was a fairy queen known throughout Ireland, while another goddess, the fair-haired Clídna, became queen of the Munster fairies. The fairy kings Midir and Finnbheara correspond to figures of the old Tuatha Dé Danann. Midir had been a proud chieftain of the old gods, whereas Finnbheara was known more in his role as a fairy king, who spirited away beautiful brides of Ireland to his enchanted palace. Similarly, the legendary Welsh Gwyn ap Nudd was a mythological ruler of the divine otherworld who appears in Welsh folklore as a king of the fairies.

In the ancient tales, the paths of humans and the Tuatha Dé Danann constantly met when the "others" came among men for a time, in the form of humans, or as birds or deer, or unseen. Mael Muiri included in his *Book of the Dun Cow* a part of "The Intoxication of the Ulstermen" (*Mesca Ulad*), a story from the Ulster Cycle in which some of the Tuatha Dé Danann came to fight alongside humans to assist them in a battle and excite their courage. The gods were splendid, and they were so light that where they trod the dew on the grass was not touched. The Dagda himself was among them. This chief of all the Tuatha Dé Danann is depicted as an immensely tall man in a long brown cloak, fighting with nine other warriors on each side of him. In his hand was a huge club with which he could smite men down, but the other end of the club was a wand that brought fallen warriors back to life. None of the fighting men could see this god or any of the other supernatural warriors among them.[6]

More often, the relationship between the Tuatha Dé Danann and humans was a hostile one, the folk emerging from their mounds to harass humans and steal cattle, wives, or children, especially the children of kings. One young prince, the only child of the king of Leinster, and grandson of the king of Connacht, was playing at hurling with friends near a sídh when two women in green cloaks came towards him and took him to their underground dwelling. There he stayed in captivity for three years until he was able to escape, along with a hundred and fifty other boys.[7]

The Irish heroes had a special relationship with these immortal folk. Most of them could trace their lineage back to the Tuatha Dé Danann, and the important heroes had a father, a mother, or a wife of that race. This is true of the hero Finn. A subject forming a large part of the early Irish sagas, as well as many folk tales, involves the warrior and seer Fionn mac Cumhaill, or Finn, and his band of fighting men known as the Fianna of Ireland. These tales were once so popular that a twelfth-century scholar observed that poet storytellers at that time could recite a hundred and twenty tales about these men who defended the kingship of Tara.[8] Finn was a figure in Irish narrative very early. He is first mentioned in bardic poems from the sixth and seventh centuries,[9] and there are references to his son, Oisín, that are almost as old, dating from the seventh and eighth centuries.[10] Bands of men such as Finn's, made up of young warrior outlaws and hunters who lived outside the clans in the wilds of Ireland, actually existed in pagan and early Christian times and were called *fiana*, but all of the stories in the early literature about fighting men called the Fianna refer only to this band of Finn's men. These are stories filled with heroic deeds and supernatural encounters.

Finn was descended from a Tuatha Dé Danann king, and he seems to have existed near the very edge of that other realm. One night, on watch outside a stronghold he came upon three beautiful women of the mounds, who, when they saw him, fled into a green fairy hill. Another time, he threw his spear, and when the man it hit disappeared he knew, then, that he had hit someone from a fairy mound. In one tale, Finn and six of his warriors followed a fawn to a mountain of a sídh, where the animal went into the ground, and his men discovered a fairy palace nearby where there were treasures and valuable items of crystal and white gold. There were many such incidents. One day, when Finn was hunting, he rested on an earthen mound and noticed near him a small fair-haired man playing a harp. He had been cast out of his sídh and Finn was the first human he met. His music was so exquisite and beguiling, like all the music played by the Tuatha Dé Danann on their harps and dulcimers, that Finn kept that musician, the little Cnú, with him forever. In one story Finn's own son, Oisín, became a king in the otherworld.

In several tales, Finn took a fairy wife. Deer and hunting lore are a large part of Finn's stories, and the mother of his son Oisín belongs to this lore. There are variants of Oisín's story, some of them in bits of narrative in ancient poems. The more complete story is in folklore, as the legend that is outlined below. In all of the versions, however, Oisín's mother is a daughter of the Tuatha Dé Danann who shape-shifts into a deer.[11]

Oisín's Story[12]

Finn was returning home from hunting one day with his two hounds when a fawn started up before them. The dogs followed it and chased it all the way to the Hill of Allen where Finn lived, but never harmed the animal. Finn understood, then, that this was no ordinary creature. The fawn came into the house, and all that evening it sat at Finn's feet and then stayed right by his bed at night. When he woke in the morning, he found a young woman lying beside him. This was Sadb, one of the fairy people. A dark druid of that race had transformed her into a deer when she rejected him as a suitor, and she had fled to Finn for protection.

Finn and Sadb stayed together as man and wife, and she was with child when Finn had to leave her to join with his warriors fighting raiders. On his return home, Sadb was gone. The same evil enchanter had abducted her, transforming her with his wand back into a deer once more, and Finn was never again able to find her to reverse the spell.

One day in the hills Finn's dogs discovered a small boy who knew no words of human speech, and Finn brought the child home with him. Eventually, the boy was able to tell Finn that as long as he could remember he had lived in a cave in the hills with a deer for company. But a man had appeared one morning with a wand, and the deer followed him away from the cave leaving the boy behind. The child had been unable to move from the spot to go with them. With this story, Finn knew that the boy was his own son and named him Oisín, meaning "little deer."

Oisín grew up to be the greatest poet in Ireland as well as one of the fiercest warriors of the Fianna, and several of the traditional stories of the Fianna were written as poems told by Oisín. A well-known story tells of Oisín's journey to the otherworld with the fairy Niamh. After what seemed just a short time in fairyland but was centuries in the mortal world, he returned home. Immediately upon getting down from his horse and touching the earth, Oisín became a very frail old man, who was carried to a monastery where he related the events of his long life. Just before he died, he met Saint Patrick, who listened to his tales of the Fianna and all the wonders of the older days.

As in these early narratives, for centuries people held an enduring belief that their world was alive with something else, other beings, many of them the Sidhe or fairies, who lived close by them in the green hills or wild bog places. These were the hidden people, as the Tuatha Dé Danann had been the hidden people of long ago. Lady Gregory describes the Sidhe of Irish folklore: "They are shape-changers; they can grow small or grow large, they can take what shape they choose; they appear as men or women wearing clothes of many colours, of today or of some old forgotten fashion, or they are seen as bird or beast ... They go by us in a cloud of dust; they are as many as the blades of grass. They are everywhere; their home is in the forths, the lisses, the ancient round grass-grown mounds."[13]

The frequent occurrence of these beings in folk tales indicates how pervasive the concept was. Here, fairies were referred to, respectfully, as the "gentle people," "fair folk," "good people," or "noble people." They could bring families good fortune, but could just as easily be capricious, even malevolent, spoiling crops or burning homes. They were rarely seen, but if they were it was likely by someone very old, or on a particular night of the year, such as the eve of May Day or Midsummer when the fairies were known to be active in the human world. In a tale about the fairy queen Áine, people had gathered on her Knockainy Hill as they always did to celebrate their Midsummer festival, beginning with a procession to the hill illuminated by torches and followed by games. When some girls stayed late after the others had all left, Áine appeared and asked them to leave so that her people could have the hill to themselves. She then asked the girls to look through a ring, and when they did they could see on the hill a crowd of fairy people gathered to celebrate, too.[14]

Folklore fairies were portrayed as dancing at night on the hills. A person called to join them would not be able to refuse, and even merely overhearing the music of their pipes and fiddles, or stepping into their ring of dancers without seeing them, someone could be haunted or taken away. An Irish ballad, "The Fairy Thorn," depicts the horror felt by girls who had climbed up the crags to a fairy hawthorn, where they felt their friend Anna Grace being pulled away from them. Anna Grace was never seen again. Once in their world, if a person tasted fairy food or drink he was in danger of forgetting his former life and staying with them forever, just as Connla was forever altered after tasting the fairy's apple.

Fairy stories depict these folk possessing milk-white horses that gallop over the hills, or even over waves. They also seemed to have vast amounts of gold and other treasures in their caves beneath the hills, since occasionally a large amount of fairy gold was given to a mortal as payment for a very simple kindness. Good luck always came with such a gift. Sometimes, though, the fairy payment worked the other way, and a payment of gold coins turned into dried-up leaves or cockle shells. Fairies had the power to make someone's life into a blessing, as fairy godmothers did, or into a curse, a theme played out in some of Madame D'Aulnoy's fairy tales, "Princess Mayblossom" and "The Blue Bird," for example, in which the magic of benevolent fairies was needed to overcome the evil enchantments of wicked ones.

Conditions of any bargain with the fairies were hard. From time to time, a human was forced into a promise that resulted in losing an only son or first-born child to them, which was another way they could take a human child. One thing that fairies appeared especially to care about was honour in keeping to a bargain; a promise to a fairy had a sanctity about it like a sacred oath.

All of these fairy tale themes – invisibility, enchantments, spell-binding music, abductions, fairy food or drink, horses that ride on water as well as on land, fairy gold, the sanctity of a promise – are concepts that we find over and over again in the earliest stories. Fairy folk were most like the old Tuatha Dé Danann in the sense that they lived in their own supernatural world, separate from the world of humans, close to it, parallel to it, but in another dimension where they never died and the passage of time did not exist. Although fairy tales are strange, humble little stories that appeal to children, they portray ancient ideas.

Fairies emerge from the same fairy mounds as the old divine race and are similar in all of these ways, and yet there are many folk and fairy tales in which they could not be more different. What falls under the banner of "fairies" is everything from a banshee to a leprechaun. The banshee (whose name means *ban* "woman" and *shee* "fairy") is either a pale wraith or a hideous ghostlike woman, who appears on the hills to wail and fore-warn of an impending death. Leprechauns, of course, are little men in leather aprons whistling and hammering as they work at their trade, which is making shoes. Many fairy folk are far from beautiful, being small, thin, wan, and even quite ugly and deformed. One of these is the old Scottish Habetrot, a disfigured fairy who did a princess's spinning for her. That fairy took the maiden's flax deep into a cavern under the ground where a strange sisterhood of women sat spinning the whole day long until all the flax was made into yarn. Fairy women appeared to be excellent spinners of wool and flax. A male spinning fairy was the hideous Tom Tit Tot, who spun for a maiden an enormous amount of flax into skeins working deep in his old mine pit, but who also threatened to steal her away unless she could say what his name was. Some tales such as "Tom Tit Tot" portray fairies that are not only grotesque, but are spiteful and malicious, and whose stories are altogether quite sad.

There are a great many folk tales of newborn babies, not yet baptized, who are stolen and replaced in their cradles with weak and starving fairy children called changelings, which stay small, sickly, and deformed. There are also stories of healthy young mothers taken away from their families to attend upon fairies who require the care of a mortal midwife and human milk for their babies. A woman who helps the fairies in this way may be given a little bag with instructions not to open it until she returns home. Then she finds it is full of fairy gold, and the family can live on that until the end of their days. In one of these tales, "The Fairy's Midwife," a woman is summoned at midnight by a strange, ugly, little man to attend to his wife. After the baby is born, the midwife rubs some fairy ointment on her own eye, and then the young mother of that peculiar little family appears all of a sudden to be a beautiful lady dressed in white, and her baby is swaddled in cloth of silvery gauze. Then the woman knows that she is among the fairies.[15] The midwife stories suggest a supernatural race that is weak and in need of human aid.

Possibly, the old folklore becoming reconciled with prevailing Christian beliefs accounts for a folk tradition that often depicted fairies as weak and frightful-looking, or as spirits of the pagan dead from long ago, as souls of babies not yet baptized or of the heathen. Some tales describe a group of fairies, a long cavalcade of them, departing from an area and going to live in a wilder place, or simply abandoning the human world altogether, usually because of a new church cross or the persistent sound of church bells that is so hateful to them. They form, then, a strange company of tiny, ugly forms in old-fashioned jerkins or red caps, riding on shaggy horses.

Even though a Bible was one thing that a fairy could not tolerate, a folk tale theme is the fairies' concern for their own salvation. There are tales such as this Scottish one. On a Sunday evening in summer a man was reading his Bible at a quiet spot near the shore, when a beautiful little lady dressed in green approached him and asked if the Holy Scripture held any hope of salvation for folk such as her. When the man replied that salvation was only for the children of Adam, she shrieked in despair and plunged into the sea.[16] These desperate creatures have regressed a long way from the compelling, proud, and powerful fairies in the stories that were told so long ago.

6

Elves

Elves also have a place in the long history of storytelling traditions of northern Europe. These creatures are easily found in Scandinavian, Scottish, and a few German folk and fairy tale books. In Denmark and Iceland, however, elves were particularly a favourite subject matter. In Iceland, for centuries, the dream world seemed more real than in other places, and here the elves, who were among the hidden people, *huldufólk*, lived in the hills and rocky places around the farms where they occupied a large part of culture and tradition. And they still do.

Much like the fairies, the elves in folk tradition are either long-living or immortal, use magic and enchantments, and although seldom seen can be present anywhere. They live inside the earth, most often in mountains or near rocks, sometimes close to humans, but similar to the fairies' theirs is a separate world altogether. Although generally thought of today as little people, in the nineteenth century folk and fairy tales they are often not small. In Scandinavian tales, most are as tall as humans and the women very beautiful; Danish elf maidens are so incredibly lovely that a human could lose his senses if he saw one. Swedish stories often portray them as maidens living in a forest with an elf king. In Scotland, the human-sized elves live in a fairyland called Elfame. Most elves in old Icelandic folk stories appear to be just like humans, except for their secret lives and families beneath the ground and their aversion to the humans' churches. In *The Folk-Stories of Iceland*, Einar Sveinsson finds these elves to be a mirror-image of humans, although they should be regarded dubiously: "They still needed careful handling, were dangerous even, but there is a splendour and beauty about them. Their clothes are colourful and elaborate, they often possess rich and rare jewels. They are generally said to live in places where there is great natural beauty, where there are green slopes and hills, rocks and crags, beautiful smooth stone slabs. They do not live solitary lives like trolls, but are whole peoples ruled over by kings."[1]

A theme of some of these stories is humans who take elf women as brides, and inevitably, these marriages are difficult. We can see in this tale from Lapland that the fair and long-living elf women never completely belong in the human world, but are constantly being pulled back to their own.

The Elf Maiden[2]

A young fisherman, stranded alone at the end of summer on a remote northern island, married an elf girl he found there. He first saw her when she came to the island with her family for a picnic. He was so very happy that day that he would finally have company, although as they stepped on shore they all seemed to him to be very strange and timid. As soon as the family saw the young man standing among the trees, however, they hurried back to their boat, forgetting one daughter and leaving her behind. In an instant, the boat and everyone in it vanished.

He was worried how the two of them were going to manage alone, but she assured him that her family would provide for them and all would be well. They were happy together, sleeping in a little wooden fishing hut or on the soft moss. And the girl fulfilled her promise. Food was plentiful; they caught fish, and ate game and berries, although he was never quite sure how these came to be on the island. One fall night, a house appeared in the birch trees for them to live in, they found cow-stalls complete with milk pails and stools, and then cows magically arrived. They had everything they needed to live through the long dark winter until summer came again, and they felt very blessed.

The young man and his wife lived happily together, except that from time to time the girl simply vanished from his sight for a while and never told him where she had been. One day when he complained of this, she told him that she was bound to leave him soon forever, even though it would be against her will, and there was only one way to stop her. The girl's wish to stay a while longer with her husband was so strong that she pleaded with him to put an iron nail in the threshold so she would not be able to cross it – and so he did.

The iron nail in this story was something from the human world that neither elves nor fairies could tolerate; there was powerful superstition about anything made of iron.

In some Norwegian and Swedish folk stories, an elf tries to trick a maiden working alone in the summer mountain pastures into marrying him, perhaps by taking on the exact likeness of her human sweetheart. But in similar Icelandic elf stories, such as "The Girl at the Shieling," there is a true enduring love between a girl and an elf she meets when she is working at a summer farm in the high pastures. In this tale, the couple can live neither in her world nor in his. Her baby is taken by the elves, and both the girl and the elf die afterwards from sorrow and longing.[3]

In other stories of these mortal and elf unions, a spell or a curse is put on an elf woman, usually by her stepmother, which forces her to live for a certain time with a human until the spell is broken and she can return again to her own family. Evidence that this is an old theme is a story in the Icelandic *Saga of King Hrólf Kraki*. In the introduction to his translation of the saga, Jesse Byock explains that the story was based on an oral tradition of legends of sixth-century Danish kings. One of these is King Hrólf's father, Helgi.

Skuld's Story[4]

One winter night, at Yuletide, King Helgi was alone in his hunting lodge, when a poor, tattered old woman appeared at his door. He brought her inside to warm by the fire, and he even offered her his bed for the night, though he was repelled by her ugliness. Some time later, Helgi was surprised to see in the faint light of the house that she had become the fairest woman he had ever seen, dressed in silk. She was an elf woman, and he had broken her stepmother's curse that kept her in the form of an ugly hag until she slept in a king's bed. She had travelled far to the homes of many kings, and Helgi was the first to ever show her this kindness. After this one night, the elf woman left, freed from the spell. But three years later, some men rode up to King Helgi's house and set down a small child; this was Skuld, a half-elf child and his daughter.

The child stayed with the king's household where she grew up to have a wild heart. She became a sorceress with ambitions to rule the country. During Yule celebrations at the court of her half-brother, King Hrólf, Skuld called upon an army of elves and other supernatural creatures to fight alongside her, and they overtook his castle. The half-elf became queen of Denmark.

The elves in these northern tales, especially the beautiful sorceress Skuld, are a very long way from more familiar fairy tale elves, who could never have been mistaken for humans; for one thing, they were much smaller. Some appeared at twilight or could be seen in moonlight as a brightness shining against the darkness, and then everything about them seemed luminous. Others lived in groves of trees, as in the German tale "The Elfin

Grove." Many elves were good-natured as long as they were left alone, and some even helped with farm work and with sewing, baking bread, or other household chores, most often coming at night when the family was in bed, similar to the elves in the Grimms' popular fairy tale "The Elves and the Shoemaker." The elves in this tale came every night into the house of a poor honest shoemaker and stitched up his leather into fine shoes that he could sell the next day. This happened often enough for the shoemaker to become rich, but when the shoemaker's wife acknowledged their work by sewing them new clothes, they disappeared.

An elf might appear before a woodcutter in the forest and ask to share his food or for assistance in some way such as settling a dispute or dividing a treasure, and a person who helped an elf was frequently paid with a large amount of coins or jewels. Other stories indicate that elves had trouble with childbirth or needed milk for their children, and then any human service was rewarded generously from the great riches and magnificent things, particularly silver, that elves kept beneath the ground. In an Icelandic tale, an elf woman appeared in a dream to a peasant's wife and begged for milk for her child. For some time, the woman left a bowl of milk outside each morning, and when she returned home from the fields in the evening it was empty. As payment, one morning she found under her pillow a beautifully wrought silver belt.[5] As with fairies, however, people were careful never to offend elves by neglecting to do as they requested, for as easily as being helpful and generous, they could be malicious, inflicting illness or a bad harvest, even stealing children. There are many stories of elf changelings.

These portrayals, in which elves are malevolent, appear more often in German and English folk traditions. Although most elves were not by nature hostile to humans without reason, their vengeance in the case of an offence could be out of all proportion to the cause. Then their potentially dangerous nature, along with their inclination to steal people away, was a deadly combination.

One aspect of the "otherness" of elves was their haunting music, whether the sound of a horn, a song, or a fiddle tune, and even this could be dangerous to humans. The Norwegian *huldre* women entranced humans with their songs. When elf fingers played a pipe, everyone who heard it, even old folk, couldn't help but dance. There are folk tales of a fiddle tune learned from elves so powerful that anyone hearing it was obliged to dance on and on without rest until someone cut the fiddle strings. Elves in Danish folklore could dance a man to death. There is a long literary tradition on the theme of music similar to fairy and elf music that could hold a person under a spell or draw him away from the world altogether.

Goethe's eighteenth-century poem, the tender and tragic "Erlkönig," gives an account of a king of the Alders, an elf king haunting a forest who beckoned to children and lured them to their death. The connection was strong between elves and the dead, and the word "elf" could refer to a ghost. In *Nyal's Saga*, for example, when Nyal's sons are about to murder Sigmund, they refer to him as a "red elf," in other words, as a being already dead and from the underworld.[6] In some places in western Norway and Iceland, where people believed that their souls would be taken into the mountains when they died, that they would "die into the hills," it followed quite naturally that elves were believed to reside in mountains and in old burial mounds.[7]

Included in these darker aspects of elf lore is the early concept that some diseases were attributed to elves. Old English texts of folklore and medicine include charms, or incantations, to ward off elf attacks, to cure dire afflictions and pain caused by elves, and to heal injuries in men and cattle from elf-shot (an invisible arrow or tiny spear). These charms and cures are evidence of a lingering belief in late Saxon England, in the tenth and eleventh centuries, in elf-beings that had the potential to inflict serious harm. In her book on these elf charms, Karen Louise Jolly considers the place of elves in the early Christian imagination.[8] She reasons that ideas from ancient Germanic folklore about spirits such as elves that were all around in the landscape endured in a Christian era: "In a world where everything was alive with spiritual presences, where the doors between heaven and earth were open all around, then saints, demons, and elves were all equally possible. Such was the world of late Saxon England."9 The notion of elves endured as a part of popular belief, and as folklore survived through the centuries – to emerge in folk and fairy tales.

Early elf lore is found in the poems of the Icelandic *Poetic Edda*, the mythic verse of ancient Nordic culture, and here the elves are mythological beings. These poems present a complex pantheon of northern gods and other supernatural races, and among this pantheon are five main groups. There are the Æsir, the wisest and most ancient gods such as Odin and Thor. There are Vanir, who were nature gods, such as Frey, the god who brought peace and plenty, and Njörd, who aided men with seafaring and fishing. Then there are three groups we are familiar with from fairy tales, the álfar or elves, the dvergar or dwarfs, and the jötnar or giants.

Here in the Eddic poems, we come upon the most surprising thing of all about the earliest elf ideas. Definitely, we do not find here the tiny, pointy-hatted creatures that we meet in children's stories. Several poems present the elves as a divine race. One thing that becomes apparent in the poems is that, over and over, the elves, or *álfar*, are mentioned together with the highest gods, the Æsir. The phrase "Æsir and álfar" appears at least ten times.10 Some examples will give the idea. In "The Lay of Grímnir" (*Grímnismál*) are the lines, "The land is sacred which I see lying, / near the Æsir and elves."11 The gods and elves live together in a holy land. The pairing appears in "The Flyting of Loki" (*Lokasenna*). The god Loki approaches a hall where the gods and elves are inside drinking ale together. Because the gods are angry with Loki, he won't go in, but he asks a servant at the door what they are all talking about. The servant answers that they are discussing weapons and mighty deeds of war, and he adds, "among the Æsir and of the elves who are within, / no one has a friendly word for you."[12] Another poem, "The Sayings of Hár" (*Hávamál*), refers to runic wisdom. The speaker, Hár, who is Odin, knows a spell that he can use to distinguish between gods and elves: "Æsir and elves, I know the difference between them / few who are not wise know that."[13]

The many pairings of gods and elves indicate that they were thought of as being together and similar. The image of these elves is that they lived near the gods in a hallowed place, and it was difficult to tell them apart from gods. Together, they feasted and drank ale in the halls of Ásgard; they shared talk of glorious deeds; elves were wise like the gods and understood ancient runes. Their welfare was bound together with that of the gods, and they would share the same destiny at the time of Ragnarök, the final apocalypse. Elves seem in these early poems, from their associations with the Æsir gods, to be minor gods themselves.

Besides these ancient poems, there is another source of elf ideas. In the thirteenth century, Snorri Sturluson composed the *Prose Edda* to document old Icelandic lore so that it would not be forgotten by poets. In the first section of this Edda, "The Deluding of Gylfi" (*Gylfaginning*), the god Odin is questioned about the gods and all of the elflike beings who live with them. Odin says that near Ásgard, home of the Æsir, is Álfheim where the light elves live. These elves are fairer than the sun to look upon, and the fairest of them is Delling. This elf is lord of the rosy dawn and elf of the morning, and is the lover of Nat, an ancient northern night-goddess. Delling resides in the east where the sun rises every day, so that Odin calls the sun "glory of the elves." Another name for sunshine is "elf's beam." These bright, sky-dwelling elves are like the fair, shining elves of folk tradition. The gods gave Álfheim, where the elves live, as a gift to the Vanir god Frey when he was very young, and this god was raised by elf-princes to become lord of the elves and king of their world. This Frey was a popular god, connected with the sun and with peace, prosperity, and good harvests, and he had a strong cult following in many parts of Scandinavia.

Odin says that there are also dark elves, who live deep in the earth near the gates of the lower world. These elves are associated with the dead and with ancestors, reminding us of the elves in folklore that reside in burial mounds and in mountains. In several poems, these elves create treasures for the gods. One elf in particular, called Dáin, works together with the dwarf Dvalin to create these magical things, and together these two are the finest of ancient artisans. In "The Lay of Grímnir," Dáin is referred to as "the dead one" and Dvalin as "one who is delayed." The elf Dáin and the dwarf Dvalin are also together when Odin teaches them the runes, which were the foundation of all wisdom. They teach this wisdom to their own races, just as Odin taught it to the gods, and this is one way in which elves and dwarfs became so wise. A further bit of elf lore is in the *Völsunga Saga*. Sigurd learns that some of the norns, the goddesses who determine the destiny of everyone on earth, were descended from elves.

Although elves are mentioned in the Icelandic texts, very few appear as individual personalities, as the gods and giants almost always do. The mother of the half-elf child Skuld is one of these. Another one would be Völund, who is sometimes mentioned as being a prince of the elves or of elfish kin, except that as an artisan and smith he is more closely linked with dwarfs. But, at one time, there must have been more elf names than Völund, Delling, and Dáin. Snorri Sturluson included in his *Prose Edda* a guide for poets or skalds, "Poetic Diction" (*Skáldskaparmál*), and in this we find another "gods and elves" pairing. He explains a poetic form for writers to use for kennings, or figurative expressions, that refer to one of the gods or elves. By simply naming an attribute of one of them, the poet's audience would know which god or elf was meant.[14] The implication for us of this little instruction is that thirteenth-century poets were reciting about elves in their poems. They knew names of elves and the identifying characteristics of some of them, and their audiences were also familiar with these elves. There must have been many elf names at one time and stories to go with them, just like the many stories of gods and giants.

This little reference is a clue that there was once a body of elf tales that is now lost. What a loss it is that these tales didn't survive!

Since these references to elves are as a race of beings with a close affinity to the gods, it is interesting to wonder what belief system they belonged to. Could they be remnants from an even older religion? The word elves, or álfar, in the old literature is not a clear-cut concept, and it is not productive or even possible to try to define the role of the elves in pagan beliefs. But there is a claim to be made that they were semi-divine beings who were at one time accepted as minor deities, living in an elf-world, Álfheim, with the god Frey, a fertility god closely connected with them.

There is a reference from late Viking times to a ritual observance to elves. In a poem composed by the Icelandic skald Sigvat Thórdarson on a journey to Gotland, Sweden, in 1018, he wrote that as a Christian he was not welcome at a farm there because people were holding a sacrifice to the elves. This late autumn ritual was called an *álfablót*, "álfar" for elves and "blót" from Old Norse meaning a blood sacrifice or offering. A similar sacrifice is described in the twelfth-century Icelandic *Kormak's Saga*. In order to cure a man's wound after a duel, a bull is killed and its blood is poured onto a hill where elves live. These blood sacrifices imply a pagan cult of elf-worship.

During the centuries when the old poems and sagas were written, there were likely differing and changing views of what elves, or álfar, were, but there was an aura of sacredness to them. These elves are far removed from the tiny creatures so often portrayed in today's popular culture, where they are scarcely distinguishable from brownies, hobgoblins, fairies, pixies, and so on. In *Lord of the Rings*, Tolkien created something much closer to the old northern ideas in which there was a sense of splendour, power, and brightness to the elves – something of the divine.

7

Dwarfs

At a first, quick glance, fairy tale dwarfs may appear to resemble elves; they might seem similar because of their small stature and their ability to slip in and out of rocky crevices. They, too, live underground, but here the similarity ends. The all-male dwarfs, with different origins, are entirely separate beings and have a markedly different appearance. They are amazingly strong and hardy, but they would have looked strange coming along a road, with their small, oddly shaped bodies and disproportionately large heads, half-running and half-walking on misshapen feet, their long white beards often hanging down to their knees.

Most stories of dwarfs are found today in German folk and fairy tales. Although dwarfs were certainly known in pagan Iceland and were a part of early Icelandic storytelling, I have found no Icelandic dwarf folk or fairy tales. They seem to have all but vanished over the centuries from this folk tradition.[1] As with the elves, however, we first discover them in the Icelandic Eddas, where they are called *dvergar*. The earliest dwarf lore is in one of the oldest poems of the *Poetic Edda*, "The Prophecy of the Seeress" (*Völuspá*), which was composed just before the year 1000,[2] at a pivotal time in Iceland when paganism was beginning to be replaced with Christianity. From the words of a pagan seeress in this poem, we learn that the first dwarfs were created at the beginning of time, quickened in the earth out of the blood and bones of two giants, Brimir and Bláin. The poem describes these first dwarfs emerging from deep in the earth, and the seeress lists them by name.³ Some in her long list are Thekk (Pleasant One) and Thorin (Bold One), Ráthsvith (Swift-in-advice), Mjóthvitnir (Mead-wolf), Lóni (Sea-pool), and Ái (Great-grandfather). Gandálf (Sorcerer-elf) and Vindálf (Wind-elf), with names ending in "álf," seem to have been named after elves. The dwarf names Nithi, Nyi, and Nyráth refer to phases of the moon, while names such as Nár and Náin refer to the dead. Dwarfs climbing out of the rocks were Draupnir (also the name of Odin's ring, Dripping One), Eikinskjaldi (Oaken-shield), Hár (Grey-hair), Ginnar (Enticer), and Glói (Glow). The names Bifur, Bofur, Bombur, Nóri, and Dvalin on the seeress's list are familiar to us from Tolkien's *The Hobbit* and were his borrowings from the Old Norse, as was the name of his wizard Gandalf. Chief of all the old dwarfs was Mótsognir, and next to him was Durin.

Although much smaller, dwarfs were closely allied to giants. Being made from the blood and bones of giants, the dwarfs were similar to them in their stonelike strength, their hardy resistance to pain and injury, their endurance and steadfastness. In Norse mythology, the four dwarfs Northri (North), Suthri (South), Austri (East), and Vestri (West), like giant stone pillars, held up the dome of the sky, one at each of its four corners. Dwarfs lived in rocky places and stayed close to mountain caves, since they were in danger of turning to stone if they were caught outside in sunlight, which is another way in which their nature was similar to that of giants who preferred cold, dark places and could turn to stone in daylight.

There are stories based on the theme of outwitting a dwarf by engaging him in a long conversation that delays him outside until the sun comes up, at which time he becomes stone. The dwarf Alvíss (All-wise) turned to stone this way in the Eddic "Lay of Alvíss" (*Alvíssmál*). This dwarf was in love with Thrúd, the beautiful daughter of the god Thor. Alvíss disguised himself as one of the gods and the affair was proceeding well for him, as long as Thrúd's father was occupied away from home fighting giants, but when Thor returned he was suspicious of his daughter's new suitor and challenged him to a test. Alvíss must tell him the names of the sky, moon, sun, clouds, wind, calm, sea, fire, trees, barley, and ale in the languages of the gods, giants, elves, and dwarfs. This was a difficult task Thor set for Alvíss. In most cases, the correct answers were metaphoric expressions, or kennings, that required esoteric knowledge of each race. Yet, Alvíss knew the answers. He knew, ironically, that the dwarf name for the sun was "Dvalin's doom," referring to the dwarf whose name meant "One who was delayed." Answering Thor's questions, however, occupied the whole night, so that when Alvíss's test was finally completed, his ruse of pretending to be a god was discovered. Daylight found the dwarf above the ground and turned him into stone.

Perhaps the best-known stories about dwarfs are the legends of the Nibelungs and the Völsungs, the similar medieval German and Norse epics centred on the heroes Siegfried and Sigurd. Wagner's version of the story, in his four operas, presents the Nibelungs as a race of dwarfs dwelling in their own dark realm. In the legend, dwarfs became heirs to an ancient and vast fortune of gold and jewels that was kept in a cave, watched over by one dwarf, Andvari (in the Norse version) or Alberich (German). The dwarf was forced into giving away all of the wealth, but just before he did, he put a curse on one magic ring that was part of the treasure, a curse under which the ring would eventually destroy everyone who owned it. This forms the basis of the story. The treasure passed from the realm of the dwarfs to the gods, to a giant, to a dragon, and finally into the hands of a human, Sigurd or Siegfried. To win the treasure hoard, Siegfried slayed twelve of the bravest men from Nibelungland and after that he killed seven hundred other Nibelungs. But, for a time, this strong champion was in peril of his life from the one powerful dwarf, Alberich. Finally, the dwarf swore an oath that he would be Siegfried's servant and would protect the hoard for him. There follows a series of stories involving families and their love, violence, honour, and vengeance. As the gold and the ring passed from one owner to another, death and disaster followed, until the treasure hoard had dragged families to their ruin. The fortunes of generations of strong men and women were bound up with this treasure, their fate determined by the dwarf's curse.

Dwarfs were preoccupied with gold and treasure. When two girls, Snow White and Rose Red in the Grimms' fairy tale of that name, were in the woods gathering firewood, they came upon a very little man with an old withered face, a beard a yard long, and a sack full of gold at his feet. Another day, they saw him with a sack of pearls. This dwarf had put a spell on a prince, turning him into a bear in order to steal his gold and jewels to keep with his other treasures deep in his cave.

Several medieval stories have the theme of a dwarf leading a human into his mountain cavern and holding him prisoner there. One of these is the legend of the celebrated Laurin, King of the Dwarfs, who kept a princess captive in a subterranean chamber deep inside his mountain. This is an old theme. In the *Ynglinga Saga*, Snorri Sturluson's legendary saga of the early kings of Sweden, King Swegde was lured into a dwarf's stone. This king had vowed to travel until he found Odin and the place where gods lived, and one night he arrived at a hostel at a place called Stein, where there was a stone as large as the house. As the guest was crossing from the drinking hall to the sleeping quarters in the evening, a dwarf sitting under the stone called out to the king, telling him that there was a door in the stone, and if he were to come in he would see Odin. Swegde rushed into the opening, which immediately closed behind him, and neither the door nor the king was ever seen again.[4]

This is also a fairy tale theme. "Karl Katz" is a tale of a goatherd who had ventured into a cavern searching for a lost goat, when a dwarf there led him deeper and deeper into the mountain. The goatherd did not return for twenty years.[5] In the Grimms' "Water of Life," a king's two sons were scornful of an ugly little dwarf. For their rudeness, the dwarf made the mountain gorge they were riding through become narrower and narrower until they could no longer go forward, but when they turned around the walls had closed behind them. Then the mountains must have echoed with the dwarf's laughter. In familiar fairy tales, dwarfs are portrayed as stubborn, never forgetting a slight. Yet, if treated politely, they could be helpful in giving good advice, making prophecies, or offering access to a drink that bestowed wisdom and strength. If a person had the good fortune of pleasing one, he could find a gift of coal in his pocket, which by the next morning would have turned to gold.

Dwarfs were seen wearing grey or scarlet cloaks with pointed hoods or, more often, red or blue pointed caps that seemed to give them special powers. Their caps were so important that, to recover a lost one, a dwarf would promise anything, and possibly some of their strength came from their caps, because in the *Nibelungenlied* when Siegfried put on the cap belonging to the dwarf Alberich, he suddenly found he had the strength of twelve men. Some dwarfs were invisible with their caps on their heads but visible if the cap accidentally fell off. These "caps-of-darkness" or "fog-caps" were similar to the other hats, hoods, and cloaks of invisibility found in fairy tales. In a German folk tale, a dwarf asked a miller whether he and some other dwarfs might cross over the river by way of his mill. The miller agreed, but was puzzled since he could only see the one dwarf who had spoken to him. The dwarf put his hat on the miller's head and then he saw all of them, long lines of dwarfs crossing over the river and moving towards a hollow in the mountain opposite.

These creatures often had hammers, leather aprons, and a dark, grimy appearance because they worked in mines. They were skilled miners and smiths. The familiar fairy tale "Snow White," in which a princess came to dwell with seven dwarfs in their cottage deep in a forest,[6] shows these little men leaving before dawn each day for their work, which was digging for ore in the mountains, and not returning until dark. More often, however, dwarfs both lived and worked in the mountains.

In the legends and ancient stories of dwarfs who toiled in mines deep in the earth and inside mountains, these workers in ores and metals were regarded as more than miners; they were more like magicians. In the mountains, they forged wondrous things, such as magical swords and impregnable armour, but their finest creations were crafted for the gods. The dwarf Dvalin forged for Odin a spear called Gungnir, which never missed its mark. Dwarfs also created Odin's magical ring, Draupnir, out of which other identical gold rings dropped. They made a hammer called Mjöllnir for Thor, and nothing could withstand its strike, not even giants. No matter how far Thor threw the hammer, it always returned to his hand. A wondrous thing they made was a boar that was covered all over with golden bristles. The god Frey used this boar to draw his chariot, and besides running on the ground, the boar glided over water, flew through air, and lit up the darkness like a lantern, since each of its bristles glowed like a firefly. The dwarfs also made for Frey a ship called Skídbladnir. This was so large that all of the gods with their weapons and armour could find room in it, and wherever it was going a breeze sprang up as soon as the sail was hoisted. Moreover, it was made with such artifice that, when it was not needed, it could be folded so small it would fit in a pouch.

Their most magical creation was a chain to bind up the monstrous wolf Fenrir, which would in time bring about the destruction of the gods. They made this fetter out of substances that were not always material things – the noise of cats' paws, a bird's spittle, the roots of a mountain, a woman's beard, bear sinews, and the breath of fish. These and other dwarf creations were essential to the gods, and they play a large part in the earliest stories. Thor, for one, needed his hammer for fighting the giants who were a constant danger, and he would have had a hard time without it. The dwarf-made items for the gods are "more than simple possessions," Thomas DuBois explains in *Nordic Religions in the Viking Age*: "they share integrally in each god's sacred functions."[7]

We might wonder where the dwarfs, who had come crawling out of the earth, came to have this skill. In the story of the Norse gods, as explained in the *Prose Edda*, in the beginning the gods themselves worked at the forges and created their own weapons and other things they needed out of metals and gold. But, eventually, they were ready to do their godly work, to sit on thrones and issue judgments. They decided to change underground creatures that had taken form and come to life out of the blood and limbs of giants into these dwarf-men, and they gave them human understanding. These creatures, then, became the troop of dwarfs that the seeress saw emerging from the earth, each one of them an individual with a name. The gods then left the work at the forges to them, and so the dwarfs became the primeval clan of smiths and artisans.

One little-known treasure made by dwarfs was a gold necklace, a shining torque called Brísingamen, or Necklace of the Brisings. I particularly like the story of this necklace, because it exists only by such a small thread. It is in just one manuscript, *Flateyjarbók*, which was kept for many years at a family farm on Flatey Island off the west coast of Iceland. The manuscript is not as old as some others; it was written between the years 1387 and 1394. With 450 pages, this is the thickest of Iceland's manuscripts. Today, with computers and readily available paper, it is hard for us to imagine that two Icelandic priests used the skins of 113 calves and spent seven years making this book for a wealthy chieftain. It is fortunate that the manuscript survived since it preserves some stories, such as this one, that are not found in any other sources. The Brísingamen necklace became the possession of Frey's sister, the beautiful fertility goddess Freyja, and this is how she came to own it.

Freyja's Necklace[8]

Late one night, Freyja walked alone up into the hills. She knew where the dwarf-stone was where Alfrigg, Dvalin, Berling, and Grerr lived, and this was where she was headed. She entered into a dark cave there and immediately could hear the tapping of the dwarf smiths at work deep in their cavern. As soon as she emerged from the darkness of the cave into the smithy that was bright from the fire, she saw the glorious necklace they had just made. It shone with intricate patterns that twisted and curved. She wanted that necklace more than anything, and she paid a high price for it. The dwarfs did not want silver or gold; they had enough of these. The price the dwarfs asked was that she lie one night with each of them. Four nights later, they gave the necklace to the shameless Freyja, and she returned home.

Freyja was quiet about this, as if nothing had happened. But when Loki discovered that she had the necklace and told Odin, that god was angry when he found out how she acquired it; how could Freyja, a goddess, have spent nights with dwarfs? This price she paid for the necklace did nothing to lessen her reputation for promiscuity, which was, however, a quality completely in keeping with a fertility goddess. Odin demanded that the crafty, sly Loki steal the necklace and bring it to him, which Loki did, carefully removing it from Freyja's neck while she was sleeping. When she realized her necklace was gone, she came straight to Odin, knowing this was his trickery, and then Odin set a very difficult task for Freyja to earn her necklace back again.

She must arrange to have two kings, each of them accompanied by twenty other kings, fight each other. She must put such spells and curses on the battle that if a man fell, he would stand up again and continue fighting. The strife would continue until a Christian man was bold enough to enter the conflict and slay the fighting men. The battle of the Hjadnings is the enchanted one Odin requested of Freyja, a battle that continued for a hundred and forty-three years, until the watchman on a ship bearing King Olaf Tryggvason, the first Christian king of Norway, bravely entered the fighting and slayed the weary combatants. This ended the enchanted battle and Freyja's part of the bargain.

There is a different strand to the narrative of Freyja's Brísingamen that is much older than the story of this battle, and it goes like this:[9]

After Loki removed the necklace from Freyja's neck while she slept, he decided not to give it to Odin after all, but to keep it for himself. The huge god Heimdall helped Freyja search everywhere for it. Eventually, he found the thief. A lengthy fight ensued between these two gods over the Brísingamen, until Heimdall finally won the precious item back for Freyja.

We have a fine clue that this ending to the story is close to four centuries older than the *Flateyjarbók* version, and that the tale was once well known. Long ago in Iceland, a wealthy chieftain had a hall built, with decorated wooden walls that were carved and painted with scenes from the old stories, including a scene of Heimdall and Loki fighting over Freyja's dwarf-made necklace. We know about this carved and painted scene, because some lines describing it were in an old poem of which only fragments now exist, called "House Song" (*Húsdrápa*).[10] The poem was recited, praising the decorated walls of the hall, by the Icelandic skald, Úlf Uggason, who was one of the guests at a wedding feast there in the winter of 978.

The dwarf smiths who created this precious necklace and other wondrous things were part of an ancient tradition of magician-smiths. A figure appearing in stories handed down in early times and widespread in northern Europe is a powerful magician-smith or smith-god who practised supernatural skills of metallurgy in a subterranean smithy. This wonder-smith, who was known as Weland in Old English and Völund in

Norse, could forge weapons stronger than any created by humans. This legendary craftsman is the central figure in "The Lay of Völund" (*Völundarkvida*), a very early Eddic poem (c. 900–1050).[11] Weland is a renowned smith in the Old English epic poem *Waldere*, in which the hero had a sword praised as being one that Weland had forged, and he is also alluded to in the poem *Deor*. He is mentioned in *Beowulf*, who had a coat of mail that was the finest in the world created by Weland Smith. The sword Beowulf used to kill monsters was also the work of a wonder-smith. Its blade was engraved with images of a war with giants, its golden plate was carved with runes, and it was a sword of mystic strength that became stronger with each victory.

There were other magician-smiths. In the Finnish folk poem *Kalevala*, a smith with divine status was Ilmarinen, a primeval craftsman who created in his forge objects with magical powers. Similar to these smiths, in Ireland there have been stories of Gobbán Saor for more than a thousand years. This artisan forged weapons that had perfect accuracy and always inflicted a fatal wound, but his skills went beyond metalwork. He was a renowned builder, and there were bridges, round towers, and other ancient buildings attributed to him. Gobbán Saor was the craft god known as Goibniu of the Tuatha Dé Danann, and he is identified with the Welsh divine smith, and sometimes dwarf, Gofannon. These figures suggest that a smith with divine attributes was a Celtic concept as well. Whether he was Völund, Wayland or Weland, Ilmarinen, or Gobbán Saor, whether he was a magician-smith or a smith-god, this craftsman's weapons and other creations had inherent magical strength and his skills at the forge demonstrated supernatural power. The dwarfs in their mountain caverns, so long ago appointed by the gods to their profession, clearly belong to this ancient wonder-smith tradition.

Folk traditions reflect that dwarfs had dwelt on the earth in a distant past, and it is apparent that the dwarfs we meet in fairy tales could rightly feel that they had at one time been a proud race, worthy of respect. They lived in their caves to a very old age, as unchanging as the stones of the earth, and their race would endure until the end of the world. The wise woman in "The Prophecy of the Seeress" has a vision of them in the future, at the time of the earth's final destruction, the twilight time of the gods. The wolf Fenrir eventually breaks free from the magical chain the dwarfs had made to bind him, and then he begins to run, ravenous. He will kill Odin. When the sky becomes rent apart, and all the world begins to crumble, the seeress hears the roar of the dwarfs' lament as they stand at the entrances to their caves while their world of cliffs and rocks falls around them, these old, wise masters of the mountains.

8

Household Spirits

In folk stories, the invisible beings called nissen or nisser in Denmark and Norway, tomten in Sweden, kobolds in Germany, and brownies in England and the Scottish Lowlands resembled dwarfs somewhat in stature and appearance, but these were very different creatures. Like dwarfs they were almost always male, but sometimes they had a small wife and family of their own. Where dwarfs lived independently of humans, these lived side by side with them on their farms and in their homes, sharing their hearth and food, performing helpful labour, and loyally caring for their well-being. In Swedish folklore, there was a house-tomte for every home. Even the smallest hut high in the hills had a tomte to guard it. The following story, from a Swedish folk tale translated by Martha Inez Johnson, illustrates the house-tomte's usefulness.

Singeli's Silver Slippers[1]

Martin was a shoemaker who lived with his family in a small cottage at the edge of a forest, and he and the family were so poor that he could not give his little daughter very much besides her lovely name – Singeli. But he gave her what he could, and he decided to make something very beautiful and special for her. After making her the practical wooden shoes that she needed, he carefully sewed her a pair of slippers from a goatskin that gleamed like silver. He worked sewing the slippers long into the night, and when he was finished everyone else in the cottage was asleep. Suddenly, there was a knock on the door. On the doorstep, in the darkness of the night, were fairies-of-fortune who had come to bless the little shoes that were sewn with such love. At the same time, the house-tomte was on the doorstep, too, ensuring that only good fairies came inside the cottage. When the fairies left, the shoes had become as soft as silk and had turned into real shining silver.

Singeli wore the slippers every day inside her wooden shoes as she ran up and down the mountainside caring for the goats. As the years went by, the slippers grew as she did, they never became worn, and they kept her safe from harm. No human could see them under her wooden shoes, but the house-tomte and all of the elves and trolls of the forest could see the silver shining through. Sometimes the slippers became lost when she played on the hills, and then after dark the house-tomte, who could see them shining, found them and brought them home.

When Singeli was older, she left the cottage to work as the herd girl on the king's estate. In the summer, she lived in the mountains caring for the king's cows and goats and preparing cheese from the milk, and even here there was a little herd-hut-tomte. With his help the animals did not go astray all summer and many fine cheeses were made by the end of the season. Sometimes, at night, the trolls in the hills crept close to the hut drawn by the gleam of the silver slippers, but the hut-tomte kept them safe.

One evening, near autumn, Singeli heard an anguished cry from the marsh and without stopping to put on her wooden shoes ran towards the sound. In her slippers she could run as quickly as the wind, and she arrived in time to throw a line to a young man as his horse was sinking in the mud. It happened that the young man she helped to dry land was a king. He was captivated with the girl in the silver slippers who had saved his life and decided that he would like to marry her. She became his queen; and so, as her father had wished and with the blessings of the fairies, the slippers brought Singeli happiness and fortune.

Stories depict tomten as small, rough fellows, but sturdy and dependable. Although the size of little children, beneath their caps were faces that were very old and wise. Some of them had long red beards. Others had boots with which they could run at great speeds. Often they were dressed in grey woollen coats, but seldom were they ever seen without their red pointed caps, which gave them the same ability as dwarfs to make themselves visible or invisible. Their hats were so important that some tomten had names that referred to their hats, such as Eisenhütel (hat of iron) and Hopfenhütel (hat wreathed around with hop leaves). The brownies, of course, wore brown hoods or hats.

Brownies often lived by a pool or stream near the house. Other house spirits lived in a tree, or in the stable, in a deserted loft, in the gables under the roof, or in the cellar where they watched over the ale casks. In a German story, one little fellow with remarkable prophetic and magical powers lived in a castle dungeon. Most often, these house spirits went in and out of the chimney and spent time near the hearth or behind the oven, as if this was an entrance to their underground dwelling. Usually, they stayed right with the family of the house, sometimes even in the same room.

A nisse, tomte, or brownie did domestic jobs for his master, and where he lived was where he worked. A few were useful inhabitants of a mill or boat-building yard. If treated well, a household spirit would do a great deal of work, cleaning the home and hearth, weaving and churning, cleaning out the stable, bringing food and water to the animals, and helping with harvesting and threshing. He guarded the doorway, and when something was lost, he was the one who could find it.

For all their help, these beings were willing to work for very little, being content with a dish of cream from time to time, or another small offering, such as a taste of what had been prepared in the kitchen, porridge or cake left out for them when the family went to bed. In folk tradition, it was customary for them to receive a gift at Christmas. Some would work all year for the trifling payment of a little bit of food or some tobacco left on the hearth on Christmas Eve, but what they really wanted more than anything else was respect.

It was not often that a household spirit ever left a family. He stayed for generations, and there was no one as loyal to the family as he was. He would stick with his master through all kinds of trouble. For a favourite member of the household he lent a hand with the work, but for one to whom he took a dislike he would kick the milk pail over and spread the ashes out of the hearth, making that one have to work even harder. Although in some homes he became irritating, once he was with a family nothing could be done to get rid of him; not even a priest could move him out, although that was one way to get rid of a less desirable kind of brownie called a dobie. Similar to the house elf Dobby in the Harry Potter novels, a dobie was devoted but not very clever. There are folk tales of families who moved from one house to another in order to escape such a troublesome little fellow, but he was always hidden among the household furnishings. When these had been moved into the new home, out he popped and scurried behind the hearth. Then he did nothing but torment the family, leaving the ale-tap running, setting the fowl loose, turning the milk sour, even trying to burn the house down. He could be noisy at night, making such a loud disturbance tumbling downstairs, clattering pots and pans, and setting the chairs and tables banging and rattling against each other that no one could sleep for the racket.

For their scampering about the house at night, they were sometimes thought of as taking the form of a cat, and with their special boots remind us of the sharp-witted Puss-in-Boots in the familiar fairy tale. In this story, when a miller dies and leaves the mill to his oldest son and the donkey to his second son, all that remains as an inheritance for the youngest is the devoted cat that lives in the mill. But this Puss-in-Boots is very clever and serves his new master so well that the young man finds good fortune.

Although these spirits were often heard chuckling and singing, ringing bells, or playing a fiddle, they were rarely ever seen. The presence of some was indicated by a blue light, which they carried at night. Sometimes, however, children saw them. The home spirit Hinzelmann, in German folk tales, was invisible to adults but could be seen by the children of the household when he came to play with them. At other times, Hinzelmann's presence was known by a white feather, a shape he took to accompany the family when they travelled by carriage. A house spirit in this Swedish story was seen several times, but only by the daughter of the house.

The Young Lady of Hellerup[2]

A girl lying awake in her bed one night saw in the moonlight a little fellow in a grey jacket and red cap coming across her bedroom floor. He came to ask a favour. A water tank in the kitchen had a leak. The little man's family was constantly bothered by the sound of the dripping, and it was never dry in their home beneath the floor. In the morning, the girl asked that the old water tank be moved, and from that time on all went well for the household. Some time after this, she granted another request and was paid with what looked like some bits of wood, which she threw into the hearth, but in the morning golden jewelry was shining in the ashes. Years later, she was preparing for her wedding day, which was to be a splendid event. At the same time, she became aware of sounds of work being done beneath the floor of the kitchen, at night when everyone in the house was asleep. When the wedding day arrived, and the bride was brought into the hall where the guests were waiting, she happened to look at the fireplace, and there she saw a group of fairy people gathered for a similar ceremony. There was a little bridegroom and bride, and everything was proceeding just as it was in the big hall, but none of her family or guests were aware of the wedding taking place in the hearth.

Stories such as these are widespread, appearing in folk and fairy tale collections from Norway, Sweden, Germany, Scotland, and England.[3] Unlike elves and dwarfs, however, house spirits are very hard to find in the ancient Norse myths and sagas. One appears in a tale depicting the early conversion period. This is a hearth or harvest spirit called ármadr, who protects a pagan homestead, warns of impending problems, is worshipped for a long while, but is driven away by Christian prayers.[4] The stories of home spirits are simple and often amusing tales belonging to local lore, usually attached to a single small village or to a farm. Although there is so very little evidence of these household spirits in ancient narratives, and they are not frequently found in fairy tales, they have for centuries been a large part of storytelling. Folk tale traditions about these souls are so prevalent and consistent that they likely have ancient origins, but where did the idea come from? The notion that families left bits of food for them, especially at Christmas, like little offerings to a hearth god, seems very old and pagan.

In accounts from early Scandinavia, there is evidence that family guardian spirits had a role. Deities known as *dísir* were sometimes connected with a single family in this way. "It becomes apparent that the mythical world must be extended beyond the company of the powerful individual gods to that of supernatural guardians and protectors of a lesser kind, with whom a covenant might be made," explains Hilda Ellis Davidson in *The Lost Beliefs of Northern Europe*. There are examples of "local guardian spirits, either male or female, attached to a family."[5]

"While some deities dwelled in field and forest, others lived beneath the floorboards of human dwellings,"[6] maintains Thomas DuBois in *Nordic Religions in the Viking Age*. These kinds of protecting spirits would have been important to families who lived for centuries on the same land and in the same home, in isolated places in the mountains, or in remote coastal regions. Such guardian spirits would have played a greater role and provided even more comfort in daily life than the gods Odin, Thor, and Frey, but it would be unlikely for such local spirits connected to families to make their way into mythology. And, in a Christian culture, these may have become unpopular subject matter.

An indication that some folk belief in household spirits existed in the fourteenth century is a passage from the teachings of the Swedish nun Saint Birgitta.[7] She stayed in the home of a family that did not attend church, and during her time there had a revelation. The nun heard a voice, which told her that the family still worshipped one of the household spirits, residing in the kitchen, that had belonged to the previous inhabitants of the home. She spoke out after that, condemning all lingering worship of such house spirits and warning against making offerings to them. In Sweden, a tomte belonged to the farmstead rather than to the family itself, and he may have been connected with a protecting spirit of the first settlers on the farm. It is possible, even likely, that the household spirits of folk and fairy tales are vestiges of old folklore such as this.

In Scandinavia, household spirits have become associated with Christmas. The Norwegian and Danish Christmas elf is Jule-Nisse – "Jule" meaning Yule or Christmas and "Nisse" referring to one of the home spirits. In 1881, the Swedish folklore scholar Viktor Rydberg wrote the poem "Tomten." In this poem, a tomte remains alone outside the house one cold Midwinter Night while the family sleeps soundly within. The faithful spirit walks the homestead watching over the animals and people on his farm, ensuring that all stay safe and well. The idea of the little tomte, with his grey woollen coat and red hat, is a part of Swedish Christmas tradition. Rydberg also wrote the very popular tale "The Adventures of Little Vigg on Christmas Eve." Here a boy embarks on a Christmas Eve journey on a sleigh with a little old tomte, who leaves presents for the people on the farms and in the houses they pass, even the king's castle. Rydberg's poem and story transformed the house-tomte character into "Jultomte," a Swedish version of Father Christmas, St Nicholas, or Santa Claus. This association with Christmas ensures that nissen and tomten will continue to have a place in the folk imagination for a very long time.

9

Water Dwellers

S o far, we have discovered that fairies, elves, dwarfs, and different kinds of home spirits were beings closely connected with features of the landscape: its hills and mounds, rocky places, cliffs and caverns, mountains, even fields and farmsteads. Now we turn to lakes, rivers, and the sea.

Mermaid mythology is ancient and, unlike the others, is widespread, ranging from Japanese, Chinese, and Russian mermaids, a Babylonian merman, the Syrian mermaid moon-goddess, to images of mermaids in medieval bestiaries. Legends and folklore about sea-maidens are found in every country of northern Europe, but in each region they have a different name and their stories vary slightly. In England, we find lovely, graceful mermaids who come sometimes from the deeps to lie on rocks and breathe the sea mist. In Cornwall, these creatures are called merry-maids, and in Brittany, morgans. The similar Irish mermaids, or merrows, live on dry land in a place under the sea and have magic caps that allow them to pass through the water. But where the merrow maidens are fair to look at, the green-toothed and green-haired male merrows are not. In Welsh stories, there are not mermaids as such, but lake fairies, who live in lonely mountain lakes and ponds. In Scotland, especially the Scottish Orkney and Shetland Islands, seal-people, or selkies enter into a large part of the folklore. These gentle creatures, which are seals in the daytime but can turn into men and woman at night, have an unearthly beauty when they emerge silently from the sea, remove their sealskins, and dance on the sand.

Scandinavian stories have necks or näcks, water creatures that live either in the sea or in freshwater lakes and rivers, where the rapturous, silvery notes of their harps can sometimes be heard. In Sweden, the sound of their fiddle tunes can be dangerously haunting. German stories have meerfrau or nixies, who sometimes come to shore to a market or a fair, while German undines are other water spirits who like to associate with humans and join in their dances. When an undine leaves her world to marry a human, she obtains a human soul and with it all of the difficulties and sorrows of human life. Hans Christian Andersen's fairy tale "The Little Mermaid" was derived from undine folklore. A popular French story with many versions is *Mélusine*, a medieval tale of a fairy who marries a knight on the condition that he never see her on one day of the week; that day she is part serpent or fish.

Although usually solitary, occasionally three sea-maidens appear together, or, there is a whole group of sea folk, who seem to be just like humans as they emerge from the sea to dance and gather the eggs of sea birds. On shore, they usually appear wearing clothes, but unusual attire, the men perhaps with red hats (a fairy colour), and the water-maidens in colourful, patched gowns and red caps, too, over their long hair. On land, these sea folk appear human except for some small sign that they are not, such as a delicate membrane between their fingers, a tangle of green seaweed in their hair, or a wet skirt. Most sea-maidens in folk tales do not have a fish tail.

In Irish stories, mermaids have magical abilities similar to the Tuatha Dé Danann; they can prophesy the future, grant wishes, and work wonders such as healing. And, indeed, one of the realms of that divine race was the submerged "Land under Wave" (*Tír fo Thuinn*), "one of the many places where the Tuatha Dé Danann would have fled after their defeat by the Milesians,"[1] according to the Celtic scholar James MacKillop. This land was visited several times in the early Irish stories. One of these adventures occurred when a young man, Brian, came upon the underwater country in "The Tragic Story of the Children of Tuireann" (*Oidheadh Chlainne Tuireann*).[2] Brian and his brothers were sent on an expedition to find a particular cooking-spit from an island called Inis Findcuire, as one item on a long list of magical objects they were required to pay in compensation for a murder. The brothers spent a quarter of a year on the rough seas searching for this island, until one of them finally went beneath the waves: "And then Brian put on his water-dress, with his transparency of glass upon his head; and he made a water-leap; and it is said that he was a fortnight walking in the salt water seeking the island of Findcuire, and he found it at last."[3] In a palace on the underwater island, he came upon a group of women who were doing embroidery. They were pleased to give him the cooking-spit he needed because of his great courage in travelling to their world under the sea.

In many cultures, the prevailing idea about mermaids is that they bring disaster. They have the power to create mighty waves that sweep men into the sea. The Norse sea goddess Rán was similarly associated with waves that were dangerous to those venturing on the sea and possessed a net that she used to pull drowning men down into the deeps. In Irish lore, young men who drowned were understood to have been taken to underwater caverns where they remained captives of mermaids who would give them anything they desired – except to see the earth again. An ancient poem of a mermaid is included in a book of monastery records, *The Annals of Tigernach*,[4] which were compiled by an abbot at Clonmacnoise. This is likely the earliest Irish depiction of such a sea woman, and it indicates how very long ago mermaids existed in the Irish imagination. Possibly she is a sea goddess. Her hair is in the cresting waves as she rises and flings them into a man's boat. The annals for the year 622 document that when Conaing, son of Aedán, drowned that year, the poet Nindine sang these lines to memorialize his passing:

The sea's great pure waves,
And the sun that pursued him,
Into his weak wicker coracle they flung themselves
Together on Conaing.
The woman that cast her white hair
Into his coracle against Conaing,
It is her smile
That smiled today on Tortu's tree.[5]

The tree of Tortu that the sea woman smiled on was an enormous ash tree, one of the magical trees inhabited by pagan gods and spirits in ancient Irish lore.[6]

The following mermaid tale is a shortened version of one that was first published in 1903 in *The Gael*, a journal devoted to Irish language and culture. It subsequently appeared in Padraic Colum's *Treasury of Irish Folklore*. The fairy tale is similar to the very many mermaid stories that were told for centuries in the white fishermen's cottages up and down the Atlantic coast. It is not surprising that many mermaid stories involve fisherfolk.

The Kerry Mermaid[7]

The faint light of dawn was in the sky as Donal More's fishing boat came to shore after a night at sea. He and his men stored their fish in a hut on the beach and then secured the boat in a sheltered cove. Tired after their night's work, they started along the rocky path under a cliff towards their village. The men were thankful that the tide was receding, so they did not have to worry about the waves as they crossed over the rocks. Still, it was quite dark yet and their walk was dangerous, and so they clasped hands, with Donal in the lead.

That was when they saw the mermaid. They frightened her, and in
alarm she leaped into the water, forgetting her sea-cloak on the rock
where she had been sitting. Donal seized it and held onto it tightly.

The sea-maiden reappeared, demanding her cloak. She implored
Donal to return it, but he wouldn't, knowing that as long as he held
onto it she would follow him home. By the time they reached the
road and the mermaid was still with them, Donal's men felt pity
for her, for she was very distressed. They were also fearful for themselves and for Donal. It was surely bad luck to bring the mermaid
home. But Donal brought her to his house, which was one of the
finer homes in the village, and she resigned herself to stay there
with him. As the days passed, she seemed to be happy enough.

At this time Donal was about thirty years old, and although he
knew many pleasant and attractive girls and had more to offer a
woman than most of the men in the area, he was a bachelor. The
villagers were puzzled about what had come over their friend
Donal, living with a mermaid. They discussed it far and near, but
what they did not know is that the moment he had laid his eyes
on the beautiful woman sitting on the rock running her fingers
through her hair, he was in love with her.

The years passed, and there was not a more contented, loving
couple. They were blessed with many children, and after thirty years
the children had grown up. There were no young women as beautiful and endearing in their natures as the mermaid's daughters. Her
sons were manly and stalwart and had inherited their father's passion for the sea. The family prospered. Finally, the day came when
they were to move to a new, more comfortable home. The moving
carts were all loaded with their belongings, and everyone was seated
in the wagons when the mermaid-mother went into the old house
one last time to look at the place where she had lived so long and

been so happy. It was the place where her children had been born. In one of the rooms she spied a broken trunk. In it were old items to be discarded, some of them spilling out onto the floor.

She picked up an old, dusty cloak, and no sooner did she recognize it than she laughed so loudly that everyone in the village heard her. Immediately, she changed from an old woman to a young and beautiful girl. She forgot all about her husband and children. In an instant the cloak was on her and she ran down to the sea and was gone forever, back to her old life beneath the waves.

There are a great many stories similar to this one, of a mermaid who marries a mortal. Sometimes she first appears, soaking wet, at a fisherman's door, and he takes her in to warm by the fire. More often, like Donal, he finds her on the seashore where she has come to bathe in the shallow water and has left her sea-cloak or magic cap on a rock. In Scottish stories, this is a sealskin. When the fisherman takes the sea-garment, she has no choice but to follow him home and become his wife.

Children born of a mermaid-mortal marriage attribute good fortune to their parentage and look upon themselves as superior to others. The girls grow up to be fair, and the boys, strong and fearless. Some of them have special abilities. In one folk story, the child of a mermaid invents the ten-stringed harp, and in another the spinning wheel. Other children have their mother's gift of healing. One Welsh water-maiden, in "The Legend of Llyn y Fan Fach," teaches her sons so much about herbs and their medicinal properties that they become celebrated physicians.[8] In German tradition, the smith Weland who makes magical swords for kings is descended from a sea-maiden. The legend is told in the thirteenth-century *Didriksaga* that the grandmother of Weland appeared coming out of the sea and taking hold of a king's ship. She told the king she would bear him a son, and this son was Wade, Weland's father.[9]

Other mermaids and children of mermaids, however, seemed doomed never to be able to speak. In one tale, some girls who find a sea-maiden floundering in the water near the coast take her to their home to recover, where she stays and is a great help, weaving and spinning with remarkable skill, but she never speaks a word to them. Andersen, in "The Little Mermaid," develops this theme of a mermaid losing the ability to speak when she comes to live with humans.

Some stories of a sea-maiden marrying a mortal husband mention, not the cap, cloak, or sealskin, but instead a dowry that she brings to the match from her caves beneath the sea. Or, they describe a contract by which her husband is linked to her by inviolable bonds or prohibitions, a theme we also find in fairy and mortal marriages. In stories based on the Fianna of Ireland, one of Finn's warriors married the beautiful daughter of the king of the world beneath the waves, and the husband's promise to her was that he would never mention three times what she had looked like when she first appeared to him. At that time, she had been wild and ugly with hair down to her heels.[10] The most common prohibition in these marriages is that the wife must not be struck three times. One theme holds true for all of these stories – sea-maidens are only temporary visitors to the world of humans. Their souls belong to their own glorious, watery realm, to which they inevitably return.

There is one most extraordinary notion about sea-women. In some tales, when a mermaid comes to shore and dances as a human, her true origin is betrayed by a little cow's tail visible beneath her skirt. Water spirits had a strange association with cows, and this unusual connection is a theme found both in older stories and in folk tales, although it is more highly developed in folk stories.[11] Sometimes sea-maidens come out of the water as little hornless cows, or, they come from the sea as maidens driving white cows ahead of them and then waiting on the shore while the cows graze in a meadow. When a mermaid marries a mortal, she may bring with her from the sea a wedding gift of very fine cattle. The thir-teenth-century legend of the Welsh water-maiden who raised three sons to be skilled in medicine was seen with her cows that walked on the sur-face of the water. Many years later, when her marriage promise was broken, she called each of her cows by name, and they followed her back into the lake.[12]

In a Danish folk tale, a little girl herded her family's cows every day to a meadow. One foggy morning when she arrived, the meadow was al-ready filled with cows and horses. When her cows joined them, these other animals all rushed to the water and with a roaring sound disap-peared. Cows from the sea were superior to the cows of humans. When left to pasture with a farmer's herd, his became more prolific, ensuring that the farmer who took care of such cows would thrive. *The Silver Cow: A Welsh Tale* is a lovely children's book that is a retelling of an older folk tale of elfin ladies who haunted a lake in the Welsh hills and had in their possession droves of fine white cows.[13] While minding his family's cows, a boy played his harp on the shore, and suddenly there was a silver cow with the others, a gift from the Tylwyth Teg who lived in the lake. As long as the silver cow was cared for, the family prospered. In the original Welsh tale, when the elfin cow became old and ready for slaughter, no sooner had the butcher struck it, than a green lady appeared standing on a crag over the lake, screaming:

Come yellow Anvil, stray horns,
Speckled one of the lake,
And of the hornless Dodin,
Arise, come home.[14]

Whereupon, the stricken cow arose and with all of its progeny disap-peared. One cow only was left, which changed from white to black.

In a traditional Irish folk tale, a mermaid appeared one day at the water's edge where everyone marvelled at her beauty, and the chief carried her to his cottage. The woman quickly learned the people's language and was found to be a most wise and gentle creature. On the May Eve following her capture she asked to go back to the sea, and to the crowd that gathered on the shore to watch her disappear she requested that they return there the next May Eve, when three sacred cows would come out of the water; these three cows would ensure them healthy herds for years to come. Just as she had foretold, twelve months later, three cows, one white, one red, and one black, came out of the sea.[15] This folk tale reflects a story from mythology, in which the sea god, Manannán, had a red, a white, and a black cow come up out of the sea and walk on land, where a road magically appeared in front of each one.

How very strange this connection between cows and the sea and sea-maidens is. We know that in ancient times cows were highly valued, even venerated. For the Irish, May Day celebrated cows coming to their summer pastures, and in some legends a sacred white cow appeared on that day among the others. Sacred otherworld cows are referred to in the Welsh Triads, and other references are made to sacred cows that were abundant with milk and that provided good fortune and magical gifts as well as nourishment. Ireland's Saint Brigid, who performed miracles and wonders, as a child was nourished exclusively with the milk from one such sacred cow. However, even if there were special or sacred cows, why in stories did they come from the sea? How did sea-maidens come to possess such great wealth of cattle? One has to wonder what concept, or belief, this idea came from. Unfortunately, as far as I can determine, the answer remains a mystery.

I want to leave this chapter with one final tale. I was pleased to find that there is a mermaid story in the *Book of the Dun Cow* manuscript. We know, then, how very old this Irish story is.

Princess Lí Ban[16]

A long time ago, a sacred spring that had been left neglected over-flowed. A lake formed from the flood, which submerged the palace of the high king and queen. Everyone in the palace drowned, except for the king's two sons and his daughter, Lí Ban, who with her dog was swept away in the flood. Princess Lí Ban was transformed from the waist down, her legs taking the form of the tail of a salmon. She became a water spirit, and lived deep in the sea with her little dog that became an otter.

Three centuries later, after Christianity had come to Ireland, a monk out on the sea in a curragh discovered the mermaid singing on the waves, and the song sounded to him as the voice of angels. The sea-maiden described to the monk the events of her long life, and then she made him a promise. True to her word, she came to the shore one year later and was caught in a fisherman's net. People came from far and wide to marvel at her shape before she was taken to a monastery, where she requested to be baptized and given a Christian soul. In answer to her wish, this was done, but she died immediately afterwards. Lí Ban, whose name means "beauty of women," became known as "the sanctified mermaid" for wonders and miracles she had performed throughout the three hundred years that she lived in the sea.

This very old story expresses familiar folkloric ideas about mermaids. The ability to perform wondrous deeds was somehow inherent in them. Also, it seems that when mermaids lived with humans, they came to be in need of a Christian soul. The story includes the element of composition that recurs in the old Irish stories of people from pre-Christian times living, magically, long enough to tell their stories to monks.

In the *Annals of the Four Masters*, 558 is given as the year in which Lí Ban was pulled from the sea and taken to the monastery.[17] Entries in these *Annals* were compiled to document Irish narrative and historical material, but particularly the lives of saints. Mael Muiri wrote this story down around 1100, but it depicts a time far earlier. It depicts a time in a distant legendary past when the pagan world and the world of earliest Christianity in Ireland met. It was a time when saints and sanctified mermaids were both possible. All mermaids, however, convey a sense of belonging to a very early stratum of storytelling.

10

Giants

In the ancient imagination fairies, elves, dwarfs, and mermaids existed, but in the early Norse stories, except for gods, we read more on the subject of giants and trolls than all other denizens of the supernatural world combined. In passages from the *Prose* and *Poetic Eddas*, a story unfolds about how the world was created,[1] and in this story, in the very newness of time, there were giants. They took form at the beginning of all creation, even before there were gods. They were formed before there was earth, air, sea, or sun. Before giants, all that existed was an icy northern world of endless darkness, and a southern world, which was hot with fire and burning with glowing embers. Between the cold and hot worlds was nothing but a great void – Ginnunga gap.

It is a fitting northern concept in this creation story that life began with the melting of ice and snow. The Ginnunga gap was filled with magical forces, and as fiery air from the south melted ice from the north, drops of melted frost became alive. These fused into the shape of a primeval being who was the first ancestor of all the giants, gods, and humans – the giant Ymir. Next out of the melted frost emerged a sacred cow that licked great blocks of ice and nourished Ymir with her milk. From Ymir's huge form sprang a race of rime or frost giants, their bodies dripping with hoarfrost and with long icicles hanging from their frosty beards. Giants of this clan had names such as Hoarbeard, Wind-Cold, and The Cold and Wet One.

Out of Ymir's feet sprouted trolls, ugly creatures with three, six, or twelve heads. From the giant's chest and shoulders issued forth the first of the Norse gods, the Æsir, who were good, and fair to look upon. One of these was Bor, father of the great god Odin. Odin and his brothers killed the giant Ymir, which so angered the frost giants that they would remain enemies of the gods forever. The gods then moved Ymir's enormous body to the very centre of the Ginnunga gap, and there where the air was mild, they created from his body an earth that was habitable for humans, surrounded by mountains and the sea. They called this Midgard, or Middle Earth. Rocks and soil were made from Ymir's flesh, trees and grass from his hair, cliffs and mountains from his bones, and the briny sea from his blood.

Next, Odin created the first humans. These were a man, Ask, and a woman, Embla, named for the trees ash and elm or vine, from which they were formed. Odin gave Midgard to Ask and Embla for their home. The gods had finished their creation of earth and humankind. They then created a realm for themselves called Ásgard, and from there built a shining rainbow bridge to Midgard, so that they could easily come and go between the worlds.

Far away, at the edges of Midgard, were cold mountain worlds inhabited by giants. The giants in Norse mythology are called *jötnar*, and these had a more undefined form and were wilder and far more strange than the English word "giants" usually implies. Some were connected with the powers of nature, such as the giant Hræsvelg who took the shape of a huge eagle and produced north winds by beating his wings. Ice and driving snow were associated with frost giants. The gods of day and night were of the giant race, and the night-giant's horse, with a mane of hoarfrost, left morning fields wet from the frost that dripped from its bit.

The giants are forces of chaos, larger than the gods, and constantly fighting with them. In the introduction to his *Norse Mythology*, John

Lindow expresses the essence of the mythology's narrative: "everything in it is presented in light of an enduring struggle between two groups of beings, the gods on the one hand and giants on the other hand."[2] Further on he continues, "As dwarfs, humans, and occasionally elves look on and are sometimes drawn into the struggle, the æsir and the jötnar fight over resources, precious objects, and, especially, women."[3] The enormous importance of giants is their role as adversaries of the gods.

These hideous monsters play a more limited part in the early Celtic narratives, but here as well, we come upon them. One very old story from the *Book of the Dun Cow* is filled with giants. The composition of "Bricrui's Feast" has been dated as early as the eighth century.[4] This is the bloody tale that seems to have so distressed the scribe Mael Muiri that he wrote the words *"in dei nomine, Amen"* in the margin when he was copying it into his manuscript.

One evening, an enormous churl entered a king's hall: "Next to his skin he wore an old hide with a dark brown mantle around him, and over him a great spreading tree-club the size of a winter-shed, under which thirty bullocks could find shelter. He had ravenous yellow eyes protruding from his head, each of the two the size of an ox-vat. Each finger as thick as another person's wrist."[5]

In his right hand this monster carried an axe, and he issued a deadly challenge to the men in the hall. Whichever warrior was brave enough could try to cut off the giant's head, if the giant could come back the next night and behead him in return. One man with the name Fat-Neck stepped forward for the challenge. He took the giant's axe and cut off the creature's enormous head, but when the giant's head was cut off he didn't die! He picked up his head, clasped it and his axe to his breast, and left the hall, blood streaming from his neck. The giant returned the next evening, but Fat-Neck refused to come forward for his part of the bargain. That night, another warrior once again cut off the giant's head, but this man did not show up either for the return blow as agreed upon. By the third night, the giant was furious. That evening the hero Cúchulainn cut off the brute's head for the third time, but he was prepared to die and offered his neck to the giant's axe. The monster spared his life, and for his valour in this deadly game declared Cúchulainn a champion.

When we turn to folk and fairy tales, we find giants that are by their nature similarly fearsome and hostile towards humans. Worldwide, there are stories about huge, fierce creatures just like them and about heroes such as Jack the Giant Killer and Peer Gynt who slay them. In European tales, they are known by different names. The word ogre came into English from the French fairy tales of Perrault. Giants are sometimes ents in Britain, and in Scotland, etins. In Scandinavian tales they are often trolls, since the difference between giants and trolls in the older folk stories is not very clear. Giants live in cold, wild, and remote places, and in mountains, while trolls prefer forests and mountains closer to human homesteads where they are sometimes connected with rocks and ravines in the landscape. Trolls in more recent Scandinavian tales, especially children's stories, are generally depicted as small, with long noses and mosslike hair. Some of these trolls may seem quite good-natured and shy, living peacefully in the hills with their wives and families, but most of them, like giants, have dark tempers, and one should never dare to provoke them. In Icelandic folk and fairy tales, trolls seem to be just the same as the giants from whom they are descended.

Most giants in fairy tales appear dull and clumsy. In some comical folk tales, peaceful, rather sleepy giants do honest work such as baking bread and building bridges. In most tales, however, giants are so fierce and wild that it is almost impossible for humans to survive their wrath; and although their blows may be clumsy and awkward, there is nothing as terrifying as the rage and sheer force with which they can throw rocks and uproot trees. In several Icelandic tales, giants hurl rocks at churches, buildings that make these creatures angry. Giants and ogres can tear humans in two and usually want to eat them, but because they are so dim-witted some cunning humans can outsmart them, such as the Grimms' "Clever Little Tailor," who tricks two giants into fighting one another. Mollie Whuppie and Hop o' my Thumb, the girl and boy in the fairy tales with those names, come upon fierce, stupid giants who want to kill them and eat them up, but these children trick the monsters into beating to death their own giant daughters instead, or slitting the throats of their own ogre-children.

One thing that can be said about giants is that they come in all forms and kinds. Some giants are as large as mountains. There are giants so tall that they have no need of boats but can wade through the sea carrying objects or even people. One of these kidnapped a princess and walked about through the sea carrying her in a basket on his back. Others, however, are huge in stature but almost human in appearance. Most ogresses can take on a human shape for a time and appear identical to a beautiful princess or a bride, but then change back to their own truly hideous forms. Some giants, trolls, etins, or ogres are many-headed. Others are deformed in having only one arm, one leg, or one eye, and in this they resemble the Greek Cyclopes, who had but one eye in the middle of their foreheads. This was a recurring feature. In the Welsh Arthurian *Lady of the Fountain*, an enormous, fearsome forester with one foot and one eye controlled herds of wild animals. A huge, single-eyed hag in Scottish myth created lakes by throwing rocks and peat into the sea, and in a Norwegian tale, three trolls as tall as fir trees shared one eye among the three of them, passing it from one to the other. The mythic Irish Fomorians, an early supernatural race who became giants in folklore, were both ugly and deformed in that some of them had only one arm, one leg, or one eye. One of these Fomorians, Balor of the Evil Eye, had a single eye so terrible that no one could look at it and live. One-eyed Fomorians were responsible for the deaths of several legendary Irish kings.

Part of the strange and varying nature of giants is that, as much as most of them were so hideous, the daughters of giants could be very beautiful indeed. In some texts of the King Arthur legend, for example, Queen Guinevere's father was a giant. This notion was developed as a popular story theme. "The Battle of the Birds," sometimes known as "The Prince and the Giant's Daughter," is a fairy tale of a prince who finds himself at a giant's castle, where he falls in love with his host's lovely daughter, but this is a dangerous place. The giant sets three tasks for the young man before he can marry the daughter, tasks so impossible that they require magical assistance. This story was widely told, in many different versions, all over Europe,[6] and it is also an ancient tale.

A medieval story included in the Welsh *Mabinogion*[7] has the same giant's daughter theme. *Culhwch and Olwen* is dated from about 1100,[8] making this one of the earliest Welsh texts in prose. Coming upon this tale after reading the others in the *Mabinogion*, as Andrew Breeze expresses it so well in *Medieval Welsh Literature*, "is like travelling from a princess's court to the hall of a wild Celtic chieftain. *Culhwch and Olwen* is the oldest, most primitive, most archaic, most exuberant, and (we might add) most barbaric of the tales of the *Mabinogion*."[9]

The hero of the tale, Culhwch, was King Arthur's cousin. The knight refused to marry his stepmother's daughter, and so, as angry stepmothers were inclined to do in stories, she put a curse on him. Under this curse, he could marry no one except the one maiden named Olwen, who lived with her father, the fierce giant Ysbaddaden, in a fortress from which no challenger had ever emerged alive. Undaunted, the valiant young Culhwch set off with a group of knights on a difficult quest to find the maiden. When they came to the giant's fortress and Culhwch laid eyes on the fair maiden, he was in love: "Yellower was her head than the flower of the broom, whiter was her flesh than the foam of the wave ... redder were her cheeks than the reddest foxgloves."[10] Before Culhwch could marry Olwen, however, the giant set for him a great many virtually impossible tasks to complete. One of them involved chasing a magical boar from Ireland, through Wales, then Brittany, and all the way back to Cornwall, where the giant's fortress was. No knight alone could have completed even a small part of these challenges, but with King Arthur's assistance and some powerful magic, Culhwch's tasks were finally accomplished and Olwen was free to marry her knight and hero.

In Norse mythology, through their beautiful daughters the old race of giants merged with the gods. The god Frey married a fair young giantess, Gerd. The half-god Loki had a giantess mother, and together with an ogress had a daughter who became goddess of the underworld. The god Heimdall was raised by nine giant mothers. There were many relationships such as these.[11] Most significantly, Odin's own mother was a giantess; she was Bestla, a daughter of the frost giant Bölthorn. Together with the giantess Rind, Odin had a son named Váli. With this mythic notion of the marriages of the beautiful daughters of giants to the gods, and with the great number of gods who were either descended in some way from giantesses or were raised by them, the giant race had a significant impact on all those who lived in Ásgard.

The following is an unusual story with the giant's daughter theme, in that a god does not journey to giant land. Instead, a giantess comes to Ásgard and claims a husband. Her marriage to a Vanir god, however, is not a happy one. The first part of this story is definitely ancient. Some stanzas of a skaldic poem, "Haustlöng," written around the year 900, describe a scene from this myth as it was painted on a shield.[12] But prior even to that shield-poem, the earliest known skald, Bragi, alluded to the story, indicating that at least some parts of it were known in the late ninth century.[13] It is a true Viking Age story, and it begins with the father of the giantess.

Thjazi's Daughter[14]

In his cold mountain home, the giant Thjazi thought about the gods in Ásgard who possessed apples that prevented them from ever growing old. He yearned for some of these, and he had a plan. The next time he saw Loki, he turned himself into an enormous eagle that tormented that god until he struck at the eagle with his staff. Loki then found that his staff was stuck fast, both to the eagle and to his hand, whereupon the eagle flew off with him, promising to let him go only if Loki would bring him some of the apples, together with Idun, the goddess of eternal youth who guarded them. Loki would have promised anything, and agreed. The gods were furious when they discovered that their beloved Idun was gone, along with her apples. Without Idun's magic fruit they began to experience the signs of aging. The gods knew, then, that their very existence was threatened. Odin demanded that Loki undo this calamity and bring the goddess back.

Disguised as a falcon, Loki flew off to the icy mountains where Idun was held prisoner. With a magic spell, he turned her into a nut and, with her grasped tightly between his claws, flew towards home. But the giant had shifted into his eagle shape again and was in pursuit. Odin saw them coming, the eagle gaining fast upon the falcon. He ordered a raging fire to be built that scorched Thjazi's wings as he flew into Ásgard. When the eagle fell to earth, the gods killed it. But Loki was safe and the gods had their Idun back.

However, the giant's beautiful daughter, Skadi, was at home in the snowy mountains waiting for her father to return, and when he didn't she became angry. Wearing a helmet and a coat of mail, and armed with her sword and shield, Skadi set out for Ásgard, swearing to avenge her father's death. The gods wanted no bloodshed from this giantess. Odin threw Thjazi's eyes up into the heavens so they would shine as two stars in the sky forever. As further compensation for losing her father, he offered Skadi a husband. From among all the gods, she most wanted to marry the handsome Baldr, but was tricked into marrying Njörd instead, a god who lived near the sea and controlled the winds for fishermen.

This marriage was not a success. When Njörd had lived only a short time in Skadi's mountain home, he hated it there with the howling of wolves, and he missed his swans. And Skadi found she could not live by the sea where the screeching gulls wakened her each morning. Skadi was a proud and vigorous giantess. She left Njörd and returned to her home in her beloved mountains and pine woods, where it snowed and she could ski and shoot wild animals with her bow and arrows. Very early, the giantess Skadi became known as a ski-goddess.

Most giants, like Thjazi, wanted to steal goddesses and destroy Ásgard. In fairy tales, too, giants stole things from humans, even a very poor family's only cow. They wanted human children, and particularly they took young maidens or, as in "The Red Ettin," the daughters of kings, and carried them far away to their mountain caves and castles. In a Norwegian folk ballad, a young man rescued his kidnapped bride from the cave of a giantess high up in the mountains and escaped with her on skis. When the giantess realized the girl was missing, she hastened down the mountain after the pair, accompanied by eighteen other giants so huge and fast that they left behind them a trail of trees bent to the ground. She was right behind the couple, who had stopped at the edge of a fjord, when the first rays of the morning sun appeared over the mountaintops and turned all the giants to stone.[15]

Similar to dwarfs, dawn could be fatal to giants and trolls. Living in dark pine forests, in caves and clefts in the mountains, or wherever it was cold and gloomy, giants avoided the sun, which had the power to turn them into stone. For centuries, stone circles inspired folk tales with the theme that the stones had been giants caught dancing at daybreak. In Iceland, night-trolls were dangerous creatures of the dark who turned to stone in daylight. One of these night-trolls crept up to the window of a farmhouse on a Christmas Eve, where a girl was all alone inside except for a small child she held in her arms. The troll sang to the girl through the window, and the quick-witted girl sang right back to him. All the whole night long they sang back and forth to each other, the girl matching the troll verse for verse, and in the morning it was quiet. But, when the others returned home that day, they saw a large stone on the path between the farm buildings that had not been there before.[16]

Some giants and trolls seemed to have been made out of ancient stones come to life, and giant names were Ironstone, Bride of Stone, and Power of the Mountain. Giants used stone clubs as weapons. Some of them had stone shields and helmets, and even boats made of stone. In the same ancient shield-poem with the stanzas about the giant Thjazi are stanzas that describe different scenes on the shield; these depict the story of the giant Hrungnir, whose head and shield were made of stone, and who carried an enormous whetstone as a weapon, ready to be hurled.[17] The story of Hrungnir is another Viking Age story, and it introduces us to the giants' worst enemy and their fiercest foe.

Hrungnir rode into Ásgard one day and in the gods' hall became very drunk and unruly. The giant was boasting that he was going to drink all the gods' ale, destroy Ásgard, and take away with him two goddesses, Thor's wife Sif and the beautiful Freyja. When Thor arrived home and asked what Hrungnir was doing there threatening the gods, the brazen giant challenged him to a duel. He should not have done this. At the arranged time and place, the huge Hrungnir stood all alone on a rocky field with his whetstone on his shoulder waiting for Thor to arrive, when suddenly there was lightning and a great clap of thunder. Instantly, there stood Thor, the strongest of all the gods and the god of thunder. Thor hurled Mjöllnir, his giant-killing weapon created by dwarfs. This hammer had already broken the skulls of many frost giants and mountain giants. Now it flew through the air shattering the giant's whetstone, then, finding its mark, crushed Hrungnir's stone skull to pieces.

Thor could throw stones farther than a giant, could out-eat and out-drink a giant, and could answer more riddles in a contest of wits. He never lost a wager with a giant, and his hammer Mjöllnir never once missed its mark. Thor's encounters with giants, trolls, and monsters were a popular subject matter of the early poets, and poems about this god are filled with power and fury. From his lecture notes on the *Elder* or *Poetic Edda*, Tolkien described to his students at Oxford the impact on him of first reading these poems in Old Norse: "Few who have been through this process can have missed the sudden recognition that they had unawares met something of tremendous force, something that in parts (for it has various parts) is still endowed with an almost demonic energy, in spite of the ruin of its form."[18] Even in an English translation the wildness of these poems, the energy, is there, as in the lines from a poem below.

In "The Lay of Hymir" (*Hymiskvida*), a giant called Hymir challenges Thor to a fishing contest. When the god baits his hook with an ox head, he pulls up, not a fish, but the great Midgard serpent. This monster encircles the world of men, and together with the Fenrir wolf will destroy it at the end. Fortunately, either Hymir cuts Thor's fishing line, as in one version of the story, or the serpent just falls back into the depths.

Doughtily drew   undaunted Thór
on board the boat   the baneful worm;
his hammer hit   the high hair-fell
of greedy Garm's   grisly brother.
Then screeched all scars   and screamed all fiends,

then shook and shivered   the shaggy hills.
In the sea then sank   that serpent again.[19]

Thor eventually kills Hymir, too. Allusions in poetry to Thor fishing up this serpent date back to the ninth century and pre-conversion, Viking times.[20] It seems natural, that although Odin was the head of the pantheon of Norse gods, Thor was the most popular with the Vikings. The many stories of Thor killing giants were highly developed and widely spread during the Viking era. Included in "Poetic Diction," the reference work for poets in the *Prose Edda*, are names of giants that Thor fought and killed who are otherwise unknown, and so there must have been a great many more stories on this theme that have not survived. "You broke Leikn's bones, you pounded Thrivaldi, you cast down Starkad, you stood over the dead Gialp."[21] Those lines were written by Vetrlidi Sumarlidason, a pagan skald opposed to Christianity, who was murdered in Iceland by a missionary in 999 for his staunchly pagan writing.[22] The list continues: "There was a clang on Keila's crown, you broke Kiallandi completely, before that you slew Lut and Leidi, you made Buseyra bleed, you halted Hengiankiapta, Hyrrokkin died previously, yet was the dusky Svivor's life taken earlier."[23]

Usually, associating the stories of the gods in mythology with actual religious beliefs is not useful, since so little evidence of pre-Christian religion remains. But there is ample evidence of the worship of Thor where it was widespread in Iceland, Norway, and some parts of Sweden. In the tenth and eleventh centuries, the Vikings spread his cult beyond Scandinavia, and so Thor worship was strong even in Dublin in the eleventh century.

Carved images of Thor depict him as a huge god with a beard, either fishing for the enormous serpent or holding his hammer. Thor's hammer, the shape of a shortened cross, was a powerful symbol of the pagan

Norse religion. Archaeological finds from Viking Age sites in Denmark, Sweden, and Norway reveal hoards that were buried in years prior to the end of paganism, and in these caches are a large number of iron, bronze, and silver amulets in this hammer shape, some of them finely decorated.[24] Many of these amulets were worn around the neck in the same way that Christians wore the cross. Followers of Thor may have used these even more after the introduction of Christianity. "Thórr's hammer amulets appear to gain popularity in response to the wearing of the Christian cross,"[25] Thomas DuBois explains in *Nordic Religions in the Viking Age*. They "can in many senses be termed an 'anti-cross.'"[26] DuBois describes metalsmiths' moulds, discovered from the late Viking period, that could produce both crosses and hammer amulets, and so a single smith could provide for the needs of either Christians or Thor worshippers. The hammer shape was inscribed on early coins and carved on boundary stones, memorial and gravestones, and runic stones with inscriptions to Thor.

Thor was one of the three predominant northern gods. Each of Odin, Thor, and Frey had their own following, although women also worshipped Freyja. Odin, as a god of war, wisdom, and poetry, was venerated by kings and warriors as well as by poets and learned men. But it appears that his son Thor, who had a fierce temper, was quick to strike, and fought giants, was in many regions by far the favourite god. Thor's cult among farmers and fishermen was a challenge to the repression of paganism in areas where Thor worship remained strong, even long into the Christian age.

But we cannot assume that the god of the cult was the same as the god in the stories. From the tales of Thor, his primary role, one would think his only role, was giant killing. In the pagan imagination giants were an integral force to be reckoned with, since most of them were inherently malicious and intent on taking and destroying everything that gods and humans loved. There had to be a giant killer to combat the evil that had been embodied in them since the very beginning of time.

11

Souls and Spirits

In a saga, a farmhand and a housemaid living on an Icelandic homestead were driving cattle past a burial cairn when they heard Gunnar, the dead man in it, reciting some verses. Upon returning to the farm, they reported what they had heard to Gunnar's mother, and so, a few nights later two young men, the dead man's son and a loyal friend, also visited the cairn. They had not been waiting long when they heard the same thing. A cloud had darkened the moonlight, the cairn opened, and it seemed to be lit from within. They saw Gunnar sitting upright and clearly heard his voice: "he would rather, helm-clad, / holding to his shield aye, / fall upon the field than / flee."[1] Then the cairn closed. The dead man had spoken of his decision to die at the hands of his enemies rather than leave Iceland. Another time, some men saw Gunnar standing outside his cairn, looking at the moon and smiling.

Early storytellers, such as the author who around 1280 wrote *Njál's Saga* in which these incidents take place, were familiar with the idea of ghosts. The most eerie one might well be the revenant of a heathen shepherd, Glam, who haunted a farm in *Grettir's Saga*. But, as a ghost story, it is hard to match the tale of Helgi and Sigrún in the *Poetic Edda*.[2] After Helgi had been murdered, and Sigrún was grieving for her beloved husband, her maid saw near his grave mound a figure that resembled Helgi riding into it with a retinue of other dead men. She told Sigrún to come at once. Helgi, still covered with blood, declared to his wife that he had been allowed a journey home for only one night before departing for Valhalla. Sigrún prepared a bed, and they slept together in the burial mound. The next morning, Helgi and his men rode away, and shortly thereafter Sigrún died of sorrow, but it was said that they were born again as a prince and a valkyrie.

The apparitions in these Icelandic tales speak as if they are alive, have their own bodily form, and seem to be more solidly physical than most ghosts in present-day stories, which appear more like shadows and visions. We have no way of knowing whether the early authors actually believed in the existence of such spirits of the dead, or whether the tales were simply ghost stories similar to those that anyone might tell today, but likely the idea of ghosts had wider credibility then than now. Certainly, the appearance of such apparitions is a common theme in folk literature. The notion of restless ghosts that will not stay in their graves but wander in the hills and continue to haunt the living has been found in folk tales throughout the world, since ancient times. Drowned sailors visit their bereaved lovers, dead infants haunt their parents, and ghosts of mothers comfort their children at night.

In the early literature of northern Europe and in the later folk stories, songs, and ballads, we find other concepts of after-death spirits, besides ghosts. These do not reflect the Christian view of souls released from their earthly life to enter a heavenly realm. Instead, they represent a variety of ideas that were at one time widespread in storytelling tradition, and yet a common theme runs through them all – the soul does not expire when a person dies, but continues its existence, eventually passing into another earthly or otherworldly form. The heroes of old did not entirely cease to exist when they were slain in battle. King Arthur continued his existence as a shadowy presence on a western otherworld island. In Norse mythology, the finest warriors with fatal battle-wounds journeyed to Valhalla to be with Odin, while other fallen soldiers proceeded to Freyja's hall at Fólkvang, a field where armies could continue to fight in battles forever.

Some tales depict souls of the dead leaving the human world to join the ever-living fairies or the elves in the mountains. A person may glimpse someone familiar, yet recently dead, in the midst of a group of fairies. One of these sightings was a young man riding at midnight with a troop of fairy riders on the very day he died, still showing his death-wound. In the Welsh classic *The Sleeping Bard*, a poet walking in the mountains stopped to rest and had a vision of a rabble of women in green dresses and red caps dancing, and he thought that they were gypsies, until he recognized in their midst some old women of his acquaintance who had long been dead and buried. Then he knew that these women were now among the Welsh fairies, the Tylwyth Teg.[3]

A folk myth endures in tales, legends, and ballads of some souls, who, before finding their final resting place, were simply driven round and round in the wind, carried by it in large groups of ghosts and wraiths. When a cold wind blew on a dark night, this could be a parade of death known as the Wild Hunt roaring past, with a phantom rider leading hounds and horses and a host of disembodied souls. Church clergy condemned the notion of the Wild Hunt as pagan superstition, but the legends remain. In some of these, the phantom rider and gatherer of the dead was Odin, or the wind god Woden. In Ireland, the hunt was portrayed as a cavalcade of fairies sweeping by, and in Wales, Gwyn ap Nudd, the king of the fairies and lord of the dead, led the hunt with a pack of white hounds. In France, the huntsman was Hellequin (who later became Harlequin), riding with a troop of black horses, while in English legend Herla, a mythical king of ancient Britain, led the hunt.

Souls of some young children were drawn away to join an invisible crowd of children's souls that swept through the woods and over the fields in a single company. In a Norwegian tale, a mother who had lost her child saw one night at her little one's grave the ghosts of many children sweeping past, and at the end behind all the others was her own child, so tired it could hardly keep up with the rest. Happier than these were the dead children released from earth to live with Dame Holde, a guardian of un-baptized children as well as of the souls of children not yet born. There is a rich collection of folk material about the character of Dame Holde, who was known in different regions as Frau Holle, Hulde, Percht, and Berta. This mother-figure appears in fairy tales when children are lost, are near a pond, or fall down a well only to find themselves in her garden. She rewards those who are good, helps girls and women with their spin-ning, and protects all children, living or dead.

Over and over in fairy tales, we find the notion of a soul of the dead coming to reside in a bird. In the Grimms' "Three Little Birds," each time that a queen's evil sisters threw one of her newborn babies into a river a bird flew up into the air. In another Grimm tale, "The Juniper Tree," a stepsister lovingly buried the bones of her murdered brother under a tree. Then smoke and fire appeared, a bird flew out of the flaming branches, and it was as if her brother were still alive. In "The Rose Tree," a grieving brother buried his dead sister beneath a rose tree. One spring day the tree flowered, and among the rose blossoms was a white bird that sang and sang. Its song revealed the true story of how the girl had been murdered, for anyone who would listen.

A further story theme related to the concept of the continuing exis-tence of the soul has roots in an early belief, prevalent throughout northern Europe, that souls of dead parents and ancestors continued to play an important role in the lives of the living. Ancestor worship was a large part of pagan religion. Families venerated deceased family mem-bers as sources of help and guidance. "Amid the vagaries of life in the Viking Age, people sought and found guidance in a variety of spiritual allies," according to Thomas DuBois in *Nordic Religions in the Viking Age*. "Ancestors constituted one of the most ancient and widespread types of deity worshipped in the Nordic religion."[4] In the early literature, spirits of deceased parents and ancestors protect the family, sometimes appear-ing in dreams to offer helpful advice or warnings.

The concept of a deceased family member becoming a guardian spirit is reflected in the many fairy tales in which children are helped by a friendly animal or a bird that was once a mother or a brother. This beautiful theme of a mother's soul protecting her child in the shape of a bird occurs in the Grimm brothers' well-known "Aschenputtel," the German version of "Cinderella." There are a great many variations of this Cinderella type of fairy tale.[5] In all of them, a girl who is kind and has a good heart, yet is badly mistreated and despised by those around her, with magical help achieves recognition and wins the heart of a prince or a king. This benevolent magic often provides her with dresses so lovely that no earthly person could have created them. The version of Cinderella most familiar today is Charles Perrault's "Cendrillon," but the story was already old when Perrault wrote his tale in the seventeenth century and added details such as the pumpkin coach, footmen, fairy godmother, and glass slippers that would appeal to ladies of the French nobility.

The Grimms' "Aschenputtel," is a simpler tale. In this version, a helpful, loving spirit appears one day in the form of a white bird in a tree which Aschenputtel planted on her mother's grave and watered every day with her tears. When the time of the king's ball arrives, the evil stepmother keeps Aschenputtel at home with the task of picking lentils, beans, and barley out of the ashes, while she and her daughters attend the dances. But a crowd of doves and other birds flutter into the house and set to work to help. Then the white bird throws down from the tree splendid dresses and golden shoes that Aschenputtel can wear to the castle.

The mother's spirit helping her daughter in magical ways appears in other variants of the story. In the Scottish "Rashin Coatie," the mother's love endures in a little red calf that provides the hungry girl with food. In this tale, the maiden does not go to a castle, but in fine clothes the red calf has given her attends the church, where a young prince falls in love with her. I like this Finnish version of the story, in which the spirit of the mother continues to exist in a birch tree.

Liisa and the Prince[6]

An old man and his wife lived with their little daughter Liisa in a tupa (a cottage), near a pasture where they kept some cows and sheep. One day a small black sheep became lost, and when Liisa's mother went into the woods to look for it she met an ogress. This creature cast a spell to turn the woman into her own likeness. Then the ogress returned to the pasture with the lost sheep and looking exactly like the old man's wife! The banished mother, now an enormous ugly hag, ran and ran through the forest. Finally, she sat under a birch tree by a river and wept until her spirit left her and became the spirit of the tree.

The ogress in the form of Liisa's mother raised the child, but she dressed the girl in rags and treated her cruelly, while her new step-sister was given warm clothes and the softest bed in the tupa. When the sisters were older, the king invited everyone from far and near to his castle for a feast on three evenings during which the prince would choose a bride. But, while the stepsister and ogress went to the castle, Liisa had to stay home picking barley seeds out of the ashes of the bath-house hearth. She decided to run away, and deep in the forest the birch tree called out to her. The spirit in the tree instructed her to take one of its branches, and with this as a brush all of the barley seeds would fly out of the ashes and into a basket. Then the spirit said, "Bathe now in the river," and gave her a dress of the finest linen, shoes of the softest white leather, and a horse to ride to the castle.

On the other two evenings, the same thing happened. Liisa was left at home with an impossible task, but with her mother's help she soon arrived at the castle, where the prince marvelled at her beauty and asked her to marry him. At the end of the third evening, when

Liisa had to hurry away in order to be at home when the stepmother and sister returned, the prince asked her for a keepsake, and she gave him her small, jewelled slipper.

The next day, the king's soldiers visited every home to discover the owner of the slipper, but it took an old, wise gypsy to help the prince find Liisa and to expose the ogress's true identity. The gypsy tricked the ogress and her daughter into stepping into a tub of scorching hot tar, where they perished. Liisa's mother could then rest in peace, knowing that her daughter would be happy at last.

In his *Red Fairy Book*, Andrew Lang included a version of the same story, from the Karelia area of eastern Finland. In "The Wonderful Birch," the ogress is a witch, and she and her daughter do not die in hot tar. Instead, the cruel stepsister, in anguish at being rejected by the prince, turns herself into a golden hemlock tree. The witch, furious at the turn of events, hastens to the palace, where she uses more of her magical arts to turn the prince's new wife into a reindeer of the forest. There the young woman lives with a herd of reindeer until her husband, with the help of an old widow woman, finds her and transforms her back into his wife once more.[7]

The notion of souls and spirits continuing to exist outside the living body, where they can enter into a tree, a bird, or an animal, is seen in some tales in which a spirit leaves a body for a time. In the form of a butterfly, a soul flies about, having adventures and seeing many wonders, before fluttering back into the body. There are tales of witches or ogresses who collect human souls and keep them imprisoned in cages, and stories of giants who can take out their own souls and keep them hidden far away. Sometimes, the soul is hidden in something akin to a Russian nesting doll. A beast in the Scottish tale "The Sea Maiden" stole a princess, but he could not be killed until his soul was found. This was not easy. On an island in a loch there was a white-footed hind, and inside the hind there was a hoodie bird, and inside the bird there was a trout, and in the mouth of the trout was an egg, and inside the egg was the soul of the beast. When that egg was broken, the beast would be dead.[8]

In folk literature, spirits come in all forms. Of all of the supernatural beings that we find in folk and fairy tales, some are of variations and kinds that fit into no particular group, yet many of them seem to be as similar to nature spirits as anything. River sprites appear beside Norwegian mountain waterfalls, elf-like creatures haunt lonely places in the Welsh hills, and gentle female spirits called wood wives inhabit old German and Scandinavian forests. Tales are filled with otherworldly beings such as these, existing close to the rocks, forests, and streams of the natural world. Different but corresponding beings are found in the folklore traditions of most cultures.

Long ago, the northern European world of folk belief was similarly filled with elemental spirits. When the first settlers arrived in Iceland, during the last hundred years before Christianity was introduced, they were cautious about the spirits that at that time inhabited the island. It is well noted in family sagas, in *The Book of Settlements* (*Landnámabók*), and in laws that some of these early settlers found on their new farms land spirits or "rock-dwellers" already there attached to the land. In the pre-Christian world view, a host of spirits could be connected with all parts of nature, both animate and inanimate. These presences were not beyond the world of humans; they were nearby, in rocks and springs and forest groves. The concept of many beings that were strange, menacing, or kindly, but all of them unpredictable, played a part in the mystical experiences of a pre-Christian peasantry that was steeped in ancient traditions and superstitions.

It is not surprising that remnants from deeply held folk traditions would have become embedded in folklore, finding a new form in imaginative literature. Whatever the origin or literary basis of any of the supernatural beings found in the old stories, whether fairies, elves, dwarfs, giants, or spirits, in all of their many varied manifestations the remarkable creatures of the early imagination make up a large part of the fairy tale world.

PART THREE

Stories from the Pagan Year

12

Festival Days

Seasonal festivals were important ritual days in the pagan year, and these continued to be observed into Christian times. The early literature portrays these days as brief, mysterious times when the world of humans was touched by the supernatural and impacted by mythic events. More recently, from time to time we come upon a folk story in which events hinge on one of these old sacred days, and then, strangely, gods or goddesses never appear but fairies and elves do, and something magical occurs.

The Celtic year was divided into two parts, summer and winter, with festivals heralding each new season. The beginning of summer was Beltaine on the first day of May, celebrated with bonfires, green boughs, and flowers. Winter began with Samain, a festival of the dead, when souls of the deceased came back to visit the living on the eve of the first of November – All Hallow's Eve and our Hallowe'en. In folk belief, these were the times of the year when the supernatural world was particularly active. Halfway between these major festivals fell two others, Imbolc on the first day of February, associated with lambs and with ewe's milk, and Lughnasa, a harvest feast on the first of August named for Lug, a celebrated chief of the Tuatha Dé Danann. The Celtic festivals were based not on the solstices, the turning points of the sun's path in the sky, but on the changing seasons. They belonged to farmers' and herdsmen's calendars, and were traditions preserved primarily by rural populations; they marked the times of the year when sheep and cows were sent to the higher meadows to pasture on fresh grass, and when they were brought back to shelter for the winter.

Germanic people used the same half-year division from May to November. In central Europe and Scandinavia, Walpurgis Night on the eve of the first of May is a remnant of an old festival marking the beginning of summer, and the Feast of All Souls still marks the beginning of winter. More celebrated occasions in Scandinavia were always Midwinter Night, the festival of the winter solstice, which was observed in pre-Christian times throughout most of Europe, and Midsummer Night at the summer solstice, still a popular celebration for Scandinavians. The old festivals were always celebrated with the evening and night more than the day; nights were considered to be more of a spirit time.

Our knowledge of the observance of these days by the pre-Christian people of northern Europe is understandably limited. We know little other than that these occasions were especially commemorated. There is evidence from both archaeology and classical sources that the early Celtic and Germanic people celebrated their sacred days not in churches but out of doors, on hilltops or in forest clearings. There were many holy places. One piece of evidence for this comes to us from an observation in Tacitus' first-century *Germania*, that German people visited woods and groves consecrated to their deities dwelling there, which to Tacitus were a "mysterious presence."[1]

All through the Middle Ages, vestiges of older culture survived in the traditions of people who continued to observe these special days. As Jacob Grimm expressed it in his preface to *Teutonic Mythology*, "The festivals of a people present a tough material, they are so closely bound up with its habits of life, that they will put up with foreign additions, if only to save a fragment of festivities long loved and tried."[2] Centuries after pagan beliefs had apparently disappeared, the festivals had, in fact, simply been absorbed into the Christian faith. Samain became All Souls Day, Imbolc became Candlemas, and Lughnasa became Lammas. The first of May, which had been a Roman flower-goddess festival, came to be identified with special devotions to the Virgin Mary. Midsummer was Christianized by being dedicated to Saint John the Baptist, and some of the beloved customs of Yule, the old Midwinter festival, became part of Christmas. Lingering aspects of the older festival days were accommodated in Christian culture as folk traditions.

In the ancient legends and stories that are connected with these days, there is a mythic and folkloric strain, and in fairy tales centred on these days we find a distinctly otherworld magic. There seemed to be a small crack in the world as we know it – and anything could happen!

13

Beltaine

For centuries, the old Celtic festival of Beltaine continued to be celebrated as May Day, associated with boughs and fresh spring flowers, fiddle music and dances, a May queen, and sometimes a maypole. The day is still observed in Ireland, Scotland, and Wales. Over the years, stories centred on May Day have conveyed this as a time when the boundary between the human world and the otherworld became thin, our reality and the other one blended, and then mysterious things happened, either for good or for evil. Spirits became active. This was the fairies' trysting time, when they held dances and revels on the hills.

Several Welsh and Irish folk tales describe a lake with an island in it that exists only on May Day. On that morning, a door appears in a large rock beside the lake, and those who are brave enough to enter follow a passage under the water to the island, which remains invisible to anyone on shore. Visitors discover that the island is inhabited by a kind of fairy people of exquisite beauty, but inevitably, one May Day, a visitor puts a flower into his pocket before leaving the island, and from that day on the magic door is never to be seen. In other tales, a long-dead princess or king appears as a vision on May Day near his former castle. The following story from the south of Ireland is one of these.

The Legend of O'Donoghue[1]

One night, near the shore of the Lake of Killarney, a chieftain called O'Donoghue was holding a feast in his castle. He was entertaining his guests at the table, when suddenly he stood up. As if in a trance, he walked very slowly out of the castle and down to the shore of the lake. He kept walking. He stepped onto the surface of the water, walked on it to the centre of the lake, and then disappeared. For several years after this, he was seen at sunrise on May Day morning visiting his castle. One May Day, the crowd that had gathered to see if he would return again witnessed a strange event.

The night before had been wild and stormy, but in the morning the water was absolutely still. On the far shore a single wave formed, that grew larger and larger as it came across the lake, and behind the wave as if riding on it was a warrior on a white horse. This was O'Donoghue. Behind him were young men and women, a great company of them, all moving lightly over the water to the sound of music. When they reached the crowd, they turned and moved along the water's edge and then disappeared into a cleft in some rocks. For a while the music was still heard, but then it, too, vanished. The chieftain was never seen again.

The early Welsh stories set in a pre-Christian past are peppered with strange occurrences on the eve of May Day. Similar to most of the May Day stories, these primarily involve appearances and vanishings. For one thing, extraordinary babies arrived. Were they divine children? Pryderi, who was born on May Eve, has a central role in a group of four stories called "The Four Branches of the *Mabinogi*," which were likely written between 1050 and 1120.[2] Of the eleven traditional stories included in the *Mabinogion*, these four particularly have "a sense of 'otherness,'" and subject matter in the nature of "religious myths," according to the Welsh scholar Brynley Roberts: "Most of the main characters are, in origin, deities and a continuing theme is the relationship of Annwfn, the Otherworld, and this world."[3]

Pryderi's mother, Rhiannon, has been identified with the pre-Christian horse-goddess Epona, and Pryderi's story parallels that of Mabon, a Welsh divine-youth figure who originated with a Celtic god of music and poetry, a god known in Britain during the time it was occupied by the Romans.

The Birth of Pryderi[4]

This is how Pryderi's father first saw Rhiannon: Pwyll and his men had ventured high up on a mound that was known to be a location for unearthly occurrences, when they beheld a wonder. A lady in a robe of shining gold was riding a pale white horse along the roadway that went by the mound. She appeared to be riding slowly, yet as slowly as she was moving, none of Pwyll's men on their horses were able to catch up to her. This was the woman Pwyll would marry. When their baby was born, Rhiannon had six women carefully guard the infant. But, at midnight, everyone fell asleep, and so no one witnessed the baby being snatched from Rhiannon's side. He simply disappeared on the very night of his birth.

At the same time, in the darkness of that May Eve night, far away in another kingdom the baby appeared just as mysteriously as he had vanished from the castle. The lord of that kingdom, who had once been Pwyll's vassal, was in his stable tending to a foal that had just been born. His mare was the finest in the kingdom, and every May Eve it gave birth to a foal that always disappeared on that same night. He was determined to stay in the stable and find the cause. Suddenly, a monstrous claw came through the window and took hold of the foal. The man swung his sword and cut off the claw, then ran outside to confront the monster. It was gone, but, where the monster had been, a baby lay on the ground, wrapped in a mantle of brocaded silk.

The man and his wife raised this child, Pryderi, for four years as their own son. Eventually, news travelled to them that Rhiannon had been accused of murdering her baby and as punishment had been compelled to do public penance. They realized, then, that the infant the monster had dropped outside the stable, who had grown so fair and tall and strong beyond his four years, very much resembled Pwyll. The child must be Rhiannon's. The next day, with the child mounted on the horse that was born on the same night, they rode to Pwyll's castle. Eventually, Pryderi became lord over all of that land, Dyfed, until a time when it fell under an enchantment and he became trapped in the otherworld.

May Eve also features in the legend of the birth of Taliesin, another key figure in Welsh tradition, who, after King Arthur and Myrddin, or Merlin, is perhaps the most well-known character in Welsh literature. He was a sixth-century poet, however much debate has surrounded the authenticity of the poetry and legend connected with Taliesin. The current view is that he was a true historical figure and bard, but over the centuries a legendary persona of Taliesin developed, to whom many poems are attributed and much folklore is attached.[5] The story of Taliesin's birth belongs to this folklore.[6]

In the tale, which also accounts for Taliesin's renowned wisdom and powers of prophecy, his mother, Ceridwen, was either a shape-shifting goddess or a witchlike hag. One day, she set a blind man and a boy, Gwion Bach, to stir a cauldron that was filled with her magical brew that could impart knowledge and inspiration, but when three drops of the hot liquid landed on the boy's fingers and then he licked them, Ceridwen was angry. He had gained wisdom and visionary powers that were not intended for such as him. Gwion ran away and she chased him, for a whole year. The boy changed his shape with the seasons, so that he became a hare in the autumn, a fish in the winter, and a bird in the spring. To hunt him down, Ceridwen changed from a greyhound to an otter and then to a falcon. Finally, in the summer, she found him hiding in a barn disguised as a grain of corn, and turning herself into a black hen she ate him. He was reborn as her child, and was so beautiful that she could not bring herself to kill him. Instead, she wrapped the baby and threw him into the sea, where he drifted into a salmon weir.

On that May Eve, a youth, Elphin, was drawing fish from the weir when he found a leather bag floating in it. The bag contained the baby boy. Elphin called the child Taliesin, or "Radiant Brow," raised him as his own son, and became Taliesin's patron as the boy grew up to become famous throughout the land for his magic, prophecies, and poetry.

In Irish legend, Beltaine is a pivotal time in Ireland's history. One of the first groups of settlers landed on Irish soil on the first day of May. These were Partholón and his followers, a company of a thousand men and women. During the three hundred years that this population inhabited Ireland, they bravely fought against the evil Fomorians, but eventually the descendants of Partholón's people all succumbed to a mysterious plague. Another group of settlers, who also arrived on May Day, were the Tuatha Dé Danann, the magical, immortal folk who reached Ireland in a cloud that settled on the mountains of Connacht. They, too, became archenemies of the Fomorians. Centuries after the Tuatha Dé Danann arrived, another group of settlers landed – also on the first day of May. These were the Milesians, who displaced the old gods and whose culture remained dominant from then on. It becomes apparent that, in the legends, Beltaine does not represent simply a seasonal festival celebrating spring's return after the bleakness of winter, but something more, the commemoration of one race triumphing over another and the establishment of a new order in the land.

A Beltaine subject in the literature involves annual ritual conflicts and contests, which seem to be part of the larger mythic theme. In Welsh mythology, on every May Eve during the reign of King Lludd, two fierce dragons that represent an old battle, the Red Dragon and the White Dragon, fought, and with their strife raised a shriek that struck to the heart of Welsh people, terrifying those who heard it in every home in Wales. In another story from the same king's reign, King Lludd's beautiful daughter Creiddylad eloped with her lover Gwythyr.[7] On the very same night, before she could even sleep with Gwythyr, she was captured by Gwyn, who was lord of the otherworld, Annwfn. A battle then ensued between the human forces of Gwythyr and the otherworldly warriors of Gwyn, with fighting so savage that King Arthur himself came north to settle it. Eventually, Arthur made this peace agreement between the warring factions: Creiddylad would remain with her father's house throughout the year, and every May Day Gwythyr and Gwyn would fight to win the maiden. This fight took place every May Day, with no side ever winning. The ritual contest for a maiden every May Day between knights representing the human world and the otherworld seems an appropriately mythic May Day story. It is also compatible with a medieval practice of holding mock battles, tournaments, and archery competitions on the first day of May.

Creiddylad's kidnapping is echoed in the story of King Arthur's own Queen Guinevere, who, in most versions of the story, was abducted in the springtime. In Malory's popular version, the queen was celebrating May Day in the countryside with her companions, collecting spring flowers, when she was captured and carried off to the otherworld. The earliest mention of Guinevere's abduction is in *The Life of Gildas*,[8] written in the early twelfth century, and in this version, the king Melwas took her to his kingdom in the "summer country" and his stronghold there at Glastonbury, which has been associated with Avalon. King Arthur was prepared to fight Melwas until Saint Gildas intervened and reunited Arthur with his queen. In some accounts of the story, however, Guinevere was not an innocent, but was portrayed as being unfaithful to Arthur and leaving him willingly.

Traditions of May Day festivals in the British Isles changed little from the Middle Ages, despite attempts by the Puritans in the seventeenth century to abolish these activities in England, even with a parliamentary decree outlawing maypoles. At least as early as the seventeenth century, three popular figures from folk literature – Merlin, Robin Hood, and Maid Marian – had become identified with these festivals. These figures were connected with May Day in the same way that from time to time in the past there was a tendency for characters and events from folk mythology to become attached to this ancient day. Merlin, the old prophet and magician who could interact with the spirit world, sometimes made an appearance at May Day fairs, when an old man, strangely dressed and impersonating this character, joined into the festivities and entertained the crowd by prophesying future events.

A May Day king and queen were central characters in pageants, and for a long time and as recently as the nineteenth century, the king and queen of the May were called Robin and Marian, and May Day was Robin Hood's Day. The people gathered and danced for Robin Hood and his May bride, known as the Maiden or Marian, but most often Maid Marian. Plays enacting Robin Hood stories were a traditional part of May Day activities, and these entertainments included opportunities for swordplay and archery contests. One has to wonder at what time in the past Robin and Marian took on the identity of the May Day king and queen, or whether a figure from an ancient pageant evolved into the Robin Hood story character.

The legend of Robin Hood living in Sherwood Forest with the fair Maid Marian and having daring adventures with his band of men, including Will Scarlett, Little John, and Friar Tuck, has a long and well-known history. The earliest forms of the legend were ballads, rhymes, and songs.[9] In 1377, a drunken chaplain in *Piers Plowman* comments that he cannot repeat the Lord's Prayer but can sing the rhymes of Robin Hood. By 1450 the poems had become widely popular, and plays, stories, and ballads based on the adventures have been written throughout the centuries. Although children probably always enjoyed them, it was not until the nineteenth century that books of Robin Hood stories were produced especially for children.

Over the years, historians have sought evidence that a real Robin Hood existed, but there is not sufficient evidence to confirm any of the many attempts to explain the origins of the story. One account identifies him as the Earl of Locksley born in 1160, another as an Earl of Huntington who lived in the reign of Richard I. A third account suggests that he was born in Yorkshire around the year 1290 as the son, Robert, of a forester named Adam Hood. Several accounts have him christened Robert. When he went to live in the woods he beame Robin and married a girl, Matilda, who gave up for him her name, her parentage, and her father's castle to become Maid Marian of Sherwood Forest. For twenty years, the couple lived with a band of champions as outlaws and as king and queen of the forest.

A central theme in the familiar episodes is Robin's and his followers' animosity to the corrupt clergy, who were growing rich at the expense of the poor. Likely, stories with this theme originated at some time later than the thirteenth century, when the nobility and the clergy had become exceedingly wealthy and corrupt. Robin Hood is portrayed as devout with a simple and personal piety. He prays to the Virgin Mary and is a friend of honest, humble people. Robin Hood's woodland spirituality outside of the official church, and his identification with the king of the May, connected him with a more simple faith of the countryside. In 1549, a bishop recorded that his services were not attended on May Day. In fact, he found the church door locked fast. One of the parishioners explained to him that this was Robin Hood's Day, and the parish had gone to gather in the countryside for Robin Hood. May Day was a time to celebrate a new season with the woodland king and queen and to remember folk culture and traditions from the past.

14

Samain

The eve of the first day of November, the Irish Samain, was the other central day in the Celtic calendar, marking the beginning of winter and also the Celtic New Year. The festival was another spirit night, but this haunted occasion was the dark opposite of Beltaine. From ancient times, all over Europe, the first of November was a festival to honour the dead. As early as the seventh century, the old pagan day had evolved in Christian tradition into All Souls Day, a day to offer prayers for the departed.

Something of the spirit of the old festival remains in the North American tradition of All Hallows' Eve, or Hallowe'en, which was introduced to America in the 1840s with the immigrants who fled the Irish famine. Today's carved pumpkins, ghosts and witches, costumed children trick-or-treating for candy are all remnants from the old Irish folk traditions and customs. On this eve of the first day of winter, the cattle had been brought home from the high pastures, the skies were cold, and the land was stark and grey. It was a night to either stay indoors or light a bonfire to ward off spirits. Traditionally on this night, warm cakes and cider were left on a table ready for any souls of the dead who would be visiting their old homes one more time. Sometimes, a turnip was hollowed out and a candle put in it to provide a beacon of light for these night visitors. A frightening face carved in it, like a jack-o'-lantern, would keep away the unwanted spirits abroad in the countryside. When gangs of mischievous boys, in masks and costumes impersonating the spirits that might be about, came to one home after another demanding pennies or sweets, they were seldom refused.

In Irish folklore, Samain was haunted by more than the dead – a whole host of spirits was on the move. Fairy mounds were open on Samain evening, and the old Sidhe, fairies, and ghosts rushed out of their hills. There are folk tales of a dance of the fairies led by the king of the dead and his queen, while other tales describe a fair held by the fairies with goods to sell: fresh berries, apples, and all kinds of fruit, shoes, bits of clothing, and jewelry. This looked just like a normal country fair, with crowds dressed in brightly coloured but old-fashioned clothing milling about and dancing. But it could only be viewed from afar; if one ventured close, it all disappeared.

In stories, this was a potent night and the energy of dark powers was strong. The following tale has two narrative themes of Samain. One is that a sacrifice to these dark powers was required, or a payment had to be made to them; and the second is that on this dark night when the fairies ventured into the world of humans, a missing bridegroom, or more often a bride, might appear with the fairy folk as they filed out of their raths or hills. This one night she might be rescued, if her husband was brave enough to step forward and seize her as she passed by. If he called her name three times this might break the spell that held her. It is not hard to find fairy tales with this theme. Every Scottish person probably knows this tale in which a brave girl goes into the woods alone on Samain to save Tamlane, or Tam Lin, while the fairy queen and her followers try every spell they know, one after the other, to keep him.

Tamlane[1]

Janet was picking wild roses, and even though she had been warned never to go into the Caterhaugh Wood, she ventured off her familiar path into it. The wood was haunted by an elfin knight, Tamlane. Near a spring, Janet saw a saddled horse with no rider, but she was not frightened until Tamlane suddenly appeared at her side. Janet returned to her father's hall the next morning, without her maiden-hood, but with a strong desire to see the elf knight again. So it was not long before she returned once again to the Caterhaugh Wood.

Tamlane had not been born a fairy. The Queen of Elfland had stolen him to be her knight and he was the Queen's favourite, but the time had arrived when the fairies were obliged to pay a tribute of a human sacrifice to the gods of darkness. Tamlane was to be the chosen victim. Only if Janet could free him would he be safe, and she would have won both her human knight and a father for her unborn child.

Janet had only one chance. The next night was Hallowe'en when the fairy court would be riding by on their horses. Tamlane told Janet that they would be passing Miles Cross at midnight. Two companies of riders would pass by, and then, with the third company, Tamlane would be riding by the side of the Queen. Here Janet must try to pull him off his horse and hold him, no matter what shape he turned into. Then she must throw her cloak over him.

The next night, Janet went alone to the crossroads. It was cold and dark, and she waited a long time for the fairies to come. Finally, she heard them, the bells on their horses jingling. First one company rode by, and then another. In the third company, she saw the Fairy Queen, and there on a white horse was her own Tamlane. Springing forward, she seized his horse's bridle and pulled him down to the ground, but fairy spells kept him from her. He became a slimy newt that she could hardly grasp. She felt him change again and he became a biting adder, but still she clung tightly to him. He became like burning fire, and then a dove in her arms struggling to escape. Then he was a great white swan that beat its wings so power-fully that it took all her strength to hold it. Finally, in her arms she saw a young man, her own knight. With this last transformation Janet threw her cloak over him and heard the wail of the Fairy

Queen when she saw that the knight was lost to her. Tamlane, free at last from the Queen's spell, was with his Janet – and the fairies vanished away.

In the tales of ancient Irish kings and queens, this night when the other-world became active was associated with all things to do with the occult, with auguries, witches and fairies, and especially with monsters. In the darkness of Samain night, the great warrior-queen of Connacht, Medb, gathered all of her druids and poets around her for them to prophesy what good or evil would happen in the next year.[2] In another part of Ireland, a wicked queen, the witch Mongfhind, became closely associated with Samain. In a fairy tale–like plot, this queen kept her stepson from his rightful place as king, by having her brother rule until her own son was old enough to usurp him. Similar to Snow White's poisoned apple, this treacherous queen then placed a poisoned drink in her brother's hand, but he asked her to drink with him. She died on that Samain night. From then on, Samain was called "The Festival of Mongfhind," since as long as this witch had been alive she had occult powers, and the women of Munster, even long after her death, continued to address their petitions to her on that night.[3]

The kings of Ireland held a Samain feast every year at Tara, where they gathered to hold court. After the meal, the kings sat around a great square table together with their druids, maintaining order inside the assembly hall, while the Sidhe and all forms of demons were powerful and threatening outside. For many years, this stronghold came under heavy attack at Samain. A three-headed monster emerged from its hill on this night to wreak havoc on the fortress and on another royal fort at Emain Macha, until, finally, the warrior-poet Amairgin killed the monster. Also, annually on this night during the reign of Conn of the Hundred Battles, Aillén, a fairy musician, burned the citadel of Tara after first lulling everyone there to sleep with music from his timpán, or dulcimer. This burning happened each year for twenty-three years, until Finn, at the age of ten, came to Tara and killed that fairy with his spear. When the boy brought the fairy's head to the gate of the stronghold and mounted it on a stake, he was declared the leader of the warriors known as the Fianna.[4]

In the legend of Ireland's history, similar to Beltaine, Samain was a time of mythic events, but these were of a dark, dangerous nature. It was on that day when the Fomorians first landed on Ireland's shores. This demonic race ruled Ireland like winter over a wasted land until their leader Cichol was finally defeated and his monstrous throng dispersed. Peace lasted for three hundred years until, again on Samain, Fomorians once more ravaged the land. This time, under their King Morc they imposed a horrible tax. Two-thirds of the children born during the year were to be delivered up to them every Samain night. Men fought Fomorians in four great battles, but never entirely defeated them. There were kings and heroes who died at Samain, including Cú Roí, a wizard-chieftain in early Irish stories, and Conaire, a legendary king of early Ireland, who perished at the hands of marauders who cut off his head.

Cúchulainn, the hero of the Ulster Cycle of Irish literature, was on a drunken spree with his men at Samain when they were ambushed and very nearly burned to death in an iron house.[5] Samain is mentioned many times in the stories of Cúchulainn. There is an enormous collection of stories about this hero, and these stories of the Ulster Cycle are very old. Some of them were possibly first written down as early as the eighth century.[6] But how old are the stories themselves? We don't know, but here is the interesting thing. These characters inhabit an Irish world so old it is hard to fathom. "Set a century before the time of Christ," Professor of Irish Studies James MacKillop writes, "the Ulster stories posit an older world than any known in other European vernaculars."[7]

From the very beginning, Cúchulainn was not ordinary. A story relating the strange circumstances of his birth is in the *Book of the Dun Cow* manuscript. One evening his mother, Deichtine, was riding in a chariot with her father, the king of Ulster. They had been following a flock of magical birds when snow began to fall, and so when they came to a house they requested shelter for the night and were invited to stay. Unknown to them, they had chased the magical birds into the otherworld. Several years after that night, Deichtine was grieving over the death of a foster-son, when Lug, a chief of the Tuatha Dé Danann, appeared to her. He told her that he was the one who had welcomed her and her father and had been their host on that snowy night. He also told Deichtine that he had put a child in her womb.[8] Strangely, Cúchulainn's divine father, Lug, was descended from a Fomorian, which indicates how very closely inter-related the human, the divine, and the monstrous were in the old stories.

Even as a small boy, Cúchulainn was renowned for his brave deeds and strength, and when he grew into manhood a "hero-light" was sometimes seen to shine around his head. Everyone loved him for his feats in fighting, his magical abilities, his wisdom, his sweet speech, and his beauty. He is described as having long red-gold curls that hung down over his shoulders. In the following adventure, he meets with three Fomorians who have come at Samain to collect their annual payment from a king. This is one incident in a much longer story, and at this point the young Cúchulainn and eight other champions are on board a ship, returning home to Ireland.

Cúchulainn and Derbforgaill[9]

On Samain night, they came to the northern island belonging to Ruad, king of the Isles, and when Cúchulainn left the ship and came onto the shore he heard the sound of wailing. When he asked who it was, he was told it was the king's daughter, the princess Derbforgaill. The king was forced to pay a heavy tribute to the Fomorians, and this Samain they made him leave his daughter on the shore for them, where they would come and take her away. Cúchulainn found the girl sitting alone on the sand. She told him not to stay or the robbers would see him, but Cúchulainn would not leave her, and presently three fierce Fomorians landed in the bay. They made straight for Derbforgaill. But before they could lay a hand on her, Cúchulainn leapt on them and killed the three of them. The last one wounded him in the wrist, and the girl tore a strip of cloth from her dress for him to bind around the wound. Then she ran to her father's house and told him what had happened.

After that, Cúchulainn arrived at the king's house where the other men were there before him, and everyone was talking about the escape Derbforgaill had, some of the men boasting that it was they themselves who had saved her. She was not sure which one of them it had been because of the darkness of the evening. Then the king asked for water to be brought for them all to wash, and when it came to Cúchulainn's turn to bare his arms, she knew by the strip of her dress around his wrist that he was the one.

King Ruad then offered his daughter to him as a wife, and Cúchulainn asked her to come to him in Ireland in one year's time. In the end, however, he did not marry her, but married another maiden, Emer, who was the beautiful daughter of a Fomorian, and for whom he had to travel to the otherworld.

Although Derbforgaill's story is so very old, it corresponds to a familiar fairy tale type. There are many tales of a lad who saves a princess from a giant, a troll, or an ogre, or from three of them. In "The Three Princesses of Whiteland" and in "Soria Moria Castle," such a brave lad rescues three princesses from three monstrous trolls with three, six, and nine heads. A fearless young man in the Grimms' "The Two Brothers" slays a ferocious dragon that requires a sacrifice every year or it will lay waste the kingdom, and that year had claimed the king's daughter. Often, as in the stories of this dragon and of Cúchulainn's Fomorians, there is a false claimant to the slaying until the true hero is revealed by a token he has kept from the encounter.

Mael Muiri included a different Samain story about Cúchulainn in the *Book of the Dun Cow*. In "The Wasting Sickness of Cúchulainn,"[10] a fairy spell was put on the hero on this day. Cúchulainn was among a crowd that had gathered at the court for a Samain assembly and feast, when a flock of birds settled on the lake. Two were circling above the water, linked together by a chain of red gold, and as Cúchulainn pursued these two to bring them down with his slingshot, he had a mysterious experience; he saw a disturbing vision that left him ill for one year. The next Samain a messenger invited him to come to the otherworld, where a fairy called Fand could cure him. She had been one of the birds who appeared to him the year before. Cúchulainn summoned the strength to travel to the seductive Fand, who declared that she loved him. His wife Emer, however, was wild with jealousy and determined to kill this fairy rival. In a different turn of events in these stories, Emer confronted the fairy herself and proclaimed her love for her husband, whereupon Fand left her human lover. Druids brought Cúchulainn and his wife a drink of forgetfulness so that they would have no memory of Fand and this encounter with the otherworld.

Samain, or Hallowe'en, seems to have been a favourite motif of the ancient storytellers. Many of these stories are full of horrors, as the old stories often are, but I decided to conclude the chapter with this one, which I much prefer. This is a Celtic Samain story that is as beautiful as any we could imagine. It is also part of the Ulster Cycle. "Dream of Angus" (*Aislinge Óenguso*) portrays Samain, which issued in the pagan new year, as a pivotal day. The tale also presents the prevailing theme we have seen in the other stories – in the magical hours of Samain evening, it was possible for the visible and invisible worlds to come together. Angus was an Irish god of youth and love, and he was a son of the Dagda, high chieftain of the Tuatha Dé Danann. Both Angus and the Dagda are depicted from time to time as living in Brug na Bóinne, which has been identified as the prehistoric passage tomb, Newgrange, in County Meath. This is also the place to which Midir and Étaín flew in the shape of swans. It appears that this site, which was ancient when the Celts arrived in Ireland, caught the imagination of early storytellers both as a place where gods lived and as an entrance to the otherworld.

Dream of Angus[11]

A maiden appeared to Angus one night, standing near the top of his bed like a vision in a dream. The next night she appeared again, this time with a harp, and played music for him. This was the princess Cáer Ibormeith. The girl was so radiant, and the dream vision so powerful, that the youth fell in love with her, but she never came to him again. Afterwards, he remained deeply haunted by her memory and became seriously ill. The king sent messengers throughout Ireland to find a girl like the one Angus had seen, and they searched for a whole year but to no avail.

Cáer was under an enchantment, in which for one year she was a human maiden and the next year she was a swan. Finally, on Samain evening, Cáer was found swimming on a lake with one hundred and forty-nine other swans, with silver chains between each pair. Angus stepped into the lake, and the moment he did he was transformed into a swan himself. The two swans, Angus and Cáer, swam towards each other and then flew into the air. They circled the lake three times singing glorious music. Then they flew away to the otherworld, the sidhe or mound of Brug na Bóinne, where Cáer remained with him forever.

15

Midwinter and Midsummer

W hereas Beltaine and Samain were primarily Celtic festivals, the winter and summer solstices, corresponding with the year's shortest and longest days, were significant events worldwide in the pagan year; among other winter solstice celebrations was the Roman Saturnalia. The solstice days of ancient Europe continued to be observed as Midwinter and Midsummer festivals, and the winter solstice is still celebrated in Scandinavia with a festival of light at the beginning of the Christmas season. Familiar Christmas customs of decorating with candles, evergreen boughs, and holly and ivy wreaths, as well as trees hung with candles or lights all have origins in the old Germanic celebration of Yule, the pre-Christian Midwinter festival that was simply advanced along a few days to fall on the same day as Christmas. In the early days of Christianity in Europe church authorities spoke out against decorating with evergreen boughs, which were associated with pagan observance. Nevertheless, the custom persisted, and the ease with which so many Midwinter traditions were assimilated into Christmas celebrations indicates how deeply rooted they were.

We find a sense of an old pagan festival in the Christmas stories of folk literature. In the imagery of folk and fairy tales, Christmas is associated, not with the Christ child and with angels, but with elves, dwarfs, household spirits, and trolls. The Norwegian fairy tale at the end of this book describes a Christmas celebration enjoyed by dwarfs and giants. A great number of Icelandic tales are Christmas stories. Here people clung to their cherished folk tales, and these particularly seem filled with old folklore. In Icelandic tales, elves were on the move at Christmas travelling to their own Yuletide celebrations, where they feasted and danced until dawn. Trolls emerged from their dark caves to hold their own strange revelries, and some hidden folk chose Christmas Eve to come among humans for a time.

The Icelandic elves, who in the folk stories were usually indistinguishable from humans and often beautiful, sometimes lived among humans and were only revealed to be elves when they refused to attend the humans' church. "Una the Elfwoman" is a traditional Icelandic tale. Usually in stories similar to this one the elf maiden is under a spell that forces her to live with humans until the magic power is broken, but we never learn why Una had to leave her own people and help a young farmer. Once a year at Yuletide, however, when the boundary between the worlds is thin, Una is able to return to her own race to join in their celebration.

Una the Elfwoman[1]

At haying season a handsome young farmer, a widower, had a large quantity of hay to be raked up, far more than his farmhands could manage. One morning he saw a young woman come into the field and begin raking with the others. She spoke not a word, but raked so quickly it seemed like magic. That night she went away, but every day thereafter came again and accomplished far more work than anyone else. When all the hay was in, the farmer thanked the mysterious young woman and asked if she would like to come to his house as a housekeeper. She agreed.

The next day she arrived at the farmhouse to begin her work and brought with her a large chest, which she put into one of the outbuildings, not wanting to keep it in the farmhouse. Una managed the house well, and the farmer was very pleased. When three years had passed, he had grown so fond of Una that he wanted to marry her – but two things puzzled him. She would never tell him where she had come from, and she refused to accompany him to church.

Each Christmas Eve it was the custom for everyone at the farm to attend a service, and for three years everyone went to the church except for Una, who stayed behind to finish the Christmas preparations. On that third Christmas Eve, one of the servants lagged behind the others, and when they had all gone on, he hurried back to the farm. This young man was skilled in magical arts and could make himself invisible. He was curious to watch unobserved how Una spent her Christmas Eve.

He found her finishing her cleaning with great haste. Then she went to the outbuilding and unlocked her large chest from which she took finely embroidered clothes, and when she was dressed in them, the servant thought he had never seen anyone fairer. From the chest Una took a red cloth, and with this under her arm ran as quickly as she could across the meadow to the edge of a swamp. She spread the cloth on the ground and stepped onto the centre of it. The servant stepped onto a corner of the cloth without Una's noticing!

The cloth sank down into the ground, passing through the earth as easily as if it were smoke, when suddenly they were surrounded by green fields and a palace where a crowd was assembled for a feast. A table was set with silver cups filled with wine, and there were trays of fine food. From one tray the unseen servant took a mutton bone and thrust it in his pocket. Dancing and revelry lasted well into the night, but as dawn approached Una sadly declared that she must leave. She spread out her red cloth and stepped on it, with the servant on a corner just as before, and up they rose again to the farmer's meadow. On Christmas morning at breakfast, the servant held up the mutton bone he had kept in his pocket, asking if anyone had ever seen such a fine rib-bone of mutton as that. Immediately Una changed colour. Without a word she vanished and was never seen again. When the servant explained what he had seen the night before, the farmer no longer wondered why Una had avoided the church.

Stranger than Christmas folk and fairy tales are the medieval stories of Yule. "Helge in the Glittering Plains" is part of the long *Saga of Olaf Tryggvason* from the Icelandic manuscript *Flateyjarbók*, and this is a story that takes place in Norway before the year 1000. In Norway, Christianity was introduced through its kings rather than by missionaries, and King Olaf, by the age of twenty-seven, had travelled to England, been converted to the new religion there, and returned to become king of Norway. This king became the subject of many stories, which are set during his short reign and the early conversion period from 995 to 1000. Helge's is a tale of a clash between two kings, one Christian and one pagan. It also depicts a place in the far north found in several narratives, called the Glittering Plains (*Glæsisvellir*), ruled by a giant king, Gudmund. This giant is portrayed as wise and skilled in magic, living for five hundred years, and being worshipped after he dies as a god. Gudmund's realm displays some of the characteristics of the Celtic otherworld.

Helge in the Glittering Plains[2]

A young northman, Helge Thoreson, was on a journey far beyond the borders of his country and had become lost in a forest. In fact, without knowing it, he had ventured north beyond the world of humans and had entered the land called the Glittering Plains. While he was wondering which direction to travel, twelve maidens, all of them dressed in red cloaks, rode by him on horses with golden trappings. These were the twelve daughters of the giant Gudmund. The women stopped and set up tents and a table on which they put gold and silver dishes. The leader of the women, Ingeborg, invited Helge to join them and to stay with her in her tent. After three days the women left Helge, but before Ingeborg bid him farewell she gave him two chests filled with items of gold and silver. He took these chests home with him and shared the fine gifts with his parents, but told no one where they had come from.

At Yule, Helge and his family were celebrating when a great storm suddenly arose, and out of the wild night two men burst into the hall, grabbed the young man, and took him away with them. No one knew who these men were or where they had taken Helge. His father reported to King Olaf the strange event that had happened. Helge was gone for a year. He returned the next Yuletide to celebrate with his family, but disappeared again immediately afterwards, and the same thing happened for several more years. One Yule, King Olaf was in attendance. Helge returned home that year accompanied by unknown men, who handed Olaf two gold horns that had been sent from Gudmund as a gift between kings. King Olaf filled the drinking horns with wine and handed them to the men. But the wine had been blessed. Immediately, there was noise and confusion. A fire broke out, and the heathen messengers ran out of the hall with Helge.

At last, one Yule when he returned home, the prayers of the Christian king finally made it impossible for Helge ever to be drawn back to the otherworld. But this time when he arrived home, he was blind. Ingeborg had picked his eyes out, so that if she could not have him, no girls in Norway would ever love him.

Stories of Christmas time, whether folk tales, fairy tales, or the older medieval stories, have a Samain quality to them. Similar to the other ancient spirit nights, when supernatural beings could move between the worlds, Christmas Eve appears as a potent time replete with giants, trolls, elves, and ghosts, and it is a dangerous time for humans. Mainly, these stories have a theme of Christmas Eve visitors. In one fairy tale, a troll comes at Christmas to steal princesses – one princess every year. In another, a fierce and ugly troll wife comes to the same farm every Christmas Eve and captures the farmer's shepherd. One elf-queen is under a curse that demands that she take the life of a human every Christmas. There are many folk tales of elves and trolls overrunning farmsteads on Christmas Eve. In one Swedish tale, a man puts a Bible over one doorway and a hymnal over the other and makes a cross on the chimney; that night the trolls can't get in, but they still make a racket on the roof. A well-known fairy tale with this theme is the Norwegian "Peer Gynt and the Trolls." Peer had heard of an isolated farm on the Dovrefell that was invaded by trolls every Christmas Eve, and decided that he would stay there and try to clear them out. He brought a polar bear with him, and between the hunter and the bear the trolls were terrified and never returned to that farm again.[3]

The medieval sagas of the Icelanders include similar stories of trolls and monsters invading the homes of humans on Christmas Eve. The supernatural world shows itself more in the *Saga of Grettir the Strong*[4] than in other sagas, and most of Grettir's hardest battles with trolls and ghosts were fought at Yule. His fiercest struggle was with a huge troll woman who was haunting a farm at Sandhauger. For several winters the troll had come to the farm when the farmer's wife and children were away attending Yule mass at a village across the river. The first time the troll came the farmer disappeared and was never heard of again. The following winter, a servant who was left minding the farm vanished. News of this haunting spread, and the next Yule Eve the powerful Grettir came to stay in the farmhouse. Around midnight the troll woman came through the door and attacked him with a large cutlass. Grettir had never fought such a beast. They struggled all night. By morning, the doors and walls of the farmhouse were smashed, and Grettir was so exhausted he could do nothing but clutch onto her waist. The troll woman dragged him outside to the edge of a chasm, when, in a last second of strength, he finally managed to lift her off her feet, grab his sword, and cut off her arm. She fell into the chasm near a waterfall. Grettir didn't stop there. He later dove down under the torrent, found the ogress's cave, killed her horrible mate, and discovered some treasure.

Perhaps the best-known Christmas visitor story is *Sir Gawain and the Green Knight*,[5] written by an unknown poet in the fourteenth century near the English-Welsh border.

The Green Knight

King Arthur and his court had been celebrating Christmas by exchanging gifts and singing carols. They were just sitting down to enjoy a feast when a giant rode into the banquet hall. He was terrible to behold. He looked like a knight, but was huge, holding a branch of holly in one hand and wielding a great axe in the other. The strangest thing about him was that he was entirely green, his face and hair, his armour, his shirt, his tunic, even his horse – all of it was green! The astonished men in the hall were struck as still as stone, convinced that this unearthly knight must be a phantom.

The Green Knight proposed a deadly Christmas game. He would allow any one of the knights gathered there to strike him with his axe, but the blow would be returned in one year. No one moved, and Arthur was about to take the challenge himself when his sister's son, Gawain, stepped forward. He took the huge axe and struck the giant's head off, but the creature reached down, picked up his head, told Gawain to meet him in one year at his Green Chapel, and rode out of the hall.

Gawain was loyal to the contract. The following year at Christmas he arrived at a castle close by the chapel, but here he faced another challenge. At no time was the knight aware that his host at this castle was the same giant, but now in a different, human form. This time it was not his courage or physical prowess that was tested, but his virtue and moral strength. While his host was away for a few days of hunting, his beautiful wife came to Gawain while he was sleeping, once, twice, three times tempting the knight. But even on the final night, when Gawain knew that he would be beheaded the following day, he fought with his conscience and did not yield to temptation.

On the appointed day, Gawain found the chapel under a grass-covered mound and stood ready for the giant's blow. The great axe went up, then down to Gawain's neck, but only nicked him. Gawain had proven his goodness and bravery; he had come to the Green Chapel in good faith, and the scar on his neck would be a constant reminder of his bravery and this terrifying encounter with the Green Knight.

In the chapter "Giants," there is an almost identical beheading game, in the much earlier story from the *Book of the Dun Cow*. In these stories both Cúchulainn and Gawain were willing to sacrifice themselves to these giants. There is no knowing what obscure winter rite or concept of dark powers is reflected in the Midwinter stories, or where the prevailing theme of encounters with trolls, giants, ghosts, and monsters on Christmas Eve came from. Perhaps these monsters represent some force of darkness similar to a giant pagan mountain-king in a tale from Lapland, "Sampo Lappelill," whose deadly power is strongest at darkest Midwinter but begins to fade away with the first faint rosy light in the southern sky. The boy Sampo barely escapes from this giant on an enchanted reindeer.[6]

More welcome Christmas visitors were the elf-figures that first appeared as part of Christmas folklore traditions during the nineteenth century. The Swedish Jultomte, and in Norway and Denmark the Christmas Jule-Nisse, don't come down the chimney, but bring Christmas presents for children right through the front door and then enjoy the gift of a bowl of porridge that is left out for them. In Finland, the Christmas elf comes from Lapland where he lives, and so, of course, his sleigh is drawn by reindeer. In other regions it is pulled by a goat or a horse. It is only the American Santa Claus, based on the Dutch Saint Nicholas, or Sinter Klaas, who uses flying reindeer when he visits every home at Christmas. All of these Christmas Eve visitors derive from the ancient idea of sacred nights as spirit nights – when supernatural beings enter into our world.

It is much more difficult to find any tales with a Midsummer theme, but those that exist seem similar to Beltaine stories. On Midsummer Night the fairies might be seen, and the Irish fairy Áine came out onto her hill with her host of fairies that night to dance. Despite early efforts to Christianize the summer solstice festival by renaming it Saint John's Day on June twenty-fourth, Midsummer Eve remained a secular occasion. From ancient times throughout northern Europe, people gathered on the hills to light fires, dance, and hold night-long vigils. This longest day is still celebrated today, particularly in Sweden where some communities gather and dance to traditional folk music around a maypole decorated with birch leaves and flowers, and in Finland where lighting bonfires is a tradition.

This popular Norse story is a Midsummer fairy tale and a masculine version of a Cinderella story.

The Princess on the Glass Hill[7]

A farmer had a meadow on the side of a mountain and a barn there in which he stored hay, but for two years on Saint John's Eve the grass was all eaten up. It was just as if a whole flock of sheep had gnawed it down to the ground during the night. This happened once and then twice, and the man was tired of losing his crop. He told his three sons that one of them must stay in the barn on Saint John's night and see what was eating the grass. For the next two years on that night one of the older boys slept in the barn, but in the night there was such a rumbling like an earthquake that they jumped up, ran out of the barn, and never looked back.

Then it was Cinderlad's turn, the youngest son who had always been despised and laughed at by his older brothers. In the night he heard rumbling and the barn creaking, and then the earth quaked so that hay was flying all around. Still, he thought he could manage to stay there, and after a quaking came that was so violent he thought the walls and roof had fallen down, everything was silent. He looked outside to see a single horse chewing grass just outside the barn door. Cinderlad had never seen such a fine horse, with a saddle and bridle and carrying a complete set of armour. The same thing happened on the next two Midsummer Nights. The older boys were afraid to stay in the barn, but Cinderlad did. Every time, after an earthquake he found a horse outside, each one finer than the previous year's and with a full set of finely made armour. The lad kept these horses hidden in the woods.

The king of this land issued a challenge. His daughter would sit at the top of a glass hill with three golden apples in her lap. Whatever man could ride up the glass hill and take the golden apples could have her for his wife – and half of the kingdom as well. The day came for all the princes and knights in the country to try to ride up the hill. All of them rode up and slipped down and rode up and slipped down, until they were too tired to continue the attempt. Suddenly, a knight wearing armour made of copper came riding towards the hill on a fine horse. No one recognized him. This was

Cinderlad who rode up the hill three times, each time on one of the Midsummer horses, each time wearing a different fine suit of armour – and the princess thought she had never seen so handsome a knight. He retrieved the golden apples, thus winning the princess together with half of the kingdom.

In this story something mysterious and unearthly happens on Midsummer Night. Perhaps as a reward for facing the supernatural Cinderlad received the three magical gifts. Einar Sveinsson, who was researching the folk stories of Iceland in the early twentieth century, describes the magic of Midsummer Night as not as dangerous as Midwinter, but certainly with mysteries associated with it. On Midsummer Night a spell that has turned a man into a bear is broken, "seals come out of their enchanted shapes, cows talk and stones dance. All life on this northern island becomes a fairy story."[8]

In the medieval stories and in fairy tales there are lingering ideas about the ancient sacred days, even though the pre-Christian beliefs in which they are rooted are long forgotten. They were spirit nights, with a definite otherworld quality. Beyond that, we can't say very much about what rites or goddesses or frightening gods were originally connected with them. In her *Gods and Heroes of the Celts*, Marie-Louis Sjoestedt concludes that the myths can't tell us about the old goddesses with their cults and obscure rites, but that this doesn't really matter: "What does matter is that for a long time the imagination of the Celts persisted in gathering around a particular feast, or a particular place, or a particular complex of ritual, a given type of mythological symbolism."[9] The pagan imagination wound itself around these old sacred days and attached stories to them. That is how the pagan imagination worked. The stories were important, and it is enough to know them. What is significant about all of this mythological symbolism is that still we see fragments of it retained as part of our culture, both in fairy tales and in our own traditions.

PART FOUR

Storytellers' Themes

16

Wishing, or Dreams Come True

Some themes and motifs seem so closely bound up with fairy tales that they could be part of the definition of these stories. The reader expects to find enchantments and friendly supernatural helpers, as well as ogres and witches. Magic happens, and there will be a happy ending. Fairy tales could be called "wish tales." Usually the story's protagonist is the youngest child or is dirt-poor, with little hope or expectation of ever having his or her hopes and dreams fulfilled. Nevertheless, endurance, resourcefulness, a good heart, and magical assistance go a long way towards fulfilling those wishes. In fairy tales a goatherd can marry a prince, and a poor farmer's son can earn half a kingdom.

Stories did not always have happy endings; this is not a concept that we find in the early literature. The rags-to-riches theme had a social relevance in folk tales and then became highly developed in fairy tales. In *Breaking the Magic Spell*, Jack Zipes suggests a particular resonance among rural populations in the juxtaposition in folk and fairy tales of extreme poverty and hopeless situations against a world of gold, jewels, fine dresses, castles, and kingdoms. When folk tales were first documented in the late eighteenth and early nineteenth centuries, the widely popular theme reflected the hunger, injustice, and harsh living conditions that had been felt for centuries by the lower classes under oppressive social systems. Zipes concludes that although we can say very little about the early oral tradition of folk tales, of this we can be certain, the tales "were widespread, told by all classes of people, and very much bound by the material conditions of their existence."[1]

Wishes and dreams in folk and fairy tales conform to the storytelling motifs of the genres, yet also reflect each different culture. In Icelandic folk tales, for example, there are fewer castles and kingdoms, but more of the normal dreams of a hard-working but poor peasantry, as expressed by Jacqueline Simpson in her *Icelandic Folktales and Legends*, "wealth may be given by elves, taken by force from ghosts, or found in a 'money tussock' or a haunted mound; marvellous cows may appear from the sea or the elves' herds; one may be given knowledge, medical skill, or farming and fishing luck by elves, or simply a fine helping of porridge by a good-natured troll."[2]

The agency of magical good fortune often appears in items such as wishing caps, cloaks, rings, and boots. A dwarf provides a hungry shepherd with a magic tablecloth, upon which any food he may wish for appears. A lad far from home is rewarded with a wishing ring that will take him back to his family or anywhere in a second. A poor soldier receives a magic purse that appears empty, but when it is turned upside down gold pieces come pouring out of it. The most important instrument in the granting of wishes is a magic wand. Such a wishing-rod was part of the famous treasure hoard of the Nibelungs. When this fortune was being taken down to be loaded onto boats on the Rhine, it took men four days to carry it all, but among all of these gems and riches, the most precious item was a single gold rod – the means by which happiness might be attained. This rod was called simply "Wish."

A wondrous wishing item is a coat in the following story. This was a gypsy's tale, told to a folklorist in Northumberland in 1915. Here the girl's dresses do not come from a fairy godmother, as in Cinderella, but from a peddler who arrives at her door, and we feel sorry for the peddler who may himself be a gypsy and deserving of better treatment.

Mossycoat[3]

A poor widow lived in a cottage with her only daughter, a beautiful nineteen-year-old girl. A peddler was in love with the girl and brought her trinkets from time to time, hoping that she would marry him. On her mother's suggestion, she asked him if he would bring her a white satin dress embroidered with sprigs of gold, and within a week he arrived at her door with the dress, which was a perfect fit. But still, the girl was not ready to marry him quite yet. Next, she asked him for a dress made of silk with the colours of every bird. Again, he came with the dress the next week and this time brought her a pair of silver slippers to go with it. Then the young woman promised the peddler that she would marry him the next morning, even though she did not love him.

Meanwhile, the mother had been spinning for her daughter a special, magical coat made of green moss and gold thread. She called it Mossycoat, and she called her daughter by the same name. It was a wishing coat. When she put it on, the girl could wish to be anywhere and she would be there that instant. If she wanted to change into a swan or a bee, she had only to wish for it to happen. By morning the coat was finished, and so the girl put it on underneath her ordinary tattered clothes, packed up her beautiful dresses, and wished to be a hundred miles away.

Mossycoat found work in the kitchen of a grand house, where the other servants came to despise her for her ragged clothes and for her fine looks. The son of the household, however, liked her very much indeed! He asked her to accompany him to a dance to be held on three successive nights. Knowing that her place was in the kitchen scouring pots, Mossycoat declined the invitation. But on the second night of the dance she put her wishing coat on under

151

her white satin dress, wished herself at the dance – and there she was. The young man didn't recognize her in her finery, but danced with her all evening. He was still under her spell on the third night of the dance when she appeared in her gown that reflected the colours of birds. Later that evening, he had his arm around her waist when he felt her rise up and then suddenly vanish. He was left holding one silver slipper that had fallen off her foot. Of course the slipper fitted Mossycoat perfectly, and so she was revealed to have been the mysterious girl at the dance. The master and mistress of the grand house were as delighted as their son, and his wedding with Mossycoat was planned for the first day possible.

Frequently, good fortune arrives simply as a gift of wishes granted. When a young herd-boy finds three magical items that belong to the elves – a red cap, a bell, and a pair of little glass shoes – the elves are so pleased at having their lost belongings found that they grant the boy three wishes. Another elf grants three wishes to a woodcutter for sparing a particular tree. A mermaid stranded in the shallows grants a fisherman's three wishes when he carries her to deep water, and a dwarf-like fellow grants a little girl three wonderful wishes only if she will stop pulling the heather off his mound, and for being so kind as to share her pancakes with him. But, this dwarf chooses the wishes for her. She will be so beautiful that there will not be another like her in the whole world, her voice will be lovely music, and she will marry a young king.[4] Elves, mermaids, dwarfs, and fairies can grant wishes; it seems to be an innate attribute of their "otherness" that they have this magical facility. Giants in fairy tales, however, seldom grant wishes, although a sharp-witted boy can trick an oafish giant into giving away a wishing hat, or wishing boots that allow him to travel seven leagues with a single step.

The familiar story motif of granting three wishes is very old. One of the many giants in the story "Bricriu's Feast" granted Cúchulainn's three wishes. The hero was on night watch outside a fort when he saw a giant approaching, yet before the giant could seize him, Cúchulainn leapt up quick as a hare and was in mid-air with his sword poised over the monster's head when the giant asked to be spared. "For my three wishes," Cúchulainn said, and they were granted – to be sovereign over Ireland's heroes, to be declared champion without dispute, and for his wife to take precedence over all of Ulster's ladies, forever. In another story, a mythical Ulster king, Fergus Mac Léti, fell asleep near the coast, where some water-sprites tried to drag him into the sea. He took hold of them, and for their freedom they granted him three wishes – one of which was to be able to breathe underwater.

In fairy tales, making a wish is never inconsequential. Impatient with his seven sons, a father utters, "I wish they would all be turned into ravens," and immediately there is a whirring sound in the air as seven black ravens circle above the father's head and fly away. There are wives and children in folk and fairy tales who are invoked into existence by being wished for. Snow White's mother wishes for a child with skin as white as snow, cheeks as red as three drops of her blood, and hair as black as the ebony window-frame. Soon after, she gives birth to just such a little girl. A sense of something magical accompanies such wish-children.

Today, children make wishes when they blow out birthday candles or throw coins into wishing wells or fountains. The definition of a wish as something desired or hoped for seems to be a more restricted meaning of the word than it had in earlier times. Jacob Grimm studied extensively the use of the word in the oldest German texts and found a different meaning for *wunsch*, the German "wish": "The sum total of well-being and blessedness, the fullness of all graces, seems in our ancient language to have been expressed by a single word, whose meaning has since been narrowed down; it was named *wunsch* (wish)."[5] Wishing was connected with destiny, well-being, and miracles. Grimm found a strong connection between the concept of "wish" and the god Woden. "Wish" implied and appealed to the will and bounteousness of the gods, particularly Woden, who in old German poetry was portrayed as a personification of the concept. This god, who could invoke all of the power and fury of nature, was the same god who brought into being all the good that men were worthy of, from victory in war to the fulfillment of love and longing in a man's heart. A wish was Woden's gift. Grimm also found that the Finnish Väinämöinen, who is the central wonder-worker in Finnish folklore, resembled Woden in that he, too, was a personification of the concept.[6]

Woden for the early Germans corresponded to Odin in Norse beliefs. This god was known by many different names, each name referring to one of his qualities or to events that had been developed in stories.[7] Odin was All-wise among the giants, he was Wanderer among humans for the many places he travelled, and other names were One-Eye, Mask, Helm-wearer, War-merry, and Broadhat. One name was simply Wish (*Oski*). Grimm expresses Odin's Eddic name Oski as "he who makes men partakers of wunsch, of the highest gift."[8] Odin had wish-maidens he sent to the aid of humans. In the *Saga of the Völsungs*, the god heard King Rerir's prayer for a child to carry on his family's heritage and sent a wish-maiden in the form of a crow with an apple of fertility for the king's wife. The child she bore was Völsung, who became the legendary king of the Völsung clan.

Odin is the god who granted victory to warriors and good fortune to kings, but he cared about all humans. He had two ravens perched on his shoulders that told him of everything they saw and heard in our world. Then, disguised in a cloak with a hood to conceal his face, Odin wandered the earth and visited the homes of men, hearing of their troubles and longings and testing their kindness. In the Eddic "Lay of Grímnir," wearing his dark blue cloak he arrived one day at the castle door of a king named Geirröd. Odin's wife Frigg had told him that this king was miserly to his guests, and Odin wanted to see if this was true. The god introduced himself as Grímnir (the Hooded One), but when asked, he declined to tell his host where he was travelling or what his purpose was. In order to make him speak, Geirröd tortured his guest by setting him between two hot fires for eight nights. The guest was ill-treated by everyone in the castle except for the king's ten-year-old son, Agnar, who took pity on him and offered him beer to quench his thirst. When the fires burned so hot that the god's cloak began to burn, Odin finally spoke, and then King Geirröd learned many things about his mysterious visitor. He learned that he had seen Æsir and elves, and that he had many names besides Grímnir, including War-Father, Much-wise, and Fulfiller of Wishes. Realizing that his guest was Odin, Geirröd leapt up to move the god from the fire, but in the urgency of the moment fell onto the sword which had been lying across his lap and died. Odin then vanished, but he determined that the young Agnar would be granted the kingship succeeding his father. This may be a very early story, according to John Lindow in *Norse Mythology*, who writes, "The poem is impossible to date, but it is not difficult to imagine something like it being performed during the pagan period."[9]

This ancient tale of Odin illustrates one of the most familiar fairy tale themes – a human is tested for his good heart and kindness, is found either worthy or wanting, and is then rewarded with good wishes or misfortunes. Even in the simple tale of the dwarf who himself chose the three wishes that he would bestow upon a little girl for her thoughtfulness, these wishes have the older sense of blessings. In a typical test-of-kindness fairy tale, a poor young man (or woman), who has met with such terrible times that he has hardly a penny or crust of bread in his pocket and only tattered rags for clothes, is obliged to leave home to make his way in the wide world. On his journey he meets an old beggar-man who is in a worse state than he is, with nothing at all to eat. When the young man has given the little that he has to the beggar, he is rewarded with a wish-cloak, magic wand, spell, or good advice that serves him well and ultimately wins him good fortune.

An ancient Irish king was similarly tested for his good will, and in this old story the familiar fairy tale pattern is apparent. The fortunes of the Irish kings depended upon the blessings of a goddess of Sovereignty who determined the right of kingship, and this goddess decided the future of Niall, a legendary king in the Irish stronghold of Tara in the late fourth century.[10] When Niall was born, he was acknowledged to be the rightful heir to his father's throne, but his wicked stepmother wanted one of her four sons, Niall's stepbrothers, to become king. In order to determine which of the five boys was the most worthy, they were sent into the forest to hunt and fend for themselves, and they became lost. One by one, the boys set off to find water, each of them eventually arriving at a well guarded by an old woman. She was a fearsome-looking crone. Every bit of her was black, and the grey, bristly hair growing from the top of her head looked like the tail of a wild horse. The woman told each boy that he could have water if he gave her a kiss. The first three boys refused. The next boy gave her the very littlest kiss and was told that two of his descendants would become king. When it was Niall's turn he kissed and embraced the hag, whereupon she immediately turned into a lovely woman with white skin and lips as red as rowanberries. The hag was revealed to be Sovereignty, who declared that Niall would be king of Ireland.

As in this legend of a goddess at a well, mystical and miraculous occurrences in Irish stories were known to happen near wells and springs. In ancient Ireland, holy wells were sacred places associated with female divinities, and later these wells became dedicated to saints. The concept of wells and springs as spiritual, sacred places gave rise to folk legends about wells that contained within them wishing-stones and water that could portend the future or had the miraculous power of bestowing wishes;

these were wishing wells. Beyond Ireland, however, magical things could happen at wells and ponds.

The German mother or goddess-figure in folk and fairy tales known as Frau Holde, or Holle, had a connection with spinning and with wells, granted wishing-gifts to children, and also tested humans. A young daughter, in Grimms' "Mother Holle," sat spinning by a well when she dropped her reel into it by mistake. Her scolding mother sent her down into the well to retrieve it, but when the girl jumped in she found at the bottom a lovely garden filled with sunshine and flowers. This was Frau Holle's underground world. The child was so helpful to the old woman, that when she eventually returned home the underground lady had covered her with gold. The greedy mother sent the girl's sister to Frau Holle to bring home more gold, but this sister was so lazy that she returned home covered with pitch.

There are a great many of these kind sister/unkind sister stories. Sometimes these are referred to as "toads and diamonds" tales, from Perrault's "The Fairies." Here a fairy in disguise at a spring blessed a girl who gave her a drink of water with pearls and diamonds that would fall from her mouth with every word she spoke. Her ill-natured sister, however, was rewarded with toads and vipers. It wasn't simply kindness that was being tested in these stories. Blessings were bestowed upon those who had no expectation of reward or of magic, those who were humble and simple, who could recognize the beauty in any human beings, and who were open to all of the otherworldly wonders that befell them. In fairy tales this bestowed good favour and fortune came in many forms, but often simply as wishes granted – and almost invariably with these wishes, there were three of them.

17

The Triple Form

In fairy tales more than wishes come in threes. A girl who was always treated horribly by her stepmother one day dropped her basket over a cliff and climbed all the way down over the rocks to retrieve it. At the bottom she was surprised to find three fairies welcoming her to their palace under the precipice. There they treated her kindly and gave her a splendid gown, and when she left them a golden star shone on her forehead.[1] Just like the fairies in this Italian tale, we come upon "threes" so often in stories that the number three may be the most frequently occurring and fundamental element in fairy tales and in all of European folk literature. There are three fairy queens or three witches, three sisters or three suitors, three giants – each with three, six, or nine heads – or three evil-hearted serpents, three roses and three riddles, three swords, three dangerous journeys, and three impossible tasks. Cinderella's ball is on three evenings. The list can go on and on. Frequently, a king has three sons or daughters, and it follows then, that the most difficult trials become the destiny of the third child. Yet, the youngest child is inevitably blessed with such virtues of kindness, bravery, and faithfulness that good fortune finds him or her. The faithful third child is a theme in many stories of the Cinderella type.

Threes are not as predictable an element in the ancient stories, but still they appear over and over. Monstrous creatures have three heads, and triple narrative patterns of three curses, three challenges, or three enemies give many of the old stories a mythic quality. The tales of the

Fianna of Ireland include a great number of episodes with elements in
threes, such as three packs of vicious hounds or three days and nights
spent in a sídh or fairy mound. In one episode, three ravens flew from the
north every eve of Samain, descended on the youth from a sídh, and
carried three boys off with them; and this happened every year until three
men of the Fianna brought those birds down.[2] Their leader Finn had a
triple aspect – triplet sons born to King Eochaid were known as "The
Three Finns of Emain Macha." The Celtic scholar James MacKillop
suggests that this triple aspect to Finn reflects a very ancient repre-
sentation of Finn, in which he is a figure known as Find.[3]

Threes of different kinds appear at the very end of Cúchulainn's life
and give an ominous overtone to this hero's last battle.[4] He could be
defeated only by witchery and magic. In order to draw the warrior out of
his stronghold at Emain Macha, a magician's three daughters used witchcraft to call up an illusion of battle outside the walls. With their magic
they created smoke and the roar of battle and the sound of weapons
falling all around. Once Cúchulainn was out on the road, he was assailed,
not by enemy forces, but by three old hags who poisoned him with dog
meat. Then he was attacked by three spears made poisonous by three sorcerers. The first spear killed his charioteer, the second wounded his horse,
called the Gray of Macha, and the third spear mortally wounded Cúchulainn. As he lay dying the hero-light that shone out of his forehead began
to fade. The crow of battle sat on his shoulder, and the Gray of Macha,
dripping blood, circled around him three times. With his teeth and
hooves, the loyal horse attacked men who came to cut off Cúchulainn's
head. After he died, the people in Emain Macha saw the soul of Cúchulainn riding in the air above them in a phantom-chariot.

The horse circling the dying hero three times evokes an old rite or
ritual, and indeed, classical Roman sources describe Celtic religious
processions circling three times. From time to time the very same circling
pattern appears in folk and fairy tales, where the formula raises an

element of the supernatural. A ghost circles around a person three times in order to gain magical power over him. An exiled princess comes to a little house protected by magic, and if she walks around the house three times forwards and then three times backwards, the door will open for her and she will be safe inside, hidden from a wicked ogress.[5] In the English folk tale "Childe Roland," this young man walks three times around a fairy knoll and immediately finds himself out of our world and into a great hall belonging to the King of Elfland, where he finds his sister who had been spirited there. In the early stories and in fairy tales, any triple repetition is a formula for magic; words spoken three times are commonly used either to speak a spell or to break one. To open a locked castle door a lad strikes it three times, or by turning around three times an ogress changes her shape. A horse neighs three times before setting out from the strand onto the sea and towards the otherworld.

The concept that a triple repetition had an intensity or some profound power was ancient symbolism. A pattern similar to the magical circling three times was expressed in Celtic art in a design with three identical forms – spirals or animals or birds – all moving in the same direction around a central point. This three-armed motif, called a triskele, which appears on many very early items such as brooches, scabbards, and the covers of illuminated manuscripts, presumably had spiritual or mystical significance. In *Celtic Art: Symbols and Imagery*, Miranda Green finds the triple form and the number three to be an important aspect in Celtic religious and artistic expression: "in Romano-Celtic religious imagery and in early written Celtic myth, the number three had a sacred and magical symbolism."[6] The concept extended beyond the Celtic; throughout the ancient world a triple entity could be a magical or sacred form.

In the imagery of pagan northern Europe, protective spirits, gods, and goddesses carved in stone can appear as three-faced heads or as three identical hooded figures.[7] The number three as an expression of something divine appears in these deities seen as a trinity and depicted as three heads or as three beings. As in this visual imagery, the most important Celtic goddesses were portrayed in Irish literature with a triple form, as three of the same goddess, or as one goddess as a tripartite being. The goddess of the Sovereignty of Ireland had a triple form in Fódla, Banba, and Ériu, three personifications of the one entity, Sovereignty. The war-goddess, the Mórrígan, also had a triple form as Mórrígan, Badb, and Macha, known together as the Mórrígna, and even the goddess Macha, herself, is represented as three women, each with the name Macha, and each reflecting a different aspect of that goddess. The Irish goddess Brigit had a threefold aspect. According to the very early, tenth-century *Cormac's Glossary*, this single goddess Brigit was represented as three sisters with the same name, all daughters of the Dagda – Brigit goddess of poetry, Brigit goddess of smithwork, and Brigit goddess of healing – each sister identified with one of the magical or divine arts.[8]

With this aesthetic of goddesses as trinities, it seems natural that in folk narrative fairies and witches would often come in threes, similar to the three weird sisters or witches in Old English literature. In the following story, three golden heads at a well speak as a trinity and as something otherworldly or even divine, when they grant blessings to a princess. The tale is from Joseph Jacobs' popular *English Fairy Tales*, but this is a very early fairy tale that was known in Elizabethan times.[9]

The Three Heads of the Well

Long ago a queen died, leaving the king a daughter who was so beautiful and kind that all who knew her loved her. At the same time in the kingdom, there was a rich widow who also had an only daughter. The king married the widow for her riches, even though she was an ugly, hook-nosed, hump-backed woman, which is how she came to live at the palace along with her daughter, a plain and ill-natured girl. The king and his new queen had not been married long when the queen began to treat her stepdaughter so horribly that the princess decided to leave home and travel far away.

For her journey, the stepmother gave her nothing but a small canvas bag containing a little brown bread, a piece of hard cheese, and some beer. After a long walk through woods and valleys, the princess came upon an old man sitting on a stone, so she sat down beside him and bade him welcome to her little bit of food. For the girl's generosity, the old man gave her a wand, with instructions that when she came to a thick hedge she must use it to strike the bushes three times and the hedge would open a pathway for her. A little further on she would come to a well. He advised her to sit at its edge, and when three heads appeared to do as they requested.

The princess continued on her way. Sure enough, she soon came to the hedge, which she easily passed through, and then to the well. She had not been sitting beside it very long when a golden head rose up to the water's surface and sang, "Wash me, and comb me, and lay me down softly." The princess took the golden head in her lap, combed its hair with a silver comb, and placed it gently on the primrose bank. A second head appeared, and then a third, each singing the same song. The princess gently combed their hair and laid those heads beside the first one. Then one head spoke to the others, saying that they must have gifts for this considerate girl. The first head said, "I will give her such beauty that she will charm the most powerful prince in the world." The second one said, "I will give her a voice sweeter than the nightingale," and the third, "This maiden is a king's daughter and I will give her such luck that she will become queen to the greatest prince that reigns."

The princess gently let the heads down into the well again and continued on her journey. She had not travelled far when a young king hunting with his men stopped and spoke with her. He instantly fell in love with the young woman with the sweet voice.

The princess's stepsister decided that she would seek her fortune in the world, too, but she would not give the old man a drop to drink and had such difficulty passing through the hedge that she was cut and her fine clothes were ruined. She treated the three heads so rudely that she was granted nothing but ill-will. Eventually, the wretched stepsister met a country cobbler who was willing to marry her, and she spent the rest of her days spinning the thread for him to use mending shoes.

The three heads floating up to the water's surface in this story certainly seem strange and macabre. But it is not a notion unique to this story. In both Irish and Welsh narrative tradition, severed and disembodied heads could speak and were depicted as having magical powers and divinity.[10]

Triple goddesses are a feature of Norse literary tradition as well. The norns, the deities who had the function of shaping human lives as they travelled about the countryside allotting destinies to newborn children, were depicted as three and identified as the maidens Urd or Urth, Verthandi, and the youngest one, Skuld. Their names translate as "Fated," "Becoming," and "Must-be." In the Eddic poem "The Prophecy of the Seeress," the wise-woman has a vision of these three. In the sparse language of this pre-Christian poem,[11] she can see the norns emerging from their dwelling under the roots of the great world-tree, Yggdrasil, which they keep watered from their well. Then she sees them shaping the lives of men by cutting rune marks on pieces of wood.

An ash I know, Yggdrasil its name,
With water white is the great tree wet;
Thence come the dews that fall in the dales,
Green by Urth's well does it ever grow.

Thence come the maidens mighty in wisdom,

Three from the dwelling   down 'neath the tree;
Urth is one named,   Verthandi the next,–
On the wood they scored,–   and Skuld the third.
Laws they made there,   and life allotted
To the sons of men,   and set their fates.[12]

The valkyrie warrior-goddesses, sent by Odin to fly over battlefields and determine which warriors would die, were depicted primarily as the three, Gunn, Rota, and Skuld (the name of a norn and a valkyrie), although we know the names of other valkyries as well. Throughout northern Europe when Christianity was introduced, praying to the Trinity of the Father, Son, and Holy Ghost would have seemed quite natural to people who had represented pagan divinities and mythological figures as trinities.

In medieval Welsh literature, the dominant idea of threes that we have seen in fairy tales and mythology takes a different turn. The resonant tendency towards grouping things and characters in threes is expressed in a uniquely different form – as "triads."[13] A Welsh triad consists of the names of three separate characters or events, usually taken from the stories of folklore and mythology, gathered together under a single title. To give an example, one is "The Triad of the Three Great Enchantments of the Island of Britain." Under this title are included the following three stories. First is the enchantment of Math, son of Mathonwy – this refers to a sorcerer from the *Mabinogion* who created a woman out of flowers with his magic wand. Second is the enchantment of Uther Pendragon – the legendary king shape-shifted with Merlin's help, so that he could sleep one night with Igraine, and that night fathered the child Arthur. Third is the enchantment of Gwythelyn the Dwarf of whom very little is now known. Long lists of these triads preserve the names of many mythic and historical figures.

This triadic format would have served medieval bards as a useful memory aid in recalling stories, and the lists of triads may have provided a kind of catalogue of tales. Likely this was their function. But more importantly, it was a way that the Welsh people documented and commemorated the tradition of their own literature and history. Allusions to triads in the very earliest Welsh poetry indicate that they had long been a part of Welsh oral tradition. The manuscripts that contain these lists of triads are extremely valuable and interesting, since they reference ancient legendary and heroic lore, a great deal of which is now lost. The triads are evidence that Wales possessed a narrative culture far richer than that which has been left to us. Perhaps it would have been equal to, or even surpassed, Ireland's own legacy.

A great many triads refer to King Arthur, his warriors, and his court. We learn, for example, that "Three Skillful Bards at Arthur's Court" were Myrddin son of Morfryn, Myrddin Emrys, and Taliesin; this triad refers to two separate legends regarding Myrddin. "The Triad of the Three Exalted Prisoners of the Island of Britain" names one most exalted prisoner, Arthur, who spent three nights in the Castle of Oeth and Anoeth, three nights in the prison of Gwen Pendragon, and three nights in an enchanted prison under a great stone. These stories suggest the popular fairy tale theme of a young man compelled to stay three successive nights in the home of a giant, or in the homes of three different giants, where each night's experience is more terrifying than the previous one. "The Triad of the Three Great Queens" lists three queens of Arthur's court, all named Gwenhwyfar (Guinevere), Gwenhwyfar the daughter of Gwent, Gwenhwyfar the daughter of Gwythyr, and Gwenhwyfar the daughter of Gogfran the Giant, who give this one queen a triple aspect.

As well as the Welsh, there were Irish triads. The *Book of Invasions* refers to sixteen triads of the Tuatha Dé Danann. In fact, triads do exist in other cultures too, although there are not lists of them. The answer to why these story themes were collected and listed in threes is lost in time. Triads may have been simply a useful code or system for bards to remember the important stories. But this was a completely natural system to use, since the triple form was a feature of Celtic artistic, mythological, and religious ideas. By being recorded in triads, stories achieved mythic status. Similarly, storytellers through the ages knew how to use patterns of threes in their stories to imbue them with a heightened mythic shape, meaning, and resonance.

18

Shape-Shifting

There was once a king's daughter, Margaret, whose jealous step-mother repeated a spell three times to turn the girl into an ugly creature. So, Margaret went to bed a beautiful maiden and woke up as a hideous serpent. She crawled out of the castle and crawled and crept until she came to a rocky place by the sea. There, unseen by anyone, she could sleep in a cave and bask in the sun. She remained there until her brother found her and kissed her three times, breaking the spell and turning the serpent back into his dear sister Margaret once more. Then the brother found the stepmother in the queen's bower and touched her with a rowan-twig – a charm against witches – whereupon she shrivelled and shrivelled until she became a toad that hopped away down the castle steps.[1]

As in this English story, fairy tales are filled with such shape-changing enchantments. A prince is turned into a white bear, and a girl into a tiny, grey mouse. Twelve brothers are changed into twelve wild geese. A spell turns a princess into a white cat until a prince cuts off her head and tail, whereupon she becomes a princess again. There are countless similar stories, and they can be found in almost every culture of the world.

In some of these, a girl is true to a promise, or honours a contract for her family, and is thereby compelled to marry an animal, even a frog, but discovers afterwards that her husband is a young man under a spell. "Beauty and the Beast" is one of these tales; a wicked fairy has turned a prince into a frightful beast, until a virgin consents to marry him. The similar Norwegian "East of the Sun and West of the Moon" has a prince held under the enchantment of an evil troll so that he is a white bear by day but a young man at night. In these tales there is usually a formula for breaking the spell, such as kissing the unnatural creature three times.

Evidence that this is an old storytelling theme is found in the many shape-changing enchantments in the earlier stories, such as "The Children of Lir" where children live in the form of swans for nine hundred years. The Icelandic *Saga of King Hrólf Kraki* has stories that are set in a time before the year 900, in early Viking days, and in one episode a prince in northern Norway has an enchantment cast on him by a troll-wife. We can see how similar this early story is to a fairy tale.

Bjorn, the Bear-Man[2]

In a northern region of Norway there lived a king and queen, parents of a son named Bjorn. The queen died – a very sad loss for the king. In time he sent some men south to find a new wife for him, but fierce storms arose which changed the course of their ship. They found themselves even farther north, in Finnmark, and there they were obliged to spend the winter. One day, the king's men came to a house where a mother and daughter lived, and they were surprised to find the women so lovely and living there all alone. The mother explained that the girl, White, was a daughter of the king of the Lapps, and that they were hiding in the house from a wicked man until White's father returned home from raiding expeditions. The men decided that White would be a good wife for their king and brought her home with them. The girl pleased the king and, although she was young while he was old, they were married without delay. The king did not know that he had married a troll.

The new wife befriended her stepson, Bjorn, who was strong and handsome. In fact, she suggested that they should share a bed while the king was away at wars, but the more she pleaded with Bjorn, the more repellent he found her. Finally, the girl was so angry with his stubbornness that she touched him with her magic wolfskin gloves. As soon as she did this, Bjorn became a savage bear by day but a man at night. He kept away from the world of men after that, and went off to live alone in the woods.

Before long, a girl who loved him very much, lovely Bera, his dearest friend since childhood, came upon him in the forest. She knew immediately that the bear was Bjorn. From then on she came every night to sleep with him in his bear cave. One morning when Bjorn had gone out of the cave as a bear, some men came over the hill, hunted the bear down, and killed him. In the course of time Bera gave birth to triplets. Bjorn's sons grew to be so strong that by the time they were twelve years old no men dared challenge them, and one of them, Bothvar, displayed fearsome bear-like tendencies!

There are a great many curious episodes of shape-changing in a story found in the Welsh *Mabinogion*, "Math Son of Mathonwy."[3] One of the sorcerer Math's enchantments was to turn two young men into a stag and a hind, then into a boar and a sow, and then into two wolves. One of these men, Gwydion, became a sorcerer himself and put a curse on an unfaithful wife condemning her to live forever in the form of an owl. Humans shifting into and out of animal and other shapes are the subject matter of some of the strangest of the old Welsh stories. The magician Merlin changed into an eagle and a salmon, and poems about Taliesin present this figure as a great shape-shifter who could change to become a star or a tree.

Shape-changing like this, without an enchantment, was a phenomenon of the Irish stories. At one time Finn had a lover Úaine, who was one of the fairy folk from the mounds, but he left her because she was always changing herself into animal shapes.[4] Finn's men were wary of another woman of the Tuatha Dé Danann, Bé Mannair: "It is she who goes in the shape of the water-spider or a whale, who transforms herself into the shape of a fly or into a person's best friend, whether male or female, so that the secrets of all are entrusted to her."[5]

Mael Muiri included a fine tale of shape-shifting, "The Story of Tuan Son of Cairill," in his *Book of the Dun Cow* manuscript.[6] The figure Tuan mac Cairill lived for centuries in the shapes of different animals and birds. His long life provides an eye-witness perspective for the story of the history of Ireland. Tuan arrived with the early settlers, the people of Partholón, and he was the only one of them to survive a plague. Living alone in the wild cliffs, he watched as new settlers arrived and history unfolded, until finally he became too old, shrivelled, and decrepit to leave his cave. One night the old man saw himself passing into the shape of a stag. Suddenly, he was young again and once more full of spirit as he travelled across all of Ireland with a great herd of stags. Tuan changed into a boar, a hawk, a salmon, and finally into a human again. After his long life as an observer of events, he could relate his first-hand account of the Fir Bolg, the Tuatha Dé Danann, the Gaels, and finally of Patrick bringing the Faith to Ireland.

Cúchulainn was a different kind of shape-shifter. This champion could work himself into such a preternatural fury that his body experienced a wild distortion or "warp-spasm," through which he became unrecognizable. One of his eyes narrowed to a sliver, while the other grew to the size of a goblet; his body stretched taller and taller and taller. Each hair of his head bristled up to a spike, a drop of bright red blood glistening at every root. At moments such as this Cúchulainn's hero-light sprang out of his head and he possessed ferocious superhuman strength.

All of these tales of humans and animals whose shapes could merge and separate, and whose souls could migrate into one form or another, mirror the old stories of the gods, who frequently shape-shifted into birds and animals. A pagan god was depicted as having this power to transform himself at will into another shape. Odin turned into a snake, a fish, an eagle, and a hawk. Loki became a salmon, a seal, a horse, a bird, a fly. Freyja could fly as a falcon. The Celtic sea-god, Manannán, was a great shape-shifter, adept at disguising his divine form as a heron or other sea bird. In the early Irish stories, when a warrior looked upon an old hag, and the next moment found she was a young maiden, and the next a sharp-beaked crow, he realized that this was a goddess he was seeing. The Tuatha Dé Danann could wander the earth in the shape of deer. The myths are filled with such stories of shape-shifting – especially tales of shape-shifting gods. It is a very beautiful, perhaps even frightening idea that a god could change into a deer or could soar like a bird, being blown about by the wind. What are we to make of all of these transformations, especially the transformations of the gods?

The world of the ancient Irish imagination seemed a more insubstantial place than it appears to us; it was fluid, changeable, and altogether more spiritual. The place of humans in it seemed not as rigidly fixed and separate from animals and the supernatural. The historian Thomas Cahill describes "the Celtic phenomenon of shape-shifting" as "an effect that the Irish seem to have taken for granted as we take for granted molecular structures: this was simply the way the world was."[7]

Norse stories have this Celtic aspect, but at the same time in these northern stories there is something different happening. In the *Völsunga Saga*, Sigmund and his son, the young Sinfjötli, came upon a house in the woods where two kings' sons lived. These princes were skin-changers who came out of their wolfskins every ten days. Sigmund and Sinfjötli saw the skins hanging and put them on themselves, so that they became wolves that howled and lived in the wild woods, sleeping under trees. As wolves they did many fierce deeds, until there came a time when they almost killed each other! Then they were ready to abandon those shapes and burn the wolfskins in the fire.[8]

This kind of shape-shifting did not require such an imaginative leap in a culture where men identified with animals in order to absorb some of their strength and fierceness. The wild Norse cults of warriors known as berserkers (the word "berserk" means "bear shirt") identified with bears to fight in the service of Odin. Other Odinic warriors were called "Wolfskins." In the view of the medieval scholar Stephen Glosecki, these warriors must have been formidable: "we tend to romanticize swash-buckling characters like the berserkers. We put them safely on the shelf of fantasy, with Jack's giant and Paul Bunyan's ox. But in the Iron Age there was nothing romantic about facing a veteran warrior whelmed by his an-imal companion, convinced of his invulnerability, encouraged by his tal-ismanic weaponry, ecstatically out of touch with pain and fear, and therefore utterly reckless in combat."[9]

It would have been easy for these men to imagine that their gods and characters in their sagas could change into these animals at will. The idea is consistent with the religious practice of shamanism in the early cultures of northern Europe. Shamans were spiritual shape-shifters. A shaman, wearing a belt or other item made of animal pelts or feathers, could become entranced and channel his spirit into another form – a bear, a fish, a bird – and travel into the spirit realm where he could communicate with ancestors and with gods. These visionary religious practitioners were mainly healers, called "dream doctors," but they could also bring back messages from the spirit world. Glosecki explored the idea that shamanic beliefs survive in old Norse and English literature. He found vestiges of shamanism in the concept of shape-shifting and in images such as Odin flying as an eagle. Odin would be considered to be a divine shaman, as would Freyja putting on her feathered cloak to fly as a bird: "Although European shamanism steadily disintegrated during the Middle Ages, it left many traces behind, scattered fragments of its rich mythos embedded in the most archaic strata of myth and epic, folklore and charm."[10]

Shape-shifting stories, which are usually animal stories, tend to reflect the role of certain animals in mythology and folklore. Wolves were espe-cially sacred to Woden and also Odin; both had wolves accompany them into battle. An animal especially revered in northern Scandinavia was the bear. When hunters in Lapland brought a bear they had killed back to the community, it was referred to as a guest or even as a bride or bridegroom. In northern tales, when a bear knocks on a cottage door, it is welcomed as a guest, called grandfather, and invited into the home to warm itself by the fire. These bear stories may suggest early notions of these animals being regarded with fear as well as with great respect. Some animals, by their natures, seemed to exist close to the threshold of the otherworld, as deer and especially fawns do in the Celtic stories. Wolves often appear in stories as death spirits haunting the dark woods where men have been murdered, as if existing in some supernatural state between the living and the dead.

In mythology, birds could easily cross the boundary from the otherworld into our own, and bird shape-shifting stories, more than any others, reflect the fragile boundary between the real and spirit worlds. When Tuatha Dé Danann appeared in the form of swans, chains of gold around their necks identified them as these immortal folk. Goddesses in both Norse and Celtic mythology shape-shifted into birds, usually either swans or crows. The Mórrígan was known as the Crow of Battle. When she wasn't standing on the battlefield chanting a poem filled with spells, she would be flying as a crow over the heads of the fighting men, swooping and screeching at them. Odin's valkyries, in the form of ravens, also appeared shrieking above battlefields. A swan was another valkyrie form. One warrior, Helgi, was a favourite of the valkyrie Kára, who turned into a swan flying over his head when he fought in battle.

Swans shape-shifting into young women is a popular story theme that is found in folk and fairy tales from many different cultures. In the fairy tale "The Swan Maidens,"[11] a duck hunter hears, high in the air, the sound of wings, but instead of ducks seven swans fly down to the water, take off their feathers, and bathe in the water as human girls. The tale is a typical one. The stories involve a swan-maiden who loses her feather plumage, appears exquisitely beautiful as a human maiden, and lives for a time with a mortal husband. However, she never really belongs in the human world, and eventually she leaves it. These tales have an aura of great antiquity. In fact, one of them appears in a poem in the *Poetic Edda*, "The Lay of Völund," one of the oldest poems in the Edda (c. 900 – 1050).[12] It presents events that occur very early in the life of Völund, the popular magician-smith, not quite human, yet not quite divine, who created rings, armour, and swords for champions and kings. The swan-maidens in this poem are valkyries and pagan spirits. They come from a place beyond the Myrkwood, which was for the northerners a dark, mythic forest at the very edge of the human world, and was the inspiration for Tolkien's Mirkwood forest in *The Hobbit* and *Lord of the Rings*.

The poem exists in a single manuscript,[13] and parts of it are in poor shape and unreadable. Fortunately, a prose introduction to the poem exists. This introduction would have been added by the compiler of the *Poetic Edda* manuscript to clarify the poem for readers, and therefore it would have been a more recent addition to the original poem by two or three centuries. The prose summary provides the following details of the story.

Three sons of a Finnish king, Völund and his two brothers, Slagfith and Egil, are living in a hunting hall in the Wolfdale valley near the sea, where they spend their days on snowshoes hunting game. Early one morning, they are surprised to find at the water's edge three maidens sitting on the shore spinning flax. These are valkyries who have set aside their swan plumages. They do not appear frightened when they see the men. In fact, each maiden approaches one of the brothers, the one called Hervor putting her arms around Völund. The maidens accompany the young men to their hall and stay there with them through eight long winters. In time, however, the women yearn to be valkyries once more, and one day, when the brothers are off hunting, they disappear. Slagfith and Egil set out on their snowshoes to find them, and search for a long time but without success. Völund remains alone in Wolfdale spending his days hunting and working at his forge, waiting for Hervor to return. He forges jewelry, including a precious red gold arm-ring, as gifts for her, but she never returns to receive them.

The lines below give a sense of the spare simplicity and yet the power of the ancient original poem. Even with so very few words, we feel the remoteness of the place, the swan-maidens' yearning, and the brothers' grief. From the poor condition of the text on the fragile, browned page, it is difficult for a translator to reconstruct the poem; the ellipses represent lines that are lost.

1 Maids from the south   through Myrkwood flew,
Fair and young,   their fate to follow;
On the shore of the sea   to rest them they sat,
The maids of the south,   and flax they spun.

2 . . .
Hlathguth and Hervor,   Hlothver's children,
And Olrun the Wise   Kjar's daughter was.

3 . . .
One in her arms   took Egil then
To her bosom white,   the woman fair.

4 Swan-White second, –   swan-feathers she wore,
. . .
And her arms the third   of the sisters threw
Next round Völund's   neck so white.

5 There did they sit   for seven winters,
In the eighth at last   came their longing again,

(And in the ninth   did need divide them).
The maidens yearned   for the murky wood,
The fair young maids,   their fate to follow.

6 Völund home   from his hunting came,
From a weary way,   the weather-wise bowman,
Slagfith and Egil   the hall found empty,
Out and in went they,   everywhere seeking.

7 East fared Egil   after Olrun,
And Slagfith south   to seek for Swan-White;
Völund alone   in Ulfdalir lay,
. . .

8 Red gold he fashioned   with fairest gems,
And rings he strung   on ropes of bast;
So for his wife   he waited long,
If the fair one home   might come to him.[14]

Alas, Völund never sees his young valkyrie wife again. The text of
"The Lay of Völand" consists of two separate poems about Völand, and
this is the end of the first one. We do not know where the author of this
lay may have heard of this stark and strangely beautiful story which he
wrote down a thousand years ago. It may have been brought from far
away. The smith-figure would suggest that it likely derived from a Saxon
song, and yet the valkyries convey a northern myth. Whatever its origin,
it is intriguing that this very old story of swan-maidens encompasses the
basic elements of most swan-maiden folk and fairy tales.

19

Omens and Prophecies

In the German epic *The Nibelungenlied*, a king with his knights and a thousand Nibelung warriors were journeying to Hungary to fight the Huns, when they came to a flood on the river.[1] One of the knights, Hagan, fully armed with his sword, shield, and helmet, was commanded to walk along the riverbank to find a ferryman who could take the men across. After he had gone a ways, Hagan heard splashing and saw maidens in the water. The garments they left lying on the shore must have been strange and marvellous, since Hagan recognized at once that these women to whom they belonged were supernatural beings with powers of prophecy, and so he asked the water-maidens how the warriors' journey to Hungary would fare.

The knight was told that they should all turn back. It was fated that every one of them would die there except for the king's chaplain. This news distressed Hagan, and he was determined that the men could prevent this from happening, but the words of the maiden were true; except for the chaplain, every knight and warrior was killed in a great slaughter. All water spirits, and swan-maidens as these probably were, had this gift of prophecy.

The medieval stories present a world more fluid and changeable than our own, and yet, in another way that might seem almost contradictory, it was a world more fixed. Fate was an understood concept. The "Lay of Völund," as sparse as this poem is, repeats the lines that the valkyries had "their fate to follow." Just as the past stretched out behind the present in a long, unchangeable form, back and back until lost from view, so too, the future stretched out ahead in an unknowable but largely predetermined way. These early stories are filled with themes that convey this – portents, dream-visions, auguries, soothsayers – all elements of old folk belief that would also become part of fairy tale lore.

The prophetic nature of dreams is an element found over and over in medieval literature; there are dreams of a hawk with golden feathers, a face in the water, a stag shot down, valkyries with swords, howling wolves, a raging river. These dreams are signs anticipating events to come. *The Nibelungenlied* is a story of tragic fate, through which women's dreams portend much of the narrative. In the beginning pages of the first chapter, the beautiful young Kriemhild, born into a noble family, dreamed that she reared a falcon that was strong, fair, and wild, but before her eyes two eagles tore it apart. Kriemhild's mother interpreted the falcon as a nobleman, who, unless God prevented it, would be taken from her daughter, and so begins that long story of proud knights who die grievously.

In Irish literature the future is presaged more frequently through visions. When a prince, Cormac, with a large company of his men, was returning home to assume the throne – his father, the Ulster king Conchobar, was dying – two disturbing sights appeared to him. First, at the edge of a river the men saw a woman who was entirely red washing a chariot and harness. Next, a young girl in a light green cloak appeared and advised the men to turn back. These proved to be prophetic visions. Cormac understood that they were going to be attacked, and indeed, at the place where they stopped that night, he and most of his men were killed.

Augury of the future through bird songs was a concept of ancient lore. In the first century, Tacitus noted that Germans, similar to Romans, were familiar with divining the future from the cries and flights of birds. He also described the future augured from the neighing of special white horses, animals that were never ridden but were cared for by German priests in sacred groves.[2] In the early literature, birds were understood to be harbingers of omens and prophetic tidings, for any who could decipher the meaning. Once Sigurd came to understand the language of birds in the *Saga of the Völsungs*, nuthatches could give him helpful counsel. On the day that the Eddic hero Helgi the Hunding-Slayer was born, eagles screamed, an omen of an important birth. Then a raven croaking in a tree foretold the child's battles ahead; the raven saw Helgi in a coat of mail, his eyes flashing fire, slaying many foes. Interpreting bird songs and omens is one of the skills taught to a young prince in the Eddic poem "The Lay of Ríg" (*Rígsthula*).[3] The prince Kon was strong and vigorous, capable of brandishing swords and riding swift horses. Nevertheless, he was more interested in charming down and snaring birds in the woods, discerning their language, and learning their wisdom. On one occasion he received valuable advice from a crow on the waging of war.

Similarly, birds sometimes appear in fairy tales explaining the past, offering advice, warning of dangers, and foretelling the future. It was helpful that a young prince had studied bird language in the Icelandic "Story of Mjadveig, Daughter of Mani."[4] The princess Mjadveig lived secluded in a hut on a stretch of land jutting out into the sea, hidden from all the world by the waves and a vast, dark forest. But she had animals and birds for company, including cuckoos that were wiser than humans, since they knew everything that had happened and would happen. The prince was sailing past her shore with his bride-to-be, when suddenly he heard a great sound of birds chirping at him all at once. He deciphered their message, that the woman in his ship was a false bride, and he should instead marry the girl in the hut. The birds were right. The prince broke the spell of the huge, ugly troll in his ship, who had taken Mjadveig's exact likeness, killed her then and there, and then rowed ashore towards the little house and his true bride. A young man in "Trusty John" also understood bird language, when three ravens croaked about calamities about to befall the king and his bride unless the king's loyal brother could prevent them, by using more bird advice.

Certain places and times were especially auspicious for omens and signs of the future, particularly any borders or thresholds, such as riverbanks, crossroads, burial mounds, or the tops of hills. It is a theme in Icelandic tales that if a person sits out at a crossroads on New Year's Eve he will see elves, and one man who stayed there, facing the elves on the road all night long, found that by dawn he had acquired the gift of foretelling the future.[5] Especially auspicious were the liminal periods of twilight and midnight, as well as the times of births and deaths.

The appearance of omens at the moment of a baby's birth, revealing the infant's destiny, is a theme of many folk and fairy tales. With the dire warning that a newborn is fated to bring about calamity, the baby is kept locked in a castle tower, set adrift in a boat, or left, wrapped in a blanket, to be eaten by animals deep in a forest. But no sooner is the baby abandoned under a pine tree, than a hunter passes by, hears its cry, and tenderly carries it home, and thus the tale unfolds with the child's tragic destiny fulfilled.

In the ancient stories, wise women, norns, and druids make such predictions at a child's birth, and one of the best-loved legends, the story of Deirdre, has this theme. This is an extraordinary, very old story, "the most stunning tale ever written in Irish,"[6] according to Jeffrey Gantz in *Early Irish Myths and Sagas.* It has been told many times. William Butler Yeats wrote the play *Deirdre* based on it, John Millington Synge wrote *Deirdre of the Sorrows,* and there are versions by Lady Gregory, James Stephens, and a host of others. The following is based on the earliest version, which is mostly in verse and was likely composed in the late eighth or early ninth century,[7] "*Longas mac nUislenn*" from the *Book of Leinster.*

The Exile of the Sons of Uisliu[8]

When Conchobar was king of Ulster, he and some of the Ulstermen were gathered one evening at the home of his chief storyteller, Fedlimid. Suddenly, a loud scream came from the unborn child of Fedlimid's pregnant wife. The frightened woman asked the druid Cathbad, who was there with the others in the room, what the meaning of this cry could be. The druid told her that he saw in her womb a woman of great beauty "with twisted yellow hair / and beautiful grey green eyes. / Foxglove her purple pink cheeks."[9] Men would fight for her, kings would woo her, and queens would envy her. But she would be a great danger. For her sake men would go into exile, and she would be the cause of death to the men of Ulster. Her name would be Deirdre, and her story would be a tale of wonder.

To prevent this prophecy coming true, the men demanded that the baby be killed as soon as it was born. Instead, the king decided that the infant would be raised in a court apart, where she would never be seen except by her nurse and foster-parents, until she was old enough to be his consort. And so Deirdre grew to be a young woman. There was no one in Ireland so beautiful, and she was to marry the king. But one day, Deirdre laid eyes on the young prince Noíse, son of the chieftain Uisliu, and then everything changed.

Deirdre fell deeply in love. Noíse was filled with dread, for Deirdre was betrothed to a great king, but with powerful witchcraft she bound him to her. The lovers escaped, along with Noíse's two brothers and a band of warriors, and they travelled away across the sea to where the king's men would never find them. There they lived in the wild woods hunting and fishing, until, after many years, news came to the couple and their companions that they could safely return to Ulster. The king had declared that all would be forgiven.

Deirdre and Noíse were eager to come home, but there was treachery!

As soon as they set foot on the green outside the fort of Emain Macha, Noíse and his men were attacked and slain; Deirdre was taken to Conchobar with her hands tied tightly behind her. Noíse's allies then raised forces against Conchobar, and the slaughter of the ensuing battle would continue for sixteen years. The druid's prophecy that Deirdre would bring death and ruin upon all of Ulster would be fulfilled.

Deirdre spent one year with Conchobar, rarely sleeping, or eating, or raising her head from her knees. She thought only about Noíse. She remembered his grey eyes, how he had cooked over a hearth on the wild forest floor, and she remembered his voice as he and his brothers sang coming through the forest. She told Conchobar, "Break no more my heart today – / I will reach my early grave soon enough. / Sorrow is stronger than the sea / if you are wise, Conchubur."[10] Enraged with her, the king gave her away to the one man she hated most of all, the man who had killed Noíse. The following day, Deirdre was forced to ride in a chariot, standing between Noíse's murderer and Conchobar. When she saw a great boulder ahead, she flung herself from the chariot, dashed her head against the rock, and died.

In Deirdre's story and in similar tales there is nothing that humans can do to change the path of fate. In a related type of tale, destiny is just as unchangeable, but rather than being predicted at the birth of a child, it is decreed for him or her by fairies-of-fortune, or in the early Norse literature by the pagan goddesses called norns. When these women of fate arrived at the home of a newborn child to set his destiny, proper hospitality towards them was critical. The story of Nornagest, from the Icelandic manuscript *Flateyjarbók*, describes what happened when a harmonious relationship with these women was disrupted. This story takes place in an era almost four centuries earlier than when it was written in the fourteenth century. It portrays a time when paganism was giving way to Christianity, when most people had converted, but some only nominally, as they secretly kept their devotion to the old gods. Olaf Tryggvason of Norway, who had been a fierce Viking before he changed into a strong Christian, became king.

Nornagest[11]

When Nornagest was born, his father, a nobleman, held a fine banquet for the three norns who arrived to visit the new baby in his cradle. Many other people were there as well, all wondering what the norns were going to say. The first two norns blessed the child and said that he would be luckier and greater than the son of any other chieftain. At that moment one of the rough men in the crowd bumped into the third norn, knocking her to the ground. Everyone was horrified! This youngest norn was so angry that she shouted at the other norns to stop their benevolent gifts. Pointing to a nearby candle, she said that the child would live only as long as the candle lasted. As soon as the flame burned out, the child would die. The oldest norn, who had spoken first, quickly blew out the candle and handed it to the devastated parents, saying that the curse could still be made into a blessing. She told them to keep the candle safe and never to light it; as long as it remained unlit the child would live. Then the parents named the child Nornagest, which meant "one protected by the norns."

Nornagest grew up to be a tall, strong young man and a fine poet; when he sang and played his harp, it was a joy to everyone who heard it. For three hundred years he did not grow old. But things changed during those years. Christianity had recently come to the north, and the old gods began to disappear. By the year 999, the Norwegian king Olaf Tryggvason had brought Christianity to Norway. It was to this king's court that Nornagest came one day and was welcomed.

That night, the king was awake and saying his prayers while all the other men in the hall slept, when he saw an elf. The creature crossed the room and stood for a time by the bed of one of the men, then vanished. The next morning the king asked who had slept in that bed the night before, and was told that it was the stranger who had arrived the previous day and given his name only as Gest. Olaf asked this man if he had been baptized, and Nornagest told him that he was converted, but not yet baptized, although, in reality, he was a heathen. Nevertheless, the king liked Nornagest and asked him to stay. Olaf enjoyed his stories of King Harald Fairhair, King Hlothver from the land of the Saxons, and others whom Nornagest had known. He particularly liked hearing the tales of Sigurd the Völsung in whose company Nornagest had travelled. Everyone loved his songs and listened to them long into the evenings.

But Nornagest had lived a long time and was tired. He told the king about the norns and the candle, which he had kept with him, and the king asked for it to be lit. If Nornagest were truly converted, he would not believe in the norns' old prophecies. So Nornagest lit the candle. The people in the room fell silent, even though they had all converted to the new religion and disclaimed the old beliefs. Their eyes watched Nornagest as the candle burned quickly and the flame flickered. The candle went out! All eyes turned to the king who looked on in disbelief. Nornagest was dead, just as the norn had predicted.

Just like the norns of this old tale, fairies who arrive to give blessings to a baby, which will determine the child's destiny, sometimes as in this story have to contradict each other's gifts so that tragedy can be averted. In all of the tales, once the destiny is set, the notion of unchangeable fate is understood. The Grimms' "Brier Rose," better known as "Sleeping Beauty,"[12] has the same story element as "Nornagest" and it is a familiar tale. When a princess is born, a fairy, or wise woman, who has been slighted cries out that the king's daughter, in her fifteenth year, will be pricked by a spindle and die. So that this evil wish cannot be fulfilled, another fairy pronounces that the princess will not die, but only sleep for a hundred years. And so it happens. At first, princes try to reach the beautiful sleeping princess, but bleed to death attempting to enter the thorn hedge that quickly grew around the castle. Over the years she is forgotten by almost everyone, until, a hundred years after her fifteenth birthday a prince easily passes through the hedge, kisses her, and she awakens along with all of the court that has been sleeping as well. The story seems to mirror an old legend of Brynhild. Odin pricked this valkyrie with a sleep thorn, so that, clad in her battle armour, she slept an enchanted sleep in a tower, unseen by anyone for many years. The curse was broken when Sigurd climbed to her sleep-chamber, removed her helmet, and kissed her.

It is relevant imagery that Sleeping Beauty's fate was determined through the use of a spindle. Supernatural women in the forms of norns, valkyries, fairies, or hags were associated both with destiny and with spinning and weaving. The valkyries on the shore near Völund's home were spinning flax. This was one of their functions. Odin's valkyries could regulate the outcome of the following day's battles by weaving the story on a grey web crossed with crimson threads, the design representing the battle and blood of the fallen. In *Njal's Saga*, twelve valkyries sang while they worked at a grisly loom – made of heads, entrails, arrows, and a sword – on which they controlled Viking armies that were fighting in far-off Ireland. Norns in the "Helgi Lay," from the *Poetic Edda*, spun Helgi's fate-threads over the whole world, stretching the ends east and west, and then gathering the threads and binding them up in the heavens. One spinning goddess was the popular Freyja, and another was Odin's wife, Frigg. These goddesses knew the fates of humans, and Frigg was portrayed in folklore as spinning while she watched the homes of earthlings. If she noticed a woman working very hard at her loom, she would send her a piece of yarn, and from that time on, no matter how much weaving the woman did, her yarn was never used up and she could experience continuing good fortune.[13]

In the ancient Irish stories, the lives of kings and heroes were bound by another factor connected to a powerful sense of fate, with a story motif that was uniquely Celtic. In *Gods and Heroes of the Celts*, Marie-Louis Sjoestedt describes the ways in which an Irish hero was a persona quite different from an ordinary mortal – in addition to his possessing courage to a "suicidal extreme": "To the valour of the warrior, the keen sense of the savage in the wilderness, he joins the magic skill of the sorcerer and the culture of the poet … Nevertheless, this triumphant personality has a master and a limit. He finds them in the impersonal and multiform doom known as *geis*."[14] This word "geis" refers to a magical bond or an injunction that is placed on a hero, rather like a spell. It is a sacred edict that something must be either done or not done. If there is more than one geis, and there often are, they are geasa, and these play a large part in Irish legends. They are a central attribute of kingship: "The more eminent a person is and the more sacred he is, the more *geasa* he has. The king's person is thus hedged around with prohibitions."[15] When a storyteller informs us that a hero has geasa that he must never violate, which have been placed on him at his birth, or later, perhaps by a druid or an evil stepmother, we understand that the hero is going to be tested. When circumstances arise that make it impossible for him not to violate the geasa, we know then, that the hero is doomed. Fate has determined that it is time for him to die.

The violation of geasa is the theme of another of the remarkable stories that Mael Muiri included in the *Book of the Dun Cow*. Along with the adventure of Connla, the wooing of Étaín, and the birth of Cúchulainn, this story belongs to the list of tales that were included in the lost manuscript *Cín Dromma Snechta* from the eighth century. This story is ancient, and it is, indeed, a strange tale.

"The Destruction of Da Derga's Hostel" (*Togail bruidne Da Derga*)[16] is the story of a legendary, first-century king. Similar to other kings and heroes in the early Irish literature, this king was not conceived in the usual way. His mother was captured by a shape-shifting bird, and the creature told her that it would impregnate her, she would bear a son, the child's name would be Conaire, and this boy must never kill birds. Soon after, his mother became betrothed to a king, and so Conaire was born a prince.

When the boy was still a youth and was being schooled away from home, the king suddenly died. At the time, Conaire was in a chariot chasing a flock of unusual, large, white-speckled birds and was attempting to shoot one with a stone, when the birds landed and removed their feather hoods. The largest of the flock told the boy that he must not shoot at birds because they were all related to him. The bird also told Conaire that it was prophesied that he was now king and he must go at once to Tara. Then the bird gave him a very long and complicated list of prohibitions. He must not hunt the wild beasts of Cerna; he must not venture beyond Tara every ninth night; he must not settle a quarrel between servants; he must not allow a single man or woman to enter his house after sunset; and there were others.

Although still a boy when he became king, Conaire's reign was peaceful and long, until he was forced to make judgments that violated several of his geasa. Then, very quickly, events occurred that forced him to transgress the rest of them – one right after the other. He knew his end had come on a Samain night when he was a guest at Da Derga's hostel. A black, ugly hag came to the door after sunset, demanding hospitality, and refused to go anywhere else. His final geis was violated. That night marauders broke in, set the place on fire, and decapitated him.

Whether there ever were prohibitions on the very early Irish kings, or whether the concept of geis was solely a narrative device of the early storytellers to introduce tricky challenges, omens, and a sense of doom into their stories, we have no way of knowing. There is nothing quite like it in folk and fairy tales. Some of these tales have prohibitions that must be respected, but invariably are broken; the forbidden box is opened, the forbidden room is entered. Still, these injunctions are not so unexplainable, so apparently random, as geasa.

Fairy tales present a different theme regarding destiny. In many stories, an old man or woman or friendly animal instructs a hero as to what he must seek and where he must travel, what obstacles he is going to encounter on his way, and where he can find the magical objects he will need to overcome his trials. The reader understands, then, that everything in the tale is going to proceed exactly as it was foretold. There is a sense in this kind of fairy tale that the outcome has already been determined. Yet, within that framework, there are some choices to be made. And, an act that is anticipated in a tale is no less noble or courageous. Although a story with omens, prophecies, and foretellings can develop for the reader a presentiment of what is going to follow, there are still many surprises as the tale progresses compellingly towards its inevitable conclusion.

20

Between Two Worlds

The old men, but more often women, in tales, who can read omens, interpret dreams, divine the future, and see events that are far away in time and place are an understood part of the fairy tale world. These masters of the supernatural, as in the Finnish fairy tale below, are usually skilled in other magical arts as well, such as knowing how to break enchantments and possessing the wisdom to confront unnatural encounters.

Vaino and the Swan Princess[1]

A young man who lived alone in a cottage beside a small lake saw nine swans one morning swoop down from the sky and settle on the water. He was amazed when they removed their feathers and swam in the form of human girls. The very same thing happened the next day, and by then he had fallen in love with one of the maidens – the girl with long golden hair and blue eyes. He knew that she must be under some spell. The young man ran through the forest to the hut of an old Lapland woman and asked of her how he could break the enchantment. After the woman had sat with her chin in her hand for a very long time, rocking back and forth and mumbling to herself, she told Vaino that he must take the swan-maiden's feather robe, and then she gave him the words of a charm to use so that the girl's heart would burn with love for him, too. Vaino thanked the woman, and the next day hid by the water and waited. That morning the charm worked. He freed the maiden, who was a princess, from a witch's evil spell. However, in order to free her eight sisters from the very same spell and to please her father, the young man had to embark on a difficult journey that took him into the otherworld, an ordeal for which he was compelled to return to the Lapland woman to seek more advice.

Figures similar to this old woman are easily found in the ancient stories. In the early Celtic and Norse literature, men and women consult with wise women, wizards, druids, and seeresses for their esoteric knowledge. These spiritual guides in all things supernatural recite spells and incantations, commune with spirits and the dead, interpret dreams and auguries, and intervene in unnatural occurrences. They function at the invisible and unknown boundary of the otherworld, and from some thin space between the two worlds are able to see into the future. The first poem of the *Poetic Edda*, "The Prophecy of the Seeress," is spoken in the voice of such a woman, who presents her visions of the gods and of the past and future of the world.

These figures in the old myths and legends conform to folklore and narrative character-types, but they also reflect the place that a few individuals, in some ways like them, held at one time in the society of real men and women. In the pre-Christian world of northern Europe, along with the kings and chieftains, warriors, farmers, and serfs, there was an important role for men and women who had acquired special knowledge and expertise to become spiritual authorities, and were believed to be practised in the art of prophecy. Priest-seers had existed since the time of the Romans. Tacitus' *Histories* and *Germania* and Pliny's *Natural History* describe encounters in Gaul, Britain, and the territory north of the Danube with priests and tribal wise women who presided over magical rites and ceremonies, spoke divine utterances and prophecies, and in times of battle pronounced magical curses. Tacitus describes one German seeress, Veleda, who lived alone in a secluded tower from which she answered any questions that were asked of her and was particularly venerated as an oracle.[2] But all German women, Tacitus wrote, had some gift of prophecy.

The Icelandic literature mentions several times a ceremony of divination called *seid* that was closely connected with the goddess Freyja. One fictional account, in the *Saga of Erik the Red*,[3] depicts a seid ritual in Greenland in the 900s that is consistent with other representations. By the late twelfth century, when this saga was written, seid was officially forbidden, but details could have been drawn from folk memory or from an illegal practice. Travelling to farms and villages as she was needed, a practitioner of this art performed a ritual of entering into a trance-like state, during which she summoned spirits to communicate with her; and in this story, the seeress Thorbjorg was requested to come to a farmstead. The community there needed to know the prospects for the season, since there had been famine and sickness for some time. As it was the custom for the ritual, a special meal was prepared for Thorbjorg's visit, and a platform built with a cushioned chair set on it. The details of the seeress's attire when she arrived at the farmhouse in the evening form one of the few long descriptive passages in the sagas, and we learn that parts of her clothing were catskin – Freyja's spirit animal.[4]

She was wearing a blue cloak with straps which was set with stones right down to the hem; she had glass beads about her neck, and on her head a black lambskin hood lined inside with white catskin. She had a staff in her hand, with a knob on it; it was ornamented with brass and set around with stones just below the knob. Round her middle she wore a belt made of touchwood, and on it was a big skin pouch in which she kept those charms of hers which she needed for her magic. On her feet she had hairy calf-skin shoes with long thongs, and on the thong-ends big knobs of lateen. She had on her hands catskin gloves which were white inside and hairy.[5]

The feast was served, and in the dark hours it came time for Thorbjorg's trance. Women gathered in a circle around the platform on which she was seated, and one of them began to sing a spell-chant, an ancient song the singer's foster-mother had taught her in Iceland. The beauty of the woman's song drew spirits to encircle the seeress, who learned from them that the famine would end in the spring. Her prediction turned out to be true. When Christianity was adopted in the Nordic countries, and sorcery and all magical practices such as this were forbidden, women may have accepted the new religion, but there remained then no one in women's lives to replace the wise women and seeresses who had been feminine spiritual guides. They became thought of as from a lost age.

In the sagas of Icelanders, some seid practitioners learned their skill in Finland or Lapland, and the sagas also refer to sorcerers and wizards from these countries, or from Finnmark, a territory in the far north of Norway where the Sami people lived. It is a possibility that the kinds of magic we find in these Icelandic stories reflect aspects of old Sami practices, but certainly, the idea that Lapland sorcerers were eminent in the supernatural arts was a medieval literary theme. In one saga, a husband and wife who were unable to have children sought help from a Lapland wizard who appealed to spirits on their behalf, and the son they bore grew up to think of himself always as a child of the old gods. Snorri Sturluson told a story of an expedition to Lapland, where the men going ashore were surprised to meet a beautiful Norwegian girl, Gunnhild, who had gone to that country to learn witchcraft or "Lapland-art" from two sorcerers. Even Odin himself, when he needed advice on magical arts, travelled there to seek the help of a wizard. The great sorcerer Väinämöinen in the Finnish *Kalevala* lived his early years in Lapland, where he travelled throughout that dark northland learning from master wizards. The excellence of wizards and wise women from Finland and Lapland was part of the folklore of these countries. And so, in "Vaino and the Swan Princess" and other northern fairy tales we come upon these people skilled in wizardry; a witch from Lapland turns a princess and all of her servants into mice, and a Lapland wizard teaches a boy how to turn himself, at will, into any bird or beast.

The early Irish and Welsh stories depict powerful literary figures who function on the boundary between the human and spirit realms. Some of these are druids. We cannot speak with certainty of the role of druids in the real pre-Christian Ireland or Wales, but in the stories they are important as prophets and advisers to kings. They are also seen as magicians, and early Irish literature is filled with things "druidic," spells and charms, wands, cloaks of invisibility; often in the stories the word "druidic" could be interchanged with the word "magic." One individual who embodies this concept of druidism is Coran, the druid in "Connla and the Fairy Maiden" who used his power of spells to defend Connla against the enchantments of the otherworld. Another druid is Cathbad, who appears in several stories and was highly regarded for his magic or *druídecht*. This druid was King Conchobar's chief adviser, and he also imposed geasa on Cormac at the time that this important early king assumed the throne. When the champion Cúchulainn was a little boy, Cathbad was his teacher, instructing him in druid lore, and the druid prophesied, correctly, that although the child would achieve fame and greatness his life would be short. Another of his prophecies foretold that Deirdre would bring ruin upon Ulster.

Female druids were also mentioned in the literature. The druidess Bodhmall, together with a wise woman named the Grey One, secretly raised Finn in the wilderness from the time of his birth. These two women taught the boy skills and knowledge he needed to become a powerful warrior-seer. Druids of the Tuatha Dé Danann had powerful magic and were known for changing themselves into deer or any other form and for calling up druidic mists. It was this kind of druid who changed Finn's wife Sadb into a deer.

Several remarkable characters feature in the very early, seventh- or eighth-century[6] "Cattle Raid of Cooley," which Mael Muiri included in the *Book of the Dun Cow*.[7] This central epic story of the Ulster Cycle is the legend of a headstrong warrior-queen of Connacht, Medb, who started a war over the issue of a single bull. While her warriors were gathering at an encampment, Medb had been to see a druid to find out how the battle would fare, when she encountered on the road a beautiful young woman, armed and riding a chariot. This woman wore a red embroidered tunic and gold-clasped sandals. Her hair was in three braids, two of them wound around her head and one hanging down her back below her knees. A strange thing about the woman was that she had three irises in each eye, but the most important detail of her description is that she held in her hand a weaver's rod made of bronze and inlaid with gold. With this oracular item connected with weaving, she was clearly a fortune teller. This was Fedelm, a poet who had studied prophecy under the renowned seeress Scáthach, and she prophesied doom for Queen Medb's army.[8] Alas, the queen scorned Fedelm's warnings, and soon Medb's warriors faced their fearsome enemy – the Ulster warrior Cúchulainn.

Cúchulainn had also trained under the woman Scáthach, "the Shadowy One," whose academy existed at the very edge of the human world. While Cúchulainn was courting the lovely Emer, the girl's father, hoping that the wild young warrior would never return to his daughter, suggested to him that he attend that training academy, and Cúchulainn agreed to go. The training camp is depicted as being in Scotland, likely on the Isle of Skye, and his journey there was long and dangerous until a lion-like animal helpfully carried Cúchulainn on its back. Still, to reach the island he had to cross the Pupil's Bridge, but whenever he leaped onto one end of it, the other end of the bridge rose up and threw him off. On his third try, with a gigantic leap onto the very centre of the bridge, Cúchulainn made it across and demanded to be trained. And so this other-worldly warrior woman, Scáthach, taught him all the arts of combat. She also foretold his future through a vision. Her prophetic poem, "The Words of Scáthach" (*Verba Scáthaige*), is cited in the contents list of the lost *Cín Dromma Snechta*, placing this part of Cúchulainn's long saga in the eighth century.

Celtic poets, when seen as figures in the early literature, were also depicted as skilled seers and prophets. Muireann Ní Bhrolcháin explains, in *An Introduction to Early Irish Literature*, that "the Celtic poet, along with saints and other marginalized characters, may be portrayed as a mantic seer or shaman."[9] In the legend that surrounds the Welsh poet Taliesin, we learn that from early childhood Taliesin exhibited exceptional powers; he could make things happen simply by uttering words. He became a magician who survived a voyage into the otherworld, and an inspired poet and prophet. Over the centuries many poems were written in the persona of Taliesin the poet-seer, among them "Taliesin's First Address," a poem of bardic lore, which lists enigmatic questions and answers about mythology and religion. A tenth-century Taliesin poem, "The Great Prophecy of Britain," predicts that the Irish, the Scots, and the Welsh will become allied together under Welsh leadership and will drive the invading Saxons out of Britain. This very early poem mentions another notable poet-seer in the Welsh tradition, Myrddin.

A prominent figure in Arthurian stories, Myrddin, or Merlin, was a magician-prophet and a truly Celtic figure. He was an adviser to King Arthur on matters both natural and supernatural and was a wizard capable of shape-shifting and calling up storms. But there is another story of Myrddin's past entirely separate from the King Arthur legend that is even, perhaps, the more interesting story.

A young Myrddin took part in the Battle of Arderydd, which was fought in the year 573 between Christian and pagan kingdoms in Cumbria in the north of England. Myrddin's king, Gwenddoleu, who was a pagan ruler and a patron of poets, died in that battle, as did Myrddin's nephew; and Myrddin was driven mad, both from the horrors of the battle and from his grief. He fled into the Celyddon Wood in southern Scotland, where he spent fifty years in solitude living as a wild man – a holy man – and communing with the creatures and spirits of the forest. He emerged from the woods transformed into a powerful prophet. Six early poems are written in the voice of Myrddin.[10] They portray a poet-prophet who has grown old and weary hiding from the world in a secret place concealed by the dark forest. In "Greetings" (*Yr Oianau*), Myrddin listens to the melody of chirping birds and the loud voices of sea birds, and predicts the future of the Welsh people. One poem is a conversation with Taliesin, in which Myrddin sees himself as the next prophet to succeed him.

It is a subject of debate whether a poet and bard named Myrddin actually existed in the sixth century. The battle was a real one. There are so many references to him in the early literature that this is possible, but we will never know. As a literary figure, however, Myrddin was a well-known poet and seer who spoke for the Welsh people and was connected with the old Celtic region of northern England and southern Scotland before it fell to the Anglo-Saxons. Prophets such as Myrddin and Taliesin, who could see into the future and could function on both human and supernatural planes, represent an important type of literary figure in the Celtic tradition.

Wizards based on these old prophet-magicians appear in fairy tales, but more often in these stories there are witches instead. Witches have a long history. From pre-Christian times wise women were honoured in communities as local practitioners who helped at the births of babies, provided herbal remedies, interpreted dreams, charmed away wounds and diseases, even created love potions. By the twelfth century, however, these women began to be regarded less highly and were ostracized. Such women lived on in lonely cottages far from society, where they came to be thought of more as sorceresses and witches, and as such they survived in folk tradition. Certainly, it is likely that some resorted to dark arts. But the more prevalent stereotype of these women as witches practising malevolent magic arose late in the Middle Ages. This idea was even more strenuously reinforced in the seventeenth century when church authorities severely crushed any remains of witchcraft.

There is a vast difference between those women called witches and the many witches in fairy tales who are long-nosed hags living in the deep forests where they cast spells and imprison children. These witches, such as "Hansel and Gretel's" wicked crone, have a prototype in fiendish hags in the ancient stories, who cast evil spells and shape-shift. These are witches who exist only in the context of stories.

21

Spells

Spells were a witch's word magic. In fairy tales, a little scrap of rhyme can turn a boy into a hare, free a bride from an enchantment, raise a strong wind, or summon a knight instantly from a faraway land. A grim ogress in a tale forces a princess into a little boat and sets her off all alone onto the sea with these words:

> Thus I lay and this I say;
> do not stop and do not stay;
> to my brother make your way.[1]

The reader is not surprised that the small craft, of its own accord, glides through the night carrying the princess straight to the home of a three-headed troll – the ogress's brother. The hostile uses of magic far outweigh the helpful ones in fairy tales, and spells are often like curses.

Once spoken, one of these spells can take flight like a bird possessed, speeding straight to the person for whom it is destined. Then, in a distant place an alarmed woman looks up from her work, a boat changes course, or a man jumps from a cliff into the sea. Such a spell is commanded to attack far away in "The Water Lily, the Gold Spinners." In this fairy tale, three girls in a remote forest hut were forced into spinning gold flax into yarn, day after day with no rest, for a wicked witch. One day, a young prince who had become lost in the forest found a small path and followed it to the hut. He secretly befriended the youngest of the maidens, and eventually, while the old woman was away, rescued her, carrying her off on his horse. When the witch realized this had happened, she was furiously angry and prepared her magic. She gathered together nine different kinds of enchanter's nightshade, bound the plants with a bewitching formula into a cloth ball, and threw it to the wind with the spell:

Whirlwind! – mother of the wind!
Lend thy aid 'gainst her who sinned!
Carry with thee this magic ball.
Cast her from his arms for ever,
Bury her in the rippling river.[2]

The prince and the maiden were by then a half-day's ride away, and were just at the very centre of a narrow bridge crossing a deep river when the spell ball flew by. Their horse reared in fright, flinging the maiden into the swift current where she entirely disappeared, to re-emerge as a yellow water lily.

More than other European fairy tales, the stories of Finland are filled with magic, and the most marvellous things might be achieved with the spoken word. A boy with his hammer and forge creates a bird from a piece of copper and then sings life-breath into it so the bird becomes alive. With a different song he restores a wild duck to its original form – a rosy-cheeked princess. In another tale, a boy knows a spell to make himself invisible, so that he can leap inside the heart of a grey rabbit running through the forest, and he can change that spell to hide himself inside the heart of a growling bear.[3]

The power of words is an ancient concept. Spell-speakers in fairy tales, similar to the old wise men and women in the early medieval literature, understood something that was intrinsic to many ancient cultures throughout the world – there could be more power in words woven together than we can even imagine, and when voiced through an incantation or song the words were even more potent.

This is a notion that did not entirely disappear. Throughout Europe, over many centuries the belief endured that words recited as charms had the power of healing.[4] In *Homo Narrans*, John Niles questions the appropriateness of the label "charms" for these short poems: "'Charm' is far too light a term to refer to these solemn rites of healing. The words of these alliterative texts are intended to ward off dire afflictions such as disease, infection, famine, infant mortality, and theft of cattle. They speak of pain in a thousand forms, and some of them seek to redress that pain through the rigors of spiritual warfare."[5] In the urgent situation of pain and illness all spiritual forces were brought to bear, Christian as well as otherwise. These little poems of healing indicate a larger concept. For a very long time there was a subtle place where both Christianity and lingering, magical folk practices could be accommodated. This place was in folk belief. In this old Finnish charm, words banish an affliction, as if this is similar to some harmful spirit, back where it came from:

> May the force of the Holy Spirit be with me. –
> All pains, all troubles
> go into a hole in brown rock
> from which you also emerged.[6]

This notion of the magical power of the spoken word found expression in folklore and folk tales. Spell-speakers could call up darkness so that an enemy's horses would lose their way in the woods. They could call up storms to overturn ships at sea, but knew other spells to calm the wind. Tales refer to Lapland sorcerers buying and selling cords into which winds were bound up with spell-knots for the use of mariners when they were stayed by calm weather. Such a knotted rope appears in a Swedish folk tale in which a hunter takes a strange ride in a Laplander troll-woman's sled that flies through the air controlled by the rope. Faster and faster it flies as each spell-knot is untied.[7]

These kinds of spells have long been a part of storytelling tradition, and there are many of them in the very early stories. There were spells on swords, and the more spells that were worked on a sword, the more magical power it had. Magic songs were blended with ale to strengthen the warriors who drank it. There were healing spells that brought fallen warriors back to full health. When Thor returned home after his duel with the giant Hrungnir, he had a piece of that giant's whetstone stuck in his head, but the wise woman Gróa arrived from Midgard to chant spells over him. These were healing spells known only to her. As Gróa chanted, the fragment of whetstone began to be released from Thor's head.[8] Another wise woman also named Gróa (who may be the same seeress) was wakened from the dead by her son. This young man was setting out to the land of giants in search of the maiden Menglöd, and he needed his mother's spells for the dangerous journey. The poem "The Spell of Gróa" (*Grógald*) lists nine spells she taught her son that he could use to protect himself: incantations against scornful words, dangerous men, raging rivers, rising seas, wind and weather, mists, and wraiths, and also a spell to give him a sharp tongue when he was speaking with giants. They were all spells the young man would use.

Odin spoke a corpse-spell, a spell for communicating with the dead, over the grave of a prophetess when he wished to ask her to interpret the meaning of strange dreams. This god drank precious mead to learn many powerful spells, and there is a long list of these in the poem "The Sayings of Hár" (*Hávamál*). In the literature of the early north, spells and magic songs were also called runes,[9] and these were closely associated with Odin. In the same spell poem, the way in which this exalted god became the first rune-master is dramatic and momentous – the god stabbed himself with a spear and impaled himself on the great world-tree, the ash

Yggdrasil. Sacrificing himself on the tree, for nine days and nights Odin hung there, without food or drink, lashed by cold winds. The god looked down, screaming with pain, and as he peered into the deep at the tree's roots, the runes in a flash were revealed to him.[10] These runes were powerful charms that Odin taught to the other gods, and to giants, and then to the elf Dáin and the dwarf Dvalin, who in turn taught them to their own clans.

Runes were wisdom understood by Odin's valkyrie Brynhild. In the *Saga of the Völsungs*, she taught Sigurd those runes that a mortal would need to know in order to become a fearless warrior and a husband suitable for a valkyrie. She taught him war-runes to engrave on the hilt of a sword, sea-runes to carve on the stern of a ship and on its rudder and oars, word-runes to wind about himself for protection, ale-runes to cut on the rim of a drinking horn, bough-runes useful for healing, and thought-runes to bring wisdom for the mind and strength for the soul. All of these runes were magical spells. Brynhild also revealed to Sigurd where the first runes had been carved – on a bear's paws, a wolf's claws, an eagle's bill, on bloody wings, on the teeth of Odin's horse Sleipnir, on the straps of a sleigh, at the end of a bridge, and on items of glass, gold, and silver.[11]

Naturally, the Irish magician gods, the Tuatha Dé Danann, knew powerful spells. Before entering into a battle with the Fomorians, one of their spell-speakers stood on the top of a hill with his back to the north wind. There, holding a magic stone and a thorn in his hand he spoke an incantation that cast an enchantment upon the enemy.[12]

A great battle of spells broke out when the Milesians advanced in their ships to conquer Ireland. Seeing the ships approach, the Tuatha Dé Danann used spells to raise a fierce wind, creating confusion on the water as the ships were tossed to and fro and forcing many of them to retreat back across the sea. One ship was broken into pieces, and many men and women drowned. The Milesian leader, Amairgin, eventually realized that this was not a natural storm – the winds were not higher than the ships' masts – but a druid wind. So, he rose up and countered with an enchantment of his own. He spoke a poem of powerful words, which proclaimed that the ships tossing on the sea would safely reach shore and that his people would find a place to live in that land with their own king. As soon as he had spoken the unearthly wind died down and the sea became calm once more. With these words Amairgin, who was portrayed in the early literature as a great poet and prophet of the Celtic race, enabled his people to land safely and to claim Ireland as their own.[13]

One of the strangest and also oldest Irish spells was uttered by the mysterious wizard-chieftain Cú Roí, who lived in an impregnable fortress in Mael Muiri's story of "Bricriu's Feast." Cú Roí was a traveller: "In whatever part of the globe Cú Roí should happen to be, every night he chanted a spell over the fort, till the fort revolved as swiftly as a millstone. The entrance was never to be found after sunset."[14] A spell could be very short – even a single word. Or, it could be long, such as a spell in the Finnish *Kalevala* extending for ten pages, which was spoken to stop the blood gushing from a wound when Väinämöinen cut his knee with an axe. That spell recounted an involved story of the origin of iron and the creation of the axe, in order to take back the axe's power and stop the blood.[15]

The greatest spell-speaker in folk literature was undoubtedly the same Väinämöinen, the central hero of the *Kalevala*. This long collection of poems from the early days of the Finnish people tells a story of magic. But, as Lafcadio Hearn expressed it, "The magic of 'Kalevala' is not like anything else known by that name in European literature. The magic of 'Kalevala' is entirely the magic of words."[16] In this epic poem Väinämöinen is a primeval sorcerer and a powerful word-master. With music and song he could cast spells on all the birds and animals and even on the sun and the moon. One day, a contest of spells ensued when Väinämöinen and a young man, Joukahainen, had a quarrel on a narrow road where neither would give way to the other. Joukahainen came from Lapland, and so he thought he knew a great deal about magic. Foolishly, the youth challenged the old seer to a match of singing spells. He proceeded to sing about birds, fish, reindeer in Lapland, and tall fir trees. Väinämöinen grew angry because these were children's spells. When he began to sing, the earth shook and the mountains trembled, cliffs fell, and rocks split in two. He sang spells of the origins of heaven, the sky, the stars, and the great constellations. He sang the cap off the young man's head and the mittens off his hands, and when he was finished Joukahainen was stuck up to his waist in a swamp – he couldn't lift a foot. The young man had a hard time freeing himself from that spot, and he realized that there was no one so awesome as a great sorcerer displaying his talents![17]

The ending of the *Kalevala* is extraordinary, and for Lönnrot, the compiler of the folk epic, the story of a newborn king signified the end of the pagan era. A shy, holy girl, Marjatta, had a baby. But the child had no father. Marjatta had been herding sheep high up on a mountain when a golden cuckoo called to her. After that she ate a berry, a magical berry that grew inside her as the baby. A pastor was called upon to baptize the infant, but since there was no father to give him a name, the old judge Väinämöinen was summoned. He decreed that this baby boy, begotten from eating a berry, should be thrown into the swamp (such was the unfortunate fate of some pre-Christian illegitimate children). As soon as he had made this judgment, the two-week-old baby spoke, condemning the old man. Immediately, the pastor baptized the child and named him "king of all the land" and "guardian of all power." Old Väinämöinen was both angry and ashamed, and he retreated to the river where he sang for the last time. The old spell-speaker chanted for himself a copper boat, in which he glided off down the rapids, and on and on, until he disappeared out of the world. But he left behind him the memory of his songs and music for the children of Finland.[18]

22

Trees

The magic of fairy tales that isn't accomplished by casting spells is often performed with the magic wands of witches, wizards, and fairy godmothers. With the touch of a wand, a hard-working girl's wooden spinning wheel is turned into shining gold, or a monstrous, three-headed beast shrinks down into a newt. These transformations happen as quickly as the stepmother in "The Children of Lir," with a touch of her wand, changed her stepchildren into swans. For the most part, fairy tale wands are used for transforming things.

A witch in the Grimms' "Sweetheart Roland" had her axe in hand ready to murder her stepdaughter, but the maiden was able to make an escape by first stealing her stepmother's magic wand. With the witch in pursuit, the girl used the wand to turn her friend Roland into a lake and to change herself into a duck swimming in the middle of the lake. The witch stood on the shore and threw crumbs to entice the duck close to her, but it would not come. At nightfall the old woman returned home, powerless without her wand. The maiden and Roland then resumed their own shapes and walked the whole night long. But at daybreak the girl used the wand to turn herself into a flower and Roland into a fiddler in order to hide themselves from the witch once more.

Wands were primary magical items, and most witches and wizards had one. The wizards in the Harry Potter novels certainly needed wands for their magic along with their powerful spells, and their wands were crafted from different kinds of wood to have unique properties. Harry Potter's was a holly wand.

Sorcerers, druids, and divine figures in the early Welsh and Irish stories transformed people into animals or birds by striking them with their wands, and they also used them to break enchantments, read omens, make divinations, and control spirits. In these stories attention was paid to the kinds of tree branches from which the wands were created. The goddess Brigit is sometimes depicted with a white wand, assumed to be from a hazel branch. Irish druids preferred yew and sometimes hawthorn or rowan wands. The Welsh magician-god Gwydion used an ash wand for his enchantments. A poem written in the persona of the old poet Taliesin is "Kat Godeu," known as "The Battle of the Trees,"[1] in which Gwydion used his staff of enchantment for one of his most magical feats – the creation of an army of soldiers from trees. This was the dilemma for which the exceptional magic was needed.

The Battle of the Trees

A farmer-magician, named Amaethon, stole a hound, a deer, and a bird from Arawn. This theft was extremely serious, since Arawn was lord and king of the otherworld. It was so grave a wrongdoing that it started a war. Soon there were raging otherworldly creatures facing the farmer and his men, and Amaethon called upon his brother, the great magician Gwydion, to help gather forces to fight them. For one thing, the men had to kill a beast with a hundred heads. The humans were outnumbered and overpowered until finally, using his staff of enchantment and all of his magic, Gwydion transformed trees into warriors. Each tree took part in the battle according to its strengths. The Alders were brave and formed the front line, unlike the Willows and Rowans that hesitated and came late to the fight. Beeches flourished in the conflict, Elms in vast numbers went straight to the centre and also took the wings and the rear, while the Ashes performed magnificently. The Hazels provided many arrows for quivers, and even the small Raspberries fought so courageously that they did not need to form their natural barricade. The Broom, at the forefront of the battle, fell wounded in the ditches. A multitude of trees fought well at that magical battle of Godeu, at which the trees, and the humans fighting alongside them, ultimately triumphed.

Seeresses and witches in Norse literature carried magical staffs like Gwydion's and used these to cast their spells. Even the Vanir gods used wands, and "Bearer of a Magic Wand" was one of Odin's names. These older wands and magical staffs were, of course, the same kinds of wands that we find in fairy tales. However, even a simple branch, a stick, or a forked hazel twig could work, too. When the god Frey's vassal, Skírnir, needed a wand to put a curse on a giantess, he went into the woods and simply cut a branch to do the job. Similarly, in the shape-changing fairy tale of Margaret the serpent, Margaret's brother used a mere rowan twig to change the witch into a toad. How did simple branches become wands of power?

The most potent wands were those made from branches that had been cut on the eves of holy days and then exposed to magical rituals. But the primary factor accounting for the old notion of the power of wands could be found in the nature of the trees themselves. There is considerable evidence from the classical Roman authors, that among the ancient Celtic and Germanic peoples many woodland groves and also individual trees were held to be sacred because of their association with deities. In *Germania*, Tacitus mentions priests taking with them into battle "totems," branches, from the groves of trees where people felt the presence of their gods, so that some of this holy presence could accompany them. Pliny explained the sacred significance of the oak tree for the Gauls, who considered that anything growing on this tree was sent from the gods.[2] When Agricola was the Roman governor of Britain in the first century, he realized the power of fundamental beliefs about certain groves of trees as sacred cult sites, and so he destroyed those groves.[3] Trees associated with gods and sacred tree symbolism extend far back into antiquity and were part of many belief systems. In her *Patterns in Comparative Religion*, Mircea Eliade discusses the importance of the tree in many early religions as a centre where the physical and cosmic worlds came together and as a symbol of a larger life force.[4] The Hebrews and even the ancient Egyptians understood that tree branches as wands had inherent or symbolic properties.

In mythology, trees with their branches and fruit are reservoirs of symbolic meaning. In *The Lost Beliefs of Northern Europe*, Hilda Ellis Davidson discusses Norse and Celtic imagery regarding the divine world, and among the great mass of often perplexing details in the stories she concludes, "Certain features concerning the world of the gods, however, seem reasonably well established. One is the importance of its centre, represented in local sacred places by a tree or a pillar, a mound or a great stone."[5] In the *Prose Edda*, when Odin was asked, "Where is the central or holy place of the gods?" he answered, "It is at the ash Yggdrasil."[6] The single world-supporting ash tree rose like a pillar up to the heavens. It was nourished from water at its roots filled with wisdom and knowledge. Around the tree's trunk was Midgard, the world of humans, and in the tree's branches four sacred deer moved about, eating shoots. The primal tree represented the meeting place of the secular and divine worlds, and it was constantly regenerating itself.

In Irish mythology some trees were acknowledged to have a special connection with the divine. These were first brought to Ireland by a god who controlled the rising and setting of the sun, the god with the long name Trefuilngid Tre-eochair. This god was a gigantic figure! He stood as tall as the forest trees, with golden-yellow hair that hung down past his waist and what seemed like a shining crystal veil all around him. He appeared one day at Tara, where the high kings were holding court, carrying in his left hand stone tablets, and in his right a single branch that had nuts, apples, and acorns growing on it. The god requested that the people of Ireland gather together at Tara, where he waited forty days for their arrival. Then he presented the Irish people with berries that they were instructed to plant in each of their regions. These became the first of the many sacred trees of Ireland.[7]

A number of enormous, wondrous trees are mentioned in the mythological lore as trees signifying the presence of the otherworld or of gods. One of these was an oak tree with acorns, apples, and nuts growing together on its branches. Another tree, high on a hill, shone the colour of gold. When the wind blew, the sound of music issued from the top of its branches and golden fruit fell onto the ground like jewels. Under these venerable trees early legendary kings were inaugurated, and a branch cut from his special tree represented a king's spiritual sovereignty.[8]

All trees in the early Irish stories, however, including each type of tree mentioned in Celtic mythology, held some mythological significance as well as spiritual relevance. The following are just a few examples.[9] Yew trees were associated with immortality, and druids often used these branches for their wands. The highly regarded ash was a tree for protection and divination, and its wood had the power to ward off witchcraft. The berries of the rowan, or mountain ash, were a source of food for the Celtic gods, particularly the berries of one sacred tree guarded by a giant. Rowan branches offered protection against enchantments. Hazel was a powerful tree for wands. Hazel trees and hazelnuts were sacred to poets as sources of mystical wisdom, and in the otherworld there were nine hazel trees that inspired poetic knowledge. Ash, oak, and hawthorn were especially associated with fairies.

Apple-laden trees and branches were powerful images from the Celtic otherworld. Bran was invited to that realm by a maiden who came to him bearing a branch from a silver apple tree. Connla was enticed there, not by a branch, but simply by the fairy's offering of an apple. In the following story of Cormac, the sea-god Manannán arrived from the otherworld bearing an apple branch. Grandson of Conn, Cormac was perhaps the most important of the legendary high kings of Ireland, and was portrayed as a wise and learned king and lawmaker.

The Adventure of Cormac[10]

Appearing at Tara as an old, grey-haired warrior, Manannán approached Cormac as the king was walking alone at dawn. The god carried on his shoulder a shining branch bearing golden apples. When the branch was shaken it produced music so delightful that anyone who heard it would not forget the sound. Cormac asked the old man about the branch and was told that it came from the Land of Promise, which was a place of truth, where there was no aging or sadness. From the moment that Cormac heard the music he wanted the branch more than anything else. Manannán offered it to him – on one condition. Cormac could have the branch in exchange for any three wishes the old man might ask for in the future. Cormac agreed, and the strange old warrior departed.

At the palace everyone marvelled at the branch. The sound of it brought joy, and yet was so soothing that anyone who was wounded or sick fell into a gentle sleep. From the time that it came into Cormac's possession no one in the kingdom knew illness or grief. At the end of one year, the old warrior arrived at the royal house with his first request. It was for Cormac's daughter, Aille. The only thing that could dispel the anguish that everyone at Tara felt when she was taken away was the magic bough. A month later the man returned and asked for Cormac's son, Carpre, and the next time he took

Cormac's wife, Ethne, away with him. These requests were too painful, and with some of his men Cormac set out in pursuit of the old warrior.

They soon rode into a heavy mist, and when it cleared they found themselves on a plain that they had never seen before. The men passed by many wondrous things, including a troop of Sidhe riders and a shining house that was thatched with the white wings of birds. The travellers eventually arrived at a royal stronghold, where they were welcomed and taken into a palace enclosure that had a well with nine purple hazel trees growing over it. There they were presented to a young king and his consort, a woman who was the fairest they had ever seen, wearing a golden helmet over her long yellow hair.

In preparation of a feast for these guests, the king had a pig brought to the palace, but the cook declared that the pig would never be cooked until four true stories had been told, one story for every quarter of it. The cook, the host, and his consort each then told a story, and at the end of each one a quarter of the pig was done. After the third story, Cormac was called upon to speak. He related the strange tale of his family's abduction and of the extraordinary sights that he and his men had witnessed in coming to that place. With this story, which although true was the strangest tale of all, the cook declared that the pig was ready to be eaten.

The men were taken inside to dine, whereupon Cormac found his wife and children at the table, and the young king, their host, revealed himself to be the god Manannán. He had brought Cormac to this otherworld castle in order to present him with a gift, a golden cup, which would break if ever lying words were spoken under it. True words would make the cup whole again. With this cup Cormac would always be able to judge between a true story and a false one, and therefore he could reign as a fair and just king. The next morning when Cormac woke, he found himself at his own royal house, and his wife, his children, the apple branch, and the golden cup were with him.

Whenever in an old story or a fairy tale there are trees and apples of silver and gold, these belong to the otherworld. Folk and fairy tales offer many images of trees that have a connection to the magical or spirit world. Fairies gather near a lone hawthorn tree, and the Welsh Tylwyth Teg dance in a circle under a yew tree in the middle of a forest. In folk tales, elves, wood-sprites, wood-trolls, and other spirits inhabited trees. Elves were sometimes connected with aspen, alder, or linden trees, or with whole groves of trees or forests, and in a few stories trees turned into elves at night and walked around. In one Danish tale, during the night a group of oak trees turned into an elf-king's soldiers.

In Scandinavian stories, a linden tree was haunted by an elf or a dwarf who put anyone who came near it after sunset into an enchanted sleep. A Swedish girl haunting the forests could be a spirit wood-wife. Or, she may be a *skogrså*. This was a truly beautiful woman who led travellers dangerously astray in the woods, although she might also grant good luck to hunters. She was beautiful from the front, and yet from the back she resembled nothing more than a hollowed-out tree trunk. In German forests there were moss-folk dressed from head to foot in moss. Some northern folk tales depict a spirit of the forest that lived in an old pine tree and might be seen striding through the woods with a fir tree on his shoulder. In Finland, the chief of all the wood spirits was Tapio, a tall god of the woodlands who had a beard and clothes of moss and a hat made of leaves. In a Finnish tale, a hunter on his skis had followed moose tracks until it grew very late and he was far from home, when he came upon Tapio's cabin. He was invited inside to spend the night and was surprised to find that it was crowded with animals – elk, bear, rabbit, wolf, and fox.[11]

The forest in fairy tales was always a vast place where one could easily become lost, and it was territory filled with mysteries. Wood spirits haunted the trees, other supernatural beings made it their dwelling place, and dangers awaited any children who were left abandoned there by parents too poor to feed them anymore. As in "Hansel and Gretel," the gloomy, pathless woodlands were a terrifying element in many of the Grimms' stories. Here, Little Red Riding Hood was first stalked by the wolf, who in the original version ate her and her grandmother up with no friendly huntsman in sight. Snow White was left alone by a hunter so far into the woods that she would never find her way home, and in "The Old Woman of the Forest," a girl, lost and alone, discovered trees that were a prince and his companions under an evil enchantment. Deep in the woods were a witch's hut, an ogre's cabin, a dwarf's cottage. In remote forest groves, children stepped into the otherworld.

23

The Invisible World

When the heroes of fairy tales venture into unfamiliar territory, they encounter the magical otherworld at every turn. Yet, as frequently as this realm is discovered, the ways there are infinitely varied. A young king in "The City East of the Moon and South of the Sun"[1] married a swan-maiden and then lost her, and he searched the world far and wide to find her again in the kingdom of her father, the Cloud-King. With the aid of a wise dwarf, helpful birds, and all the winds, he was finally carried away by a strong southeasterly wind over land and then far over sparkling seas. He travelled beyond the northern lights and out into space. Eventually, below him was an unknown land with a meadow and the Cloud-King's palace. No mortal had ever made that journey before. The divine king was so impressed with this heroic young man at his castle that he permitted his joyous daughter to return to earth with him.

The existence of an invisible otherworld to be found beyond and parallel to our own is a basic premise of fairy tales, and the same concept was inherent to the stories created so many centuries ago in the imagination of the earliest storytellers. The notion provided a remarkable setting for the ancient Irish and Norse tales, but it is not merely background; it is the essence of these stories. The invisible world is the thread running through each of the preceding chapters, and this chapter will join these threads together.

The *Book of the Dun Cow* includes several tales about this strange realm, and I hope that the reader can now understand what a treasure Mael Muiri's manuscript is. Connla travelled beyond the human world with a fairy woman in her glass boat. Another of the scribe's stories is "The Voyage of Máel Dúin's Currach" (*Imram Curaig Maíle Dúin*), possibly composed in the eighth century.[2] Máel Dúin sailed in search of Vikings who had murdered his father, when a storm came up and he and his men became lost at sea. Instead of finding Vikings they came upon fantastic places, one where the water was green crystal and another where the sea turned into clouds with underwater fortresses. The men passed by many magical islands. On one island colourful birds sang music that sounded like psalms, while on another there were giant insects. From an island abundant with apple trees, Máel Dúin cut a single branch – the fruit of that branch provided all the food his men needed to sustain them for forty days. On another island, the voyagers encountered monks who blessed them on their journey.

A fragment of another story, "The Voyage of Bran Son of Febal" (*Imram Brain maic Febail*), is found in the same manuscript. This tale contains all of the elements of the elusive Celtic otherworld, including the magical apple branch. The story of Bran is included in seven separate manuscripts, all of which use almost identical texts, and the archaic form of some words in these texts has led scholars to conclude that this story reaches far back into antiquity.

The Voyage of Bran[3]

The story begins one morning when Bran was walking outside his stronghold and he heard music behind him. The music followed him, yet as often as he looked back, he saw nothing. The sound was so soothing that it lulled him to sleep, and when he awoke, on the ground beside him lay a silver branch covered with white blossoms. Bran took the branch back to his house, where kings from all over Ireland had gathered for an assembly, when a woman from an unknown land appeared in the assembly room and sang to them.

Although all the kings heard her song describing the pleasures of her island across the sea, she sang to Bran alone. The branch she gave Bran was from one of the silver apple trees there. Another tree on her island was filled with birds whose songs called out the hours. In her land were soft fields and a white-silver plain where men and women rode golden-coloured horses, and crimson horses, too, and others that were the colour of the blue sky. At sunrise every morning a young man rode along the shore filling up the land with light. Men rowed boats out to a huge sea rock from which music swelled up like the sound of a hundred voices singing. There was laughter in her land, the best of wine, and riches of all kinds. The woman then invited Bran to sail to her gentle land, whereupon the branch that Bran had been holding leapt from his hand into hers, and she disappeared!

The next morning, Bran ventured onto the sea accompanied by three crews with nine men in each. After two days and nights on the water, the men had come to the realm of the sea-god, Manannán, who rode across the waves to meet them in a chariot. He told them that although they saw only him, there were indeed other chariot-riders on the water, whom they could not see, and where Bran could see speckled salmon swimming, calves and lambs grazed in the water as well. Soon the men arrived at the woman's island, where they were welcomed and taken to a large house replete with the finest food and with beds enough for each one of them. Bran and his men remained on this wondrous island for one year, until one among them longed to return to his own home. Then the others decided that they were ready to leave, too. The women rued this decision, warning that they would never again touch the land of Ireland. Still, the men prepared to depart.

As they neared Ireland's shore, a group of men who had gathered, seeing the boats approaching, asked the travellers who they were. Bran said that he was Bran, son of Febal, to which one of them replied, "We know no one by that name, although one of our ancient stories is the voyage of Bran." One of Bran's men leapt from the coracle, but the moment he set foot on Irish soil all the centuries that had gone by in the mortal world took their toll, and he turned to dust. Bran then told the men of the gathering of all of their wanderings and bade them farewell. And from that time on his voyages are not known.

Expeditions to places similar to this mythical island form a significant part of early Irish literature. It is the Land of Youth that Oisín visited with the golden-haired Niamh, and the realm where Manannán gave Cormac the cup of truth. This otherworld, or fairyland, that was inhabited by ever-living beings who existed beyond life and death, was a Celtic idea, and was perhaps the foundational Celtic idea. Without any doubt, it was a pre-Christian concept.

Such a place was identified by many names. In the Bran story alone it is Bountiful Land, Gentle Land, Many-Coloured Land, and Happy Plain. Whether it was the Land of Ever-Living (*Tír na mBeo*), the Land of Women (*Tír na mBan*), the Land of Promise (*Tír Tairngire*), the Land of Light (*Tír Sorcha*), the Land of Youth (*Tír na nÓg*), or Emain of the Apple Trees (*Emain Ablach*) – all terms that appear in the Irish manuscripts – it was a summer world where beings who seemed to be very much like humans lived in timeless happiness. To the Irish, it is simply "The Otherworld." In Welsh literature it was Annwfn, the summer country ruled by Arawn and Gwyn ap Nudd, where there was joy, wine, and singing, and where no one ever grew old. It was also Avalon, the Island of Apple

Trees, to which King Arthur and other heroes were transported upon their death.

Different from this otherworld of the Irish and Welsh tales was the supernatural world of the early Norse stories. These portray a mythological universe of which a picture can be put together from the Eddas, the sagas, and skaldic verse.[4] It is complex and varied, and although it was never as fixed as it is described here, a vast cosmos of different worlds emerges.

All of the worlds were supported and nourished by the tree Yggdrasil, and they existed on three levels. On the highest tier was Ásgard, the shining realm where the Æsir gods lived in their gold-roofed halls, one of which was Odin's Valhalla. To the east of Ásgard, where the dawn glowed, was Álfheim, the bright world of the elves, and to the west was Vanaheim, the realm of Vanir gods. Beneath this level, in the middle of the tree, was Midgard, where humans lived. Extending across the far eastern edge of the world of men and women lay the great Myrkwood or Ironwood Forest, where troll-women lived and into which demons were born. On the same level as Midgard lay Svartálfaheim, where dark elves lived underground, and Nidavellir, where dwarfs lived in caves and mines. Jötunheimar, the lands of giants, extended to the north, and there in the cold giant world loomed their mountain stronghold, Útgard.

Dead souls took a final journey north past Útgard and the lands of the frost giants, beyond distant realms at the very end of the world, and then downwards to the third and lowest level. Here was a pale, dim place called Hel; this was not the Christian Hell but a pre-Christian, shadowy place named for the goddess who presided there. To reach Hel one had to cross a river that separated the land of the living from the domain of the dead by a bridge guarded by a maiden, Módgud. Beyond Hel, the last world was Niflheim, a place of darkness, ice, and snow, guarded by a ghastly dog, Garm. This is the region to which dark elves escorted evil souls on a terrible nine days' journey north and downwards from

218

Midgard to where they were doomed to suffer in eternal torture. Few were ever compelled to travel to Niflheim. Several northern stories present imagery of another place, as depicted in the tale of the youth Helge, who lived with the giant king Gudmund's daughter. In the far north, beyond the ice and cold, existed a great plain and a kingdom where fair princesses lived. When it was winter elsewhere, there was sunshine in this Acre of the Not-Dead or Glittering Plains.

In the old literature, the homes of giants, trolls, elves, and dwarfs reflect these traditional mythic worlds: the shining world of the elves, the cave world of dwarfs, and the cold mountain world of giants. For the most part, humans remained unaware of these other regions around them, yet Midgard, or middle earth, connected with each of them. It is not surprising, then, that with such a world picture drawn from the early literature, we often find humans in folk and fairy tales wandering into lands just like these. A lad comes upon giants in their mountain strongholds, finds trolls near craggy precipices and ravines, or meets dwarfs close to the rocky caverns in which they dwell. He becomes aware of elves near a bright stream or in a moonlit forest far from human habitation. When a lad is carried by the wind north beyond the ice and snow, he comes to a meadow with green trees and flowers and finds there the lovely daughter of a giant.

Myths and fairy tales frequently specify journeys across water to reach other worlds. Death often required crossing water, reflecting an idea that there was water between the land of the living and the final place. The passage might be over a sea, but it could also be simply across a wide river. When Sinfjötli died in the Völsung story, Sigmund carried his dead son through the woods to a river where a ferryman waited to convey the body to the realm of the dead. Sigmund laid his son's body carefully in the boat, and then as he stood on the shore the boat, the body, and the ferryman vanished before his eyes. That ferryman is assumed to be Odin. Folk tales portray dwarfs and elves crossing over water as they leave the world of humans, when the time has come for them to return to their own world. Typically, they cross a river at night, sometimes by a bridge, and then the patter of footsteps crossing the bridge can be heard all night long.

There was a dark side to the northern otherworlds. Beyond the dwelling places of humans were realms of goblins, giants and trolls, sea-serpents, demons, and hideous evil monsters of every kind that lived in deep forests or gloomy marshes and came forth to challenge mortal heroes. Dragon-quelling stories form a part of the literature of the Middle Ages, and these terrifying creatures appear from time to time in fairy tales.[5] As old and primeval as giants, dragons hoarded gold deep in the mountains, haunted cavern pools, and emerged to lay waste the land or capture young maidens – particularly princesses. Killing a dragon was a long and brutal fight that was over only when the beast's head was cut off. Sometimes an old curse or spell was broken when such a beast was slain. The very early world of *Beowulf* was constantly ravaged by monsters and a dragon, and perhaps the most loathsome creature in all of literature was the fiend Beowulf encountered called Grendel. This monster haunted moors and fenlands, and rose from its cave under a lake's murky deeps to make visits at night to a royal hall where he killed the inhabitants. When this monster was finally slain its even more terrible mother appeared!

Humans entered otherworlds of great beauty or ghastly horrors only briefly and rarely, yet supernatural beings seemed able to come and go from our world easily, and at will. Spirits from the Irish otherworld could take the form of any kind of bird, and the human realm was subject to their invasions at any time. Long ago at Emain Macha, a large flock of birds appeared and began to eat everything on the ground around the castle until there was not a leaf or blade of grass left. It distressed the no-blemen that their land was ruined, and so with horses and chariots they followed after these birds to hunt them. They had never seen birds like these, linked together two by two with chains of silver and gold. At night-fall the birds disappeared in the darkness, and the men found a place where they could spend the night, but by then the birds had led them into the otherworld.[6]

Occasionally in folk and fairy tales there is a deer or a bird that one is compelled to follow. When Hansel and Gretel are about to perish from hunger, a bird as white as snow appears, sitting on a branch. They listen to its lovely song and then follow, as it flies ahead of them through the forest to a little house made of bread. The following tale is from the south of Ireland.

The Story of the Little Bird[7]

A monk was kneeling at his prayers one day in the monastery garden when he heard a bird singing. Its song was sweeter than anything he had ever heard before. He rose from his knees and listened. The bird flew away to a nearby grove, and the monk followed its enchanting song. Then the bird flew to another tree and another, always farther from the monastery, and the man followed, farther and farther away. At last as the sun was setting in the evening, he returned to his monastery. But he was surprised at what he saw, for everything seemed different in the garden and the once familiar monks had faces he had never seen before. While he was wondering at these things, one of the monks approached him. He asked this monk why things had changed so much since the morning. The brother of the monastery did not recognize him, but listened to his story and then told him that there was a tradition in the monastery that a monk had suddenly disappeared two hundred years before, and no one ever knew what had become of him. The singing of the bird had been enough to carry the monk out of the world of time.

Time runs differently in fairyland, and so a brief time there may be measured in centuries in the real world. There are a great many stories about this distortion of time. In one tale, a girl was invited to a celebration for an elf child and spent several days with the elves, but when she returned home, discovered that she had been gone for seven years. But time does not always lapse this way. A shepherd who joined in a fairy dance, and after that lived happily with the fairies for many years, awoke to find himself on the hillside where only a few moments had passed. Women summoned to act as midwives and to care for fairy children for a time always returned home the same night.

Everything about fairyland is enigmatic. There is no logic, and one can search the tales and myths in vain to find a coherent picture. The otherworld is a place of unsurpassed beauty, yet there can be the most monstrous horrors. Time passes strangely there. It is very far away, at the back of the north wind, or the farthest away that the wind has ever blown. It is across the western sea on a distant island, yet can be reached by entering the green fairy mounds. It is deep under the waves, and in lakes, and there are openings to it in springs and wells. But it can be entered by passing through a cleft in the rocks of a mountain, or wandering deep in a forest and stepping into an unfamiliar glade. There are many points of entry, and its borders are uncertain. In the old Celtic stories it can be entered simply by riding through a mist.

To come to the otherworld, it is enough to find oneself on a fairy mound on the eve of May Day, when the boundaries are broken down between our world and the other one, or to listen for a moment to the singing of a bird. On the shore of a lake or river, beside a waterfall, on an island – these are metaphysical places where humans meet fairies and other supernatural beings. The parallel worlds connect in a time or a space that is neither here nor there, on the days of the pagan year when it is neither one season nor the other. Boundaries are blurred at midnight, and at dusk and early dawn of each day when it is neither day nor night. The otherworld can be glimpsed in liminal places, in the thin line of any boundary or threshold, at a crossroads or the ford of a river, at the edge of a kingdom, just beneath the still surface of a pond, or in the glimmer of reflected moonlight. These thin lines in time and space can be entry points that connect our world with the other one, which lay everywhere around but always just beyond the familiar. It was not really necessary to go anywhere at all to find the invisible world. It blended with our own.

We have now taken the last steps into an ancient imagination, where the natural world and the invisible world, with its many varied inhabitants, existed together. The concept lingered for centuries as a theme of storytelling in a long oral tradition of folklore and folk tales, taking a new literary form in fairy tales. From the time of the earliest storytellers, this strange parallel world and all of the ideas associated with it have somehow touched the human psyche and intrigued the imagination.

24

A Fairy Tale Almost Forgotten

"The Dwarfs' Banquet" could easily have been lost. When it was first published many of the old Scandinavian tales had already faded from popular memory. The survival of stories from oral tradition was as precarious as the survival of old manuscripts, most of which perished until only so few now remain.

This Norwegian story was told to a bishop, Friedrich Christian Münter, who related it in Danish to Wilhelm Grimm in 1812. Because the story was Scandinavian and not German in origin, the Grimm brothers did not include it in their collection of fairy tales. But Wilhelm kept the story. Fifteen years later, he submitted it in German for publication in a yearbook of stories for children, which was being compiled by a fellow fairy tale author for the year 1827. Decades later, an Irish historian of folklore and mythology, Thomas Keightley, discovered the tale. More than half a century after it was told to Wilhelm Grimm, Keightley included it in English in his book on fairy tales, *The Fairy Mythology*, as part of a section devoted to Scandinavian stories.

The story describes a winter festival of giants and dwarfs. It also depicts the declining years of the giants after their conflicts with Odin and then with King Olaf II, here called Oluf, who was king of Norway from 1015 to 1028. This second King Olaf was canonized and called Olaf the Holy after he succeeded in the conversion of Norway to Christianity. Over the span of this Olaf's reign, the new religion was, for the most part, finally established. Everything changed with Christianity. It may have been a better world, but it was a different one. Nordic paganism became a lost religion. The rich mythos of its belief system was coming to an end, and the era of dwarfs and giants was fading away.

The following is Thomas Keightley's translation of the story.

The Dwarfs' Banquet: A Norwegian Tale[1]

There lived in Norway, not far from the city of Drontheim, a power-ful man, who was blessed with all the goods of fortune. A part of the surrounding country was his property; numerous herds fed on his pastures, and a great retinue and a crowd of servants adorned his mansion. He had an only daughter, called Aslog, the fame of whose beauty spread far and wide. The greatest men of the country sought her, but all were alike unsuccessful in their suit, and he who had come full of confidence and joy, rode away home silent and melan-choly. Her father, who thought his daughter delayed her choice only to select, forbore to interfere, and exulted in her prudence. But when, at length, the richest and noblest had tried their fortune with as little success as the rest, he grew angry, and called his daughter, and said to her, "Hitherto I have left you to your free choice, but since I see that you reject all without any distinction, and the very best of your suitors seem not good enough for you, I will keep measures no longer with you. What! shall my family be extinct, and my inheritance pass away into the hands of strangers? I will break your stubborn spirit. I give you now till the festival of the great Winter-night; make your choice by that time, or prepare to accept him whom I shall fix on."

Aslog loved a youth called Orm, handsome as he was brave and noble. She loved him with her whole soul, and she would sooner die than bestow her hand on another. But Orm was poor, and poverty compelled him to serve in the mansion of her father. Aslog's partiality for him was kept a secret; for her father's pride of power and wealth was such that he would never have given his consent to a union with so humble a man.

When Aslog saw the darkness of his countenance, and heard his angry words, she turned pale as death, for she knew his temper, and doubted not but that he would put his threats into execution. Without uttering a word in reply, she retired to her silent chamber, and thought deeply but in vain how to avert the dark storm that hung over her. The great festival approached nearer and nearer, and her anguish increased every day.

At last the lovers resolved on flight. "I know," says Orm, "a secure place where we may remain undiscovered until we find an opportunity of quitting the country." At night, when all were asleep, Orm led the trembling Aslog over the snow and ice-fields away to the mountains. The moon and the stars sparkling still brighter in the cold winter's night lighted them on their way. They had under their arms a few articles of dress and some skins of animals, which were all they could carry. They ascended the mountains the whole night long till they reached a lonely spot enclosed with lofty rocks. Here Orm conducted the weary Aslog into a cave, the low and narrow entrance to which was hardly perceptible, but it soon enlarged to a great hall, reaching deep into the mountain. He kindled a fire, and they now, reposing on their skins, sat in the deepest solitude far away from all the world.

Orm was the first who had discovered this cave, which is shown to this very day, and as no one knew anything of it, they were safe from the pursuit of Aslog's father. They passed the whole winter in this retirement. Orm used to go a hunting, and Aslog stayed at home in the cave, minded the fire, and prepared the necessary food. Frequently did she mount the points of the rocks, but her eyes wandered as far as they could reach only over glittering snow-fields.

The spring now came on – the woods were green – the meads put on their various colours, and Aslog could but rarely and with circumspection venture to leave the cave. One evening Orm came in with the intelligence that he had recognized her father's servants in the distance, and that he could hardly have been unobserved by them, whose eyes were as good as his own. "They will surround this place," continued he, "and never rest till they have found us; we must quit our retreat, then, without a moment's delay."

They accordingly descended on the other side of the mountain, and reached the strand, where they fortunately found a boat. Orm shoved off, and the boat drove into the open sea. They had escaped their pursuers, but they were now exposed to dangers of another kind: whither should they turn themselves? They could not venture to land, for Aslog's father was lord of the whole coast, and they would infallibly fall into his hands. Nothing then remained for them but to commit their bark to the wind and waves. They drove along the entire night. At break of day the coast had disappeared, and they saw nothing but the sky above, the sea beneath, and the waves that rose and fell. They had not brought one morsel of food with them, and thirst and hunger began now to torment them. Three days did they toss about in this state of misery, and Aslog, faint and exhausted, saw nothing but certain death before her.

At length, on the evening of the third day, they discovered an island of tolerable magnitude, and surrounded by a number of smaller ones. Orm immediately steered for it, but just as he came near it there suddenly rose a violent wind, and the sea rolled every moment higher and higher against him. He turned about with a view of approaching it on another side, but with no better success; his vessel, as oft as it approached the island, was driven back as if by an invisible power. "Lord God!" cried he, and blessed himself and looked on poor Aslog, who seemed to be dying of weakness before his eyes. But scarcely had the exclamation passed his lips when the storm ceased, the waves subsided, and the vessel came to the shore, without encountering any hindrance. Orm jumped out on the beach; some mussels that he found on the strand strengthened and revived the exhausted Aslog, so that she was soon able to leave the boat.

The island was overgrown with low dwarf shrubs, and seemed to be uninhabited; but when they had gotten about to the middle of it, they discovered a house reaching but a little above the ground, and appearing to be half under the surface of the earth. In the hope of meeting human beings and assistance, the wanderers approached it. They listened if they could hear any noise, but the most perfect silence reigned there. Orm at length opened the door, and with his companion walked in; but what was their surprise, to find every-thing regulated and arranged as if for inhabitants, yet not a single living creature visible. The fire was burning on the hearth, in the middle of the room, and a pot with fish hung on it apparently only waiting for some one to take it up and eat it. The beds were made and ready to receive their weary tenants. Orm and Aslog stood for some time dubious, and looked on with a certain degree of awe, but at last, overcome by hunger, they took up the food and ate. When they had satisfied their appetites, and still in the last beams of the setting sun, which now streamed over the island far and wide, discovered no human being, they gave way to weariness, and laid themselves in the beds to which they had been so long strangers.

They had expected to be awakened in the night by the owners of the house on their return home, but their expectation was not fulfilled; they slept undisturbed till the morning sun shone in upon them. No one appeared on any of the following days, and it seemed as if some invisible power had made ready the house for their recep-tion. They spent the whole summer in perfect happiness – they were, to be sure, solitary, yet they did not miss mankind. The wild birds' eggs, and the fish they caught, yielded them provisions in abundance.

When autumn came, Aslog brought forth a son. In the midst of their joy at his appearance, they were surprised by a wonderful apparition. The door opened on a sudden, and an old woman stepped in. She had on her a handsome blue dress: there was something proud, but at the same time something strange and surprising in her appearance.

"Do not be afraid," said she, "at my unexpected appearance – I am the owner of this house, and I thank you for the clean and neat state in which you have kept it, and for the good order in which I find everything with you. I would willingly have come sooner, but I had no power to do so till this little heathen (pointing to the newborn babe) was come to the light. Now I have free access. Only fetch no priest from the main-land to christen it, or I must depart again. If you will in this matter comply with my wishes, you may not only continue to live here, but all the good that ever you can wish for I will do you. Whatever you take in hand shall prosper; good luck shall follow you wherever you go. But break this condition, and depend upon it that misfortune after misfortune will come on you, and even on this child will I avenge myself. If you want anything, or are in danger, you have only to pronounce my name three times and I will appear and lend you assistance. I am of the race of the old Giants, and my name is Guru. But beware of uttering in my presence the name of him whom no Giant may hear of, and never venture to make the sign of the cross, or to cut it on beam or board in the house. You may dwell in this house the whole year long, only be so good as to give it up to me on Yule evening, when the sun is at the lowest, as then we celebrate our great festival, and then only are we permitted to be merry. At least, if you should not be willing to go out of the house, keep yourselves up in the loft as quiet as possible the whole day long, and as you value your lives do not look down into the room until midnight is past. After that you may take possession of everything again."

When the old woman had thus spoken she vanished, and Aslog and Orm, now at ease respecting their situation, lived without any disturbance contented and happy. Orm never made a cast of his net without getting a plentiful draught; he never shot an arrow from his bow that it was not sure to hit; in short, whatever they took in hand, were it ever so trifling, evidently prospered.

When Christmas came, they cleaned up the house in the best manner, set everything in order, kindled a fire on the hearth, and as the twilight approached, they went up to the loft, where they remained quite still and quiet. At length it grew dark; they thought they heard a sound of whizzing and snorting in the air, such as the swans use to make in the winter time. There was a hole in the roof over the fire-place which might be opened and shut either to let in the light from above, or to afford a free passage for the smoke. Orm lifted up the lid, which was covered with a skin, and put out his head. But what a wonderful sight then presented itself to his eyes! The little islands around were all lit up with countless blue lights, which moved about without ceasing, jumped up and down, then skipped down to the shore, assembled together, and came nearer and nearer to the large island where Orm and Aslog lived. At last they reached it, and arranged themselves in a circle around a large stone not far from the shore, and which Orm well knew. But what was his surprise, when he saw that the stone had now completely assumed the form of a man, though of a monstrous and gigantic one! He could clearly perceive that the little blue lights were borne by Dwarfs, whose pale clay-coloured faces, with their huge noses and

red eyes, disfigured too by birds' bills and owls' eyes, were supported
by misshapen bodies; and they tottered and wobbled about here and
there, so that they seemed to be at the same time merry and in pain.
Suddenly, the circle opened; the little ones retired on each side, and
Guru, who was now much enlarged and of as immense a size as
the stone, advanced with gigantic steps. She threw both her arms
around the stone image, which immediately began to receive life
and motion. As soon as the first symptom of motion showed itself,
the little ones began, with wonderful capers and grimaces, a song,
or to speak more properly, a howl, with which the whole island re-
sounded and seemed to tremble at the noise. Orm, quite terrified,
drew in his head, and he and Aslog remained in the dark, so still,
that they hardly ventured to draw their breath.

The procession moved on toward the house, as might be clearly
perceived by the nearer approach of the shouting and crying. They
were now all come in, and, light and active, the Dwarfs jumped
about on the benches; and heavy and loud sounded at intervals the
steps of the giants. Orm and his wife heard them covering the table,
and the clattering of the plates, and the shouts of joy with which
they celebrated their banquet. When it was over and it drew near
to midnight, they began to dance to that ravishing fairy-air which
charms the mind into such sweet confusion, and which some have
heard in the rocky glens, and learned by listening to the underground musicians. As soon as Aslog caught the sound of this air,
she felt an irresistible longing to see the dance. Nor was Orm able
to keep her back. "Let me look," said she, "or my heart will burst."
She took her child and placed herself at the extreme end of the loft,
whence, without being observed, she could see all that passed.
Long did she gaze, without taking off her eyes for an instant, on the
dance, on the bold and wonderful springs of the little creatures who

seemed to float in the air, and not so much as to touch the ground, while the ravishing melody of the elves filled her whole soul. The child meanwhile, which lay in her arms, grew sleepy and drew its breath heavily, and without ever thinking on the promise she had given the old woman, she made, as is usual, the sign of the cross over the mouth of the child, and said, "Christ bless you, my babe!"

The instant she had spoken the word there was raised a horrible piercing cry. The spirits tumbled heads over heels out at the door with terrible crushing and crowding, their lights went out, and in a few minutes the whole house was clear of them, and left desolate. Orm and Aslog frightened to death, hid themselves in the most re-tired nook in the house. They did not venture to stir till daybreak, and not till the sun shone through the hole in the roof down on the fire-place did they feel courage enough to descend from the loft.

The table remained still covered as the underground-people had left it; all their vessels, which were of silver, and manufactured in the most beautiful manner, were upon it. In the middle of the room, there stood upon the ground a huge copper vessel half full of sweet mead, and by the side of it, a drinking-horn of pure gold. In the cor-ner lay against the wall a stringed instrument, not unlike a dulcimer, which, as people believe, the Giantesses used to play on. They gazed on what was before them, full of admiration, but without venturing to lay their hands on anything: but great and fearful was their amazement, when, on turning about, they saw sitting at the table an immense figure, which Orm instantly recognized as the Giant whom Guru had animated by her embrace. He was now a cold and hard stone. While they were standing gazing on it, Guru herself en-tered the room in her giant-form. She wept so bitterly, that her tears trickled down on the ground. It was long ere her sobbing permitted her to utter a single word: at last she spoke:–

"Great affliction have you brought on me, and henceforth I must weep while I live; yet as I know that you have not done this with evil intentions, I forgive you, though it were a trifle for me to crush the whole house like an egg-shell over your heads."

"Alas!" cried she, "my husband, whom I love more than myself, there he sits, petrified for ever; never again will he open his eyes! Three hundred years lived I with my father on the island of Kunnan, happy in the innocence of youth, as the fairest among the Giant-maidens. Mighty heroes sued for my hand; the sea around that island is still filled with the rocky fragments which they hurled against each other in their combats. Andfind won the victory, and I plighted myself to him. But ere I was married came the detestable Odin into the country, who overcame my father, and drove us all from the island. My father and sisters fled to the mountains, and since that time my eyes have beheld them no more. Andfind and I saved ourselves on this island, where we for a long time lived in peace and quiet, and thought it would never be interrupted. But destiny, which no one escapes, had determined it otherwise. Oluf came from Britain. They called him the Holy, and Andfind instantly found that his voyage would be inauspicious to the giants. When he heard how Oluf's ship rushed through the waves, he went down to the strand and blew the sea against him with all his strength. The waves swelled up like mountains. But Oluf was still more mighty than he; his ship flew unchecked through the billows like an arrow from a bow. He steered direct for our island. When the ship was so near that Andfind thought he could reach it with his hands, he grasped at the forepart with his right hand, and was about to drag it down to the bottom, as he had often done with other ships. But Oluf, the terrible Oluf, stepped forward, and crossing his hands over each other, he cried with a loud voice, "Stand there as a stone, till the last day," and in the same instant my unhappy husband became a mass of rock. The ship sailed on unimpeded, and ran direct against the mountain, which it cut through, and separated from it the little island which lies out yonder.

"Ever since my happiness has been annihilated, and lonely and melancholy have I passed my life. On Yule-eve alone can petrified Giants receive back their life for the space of seven hours, if one of their race embraces them, and is, at the same time, willing to sacrifice a hundred years of their own life. But seldom does a Giant do that. I loved my husband too well not to bring him back cheerfully to life every time that I could do it, even at the highest price, and never would I reckon how often I had done it, that I might not know when the time came when I myself should share his fate, and at the moment that I threw my arms around him become one with him. But alas! even this comfort is taken from me; I can never more by any embrace awake him, since he has heard the name which I dare not utter; and never again will he see the light till the dawn of the last day shall bring it.

"I now go hence! You will never again behold me! All that here is in the house I give to you! My dulcimer alone will I keep! But let no one venture to fix his habitation on the little islands that lie around here! There dwell the little underground ones whom you saw at the festival, and I will protect them as long as I live!"

With these words Guru vanished. The next spring Orm took the golden horn and the silver ware to Drontheim, where no one knew him. The value of these precious metals was so great, that he was able to purchase everything requisite for a wealthy man. He laded his ship with his purchases, and returned back to the island, where he spent many years in unalloyed happiness, and Aslog's father was soon reconciled to his wealthy son-in-law.

The stone image remained sitting in the house; no human power was able to move it. So hard was the stone, that hammer and axe flew in pieces without making the slightest impression upon it. The Giant sat there till a holy man came to the island, who with one single word removed him back to his former station, where he stands to this hour. The copper vessel, which the underground people left behind them, was preserved as a memorial upon the island, which bears the name of House Island to the present day.

The giants and dwarfs in "The Dwarfs' Banquet" belong to a lost age. The decline and departure of the old races of dwarfs, elves, giants, and fairies are prevailing themes of folk and fairy tales. In this story, most of the old giants have either retreated into even more remote places or have turned to stone and become part of the landscape, the end of paganism becoming their death-knell.

Today, few people read fairy tales, especially tales such as this one that are over two hundred years old. Times have changed, and these old stories appear quaintly strange in our world. They seem to have lost some of the wonder they once had. Still, for the modern reader of fairy tales, one of the distinct pleasures can be found in the details of the stories. In this tale we see the snow and ice fields of Norway, a little house half buried underground, fish hanging over the pot on the hearth, a young mother making the sign of the cross over the lips of her baby and whispering "Christ bless you." In another fairy tale we see a girl tending goats, running up and down the mountain summer-pastures in her wooden shoes. In yet another, a young man makes his way home across shore rocks in the first light of dawn after a night of fishing out on the sea.

An understood tenet of fairy tales was always the strength of right values. These are stories of simple truths – faith in courage and a good heart is a conviction of these tales. In this story, while Aslog's father holds trust in wealth and property, Aslog and Orm discover instead the virtue of love and grow to understand that they can be happy with caring and kindness, good cheer, and enough of food and comfort to sustain them. There is a traditional happy ending to the story, when Orm and Aslog possess sufficient riches to live well. But this is not what the story is ultimately about. It is about the special Yule celebration of the dwarfs, who arrive with their blue lights from the surrounding islands to feast and to dance to the enchanting music that so captivates Aslog. And it is about one of the last of the great giants, Guru, who is able to enter the house only when a heathen baby lies within. These story elements convey the magic still lingering at the very edge of Orm and Aslog's world.

The most compelling aspect of these tales is their wild strangeness. Fairy tales are fantasy, but this is fantasy firmly rooted in old ideas and growing out of shared narrative traditions of folklore and folk tales. There is no need for the storytellers to explain the dwarfs, trolls, or fairies that populate their stories; they simply are what they are. Nor is there any need for an author to provide a time when a story takes place. It is in fairy tale time, and the welcoming invitation "once upon a time" suffices. Nevertheless, we are aware that these stories belong to the past; even when they were first written, most of them in the nineteenth century, these were tales of times gone by.

Similarly, the stories that were written a thousand years ago are set in some imagined even older age which had an appeal for these early storytellers, in a remote past when the lands were still pagan, when many gods existed, and the natural world was alive with unseen spirits of every kind – elves, fairies, ghosts, demons. The tales that came to life in the Norse and Celtic imaginations were rich with ideas about this spirit world and all its wondrous creatures.

In fairy tales we can easily find vestiges from this mythos of ancient times. Among the lakes, rivers, and deep forests of fairy tales, the mountain huts, hayfields, and fishing boats, and the very true-to-life characters with their brave deeds and adventures, occasionally there emerges a dwarf or a giant, a wizard, a mermaid, or a swan-maiden, immediately recognizable as deriving from older narrative traditions. With these story elements, born of the earliest creative impulses, fairy tales form part of a long continuum of storytelling. They provide us with a beautiful connection to old cultures, now lost, from an ancient, forgotten age.

Notes

CHAPTER ONE

1 Stories referred to are "The Fairy Dwelling on Selena Moor," in Bottrell, *Traditions and Hearthside Stories of West Cornwall*; and "The Twelve Brothers" and "The Six Swans," from the Grimm brothers' collections of tales. There are other versions of the swan story, among them Hans Christian Andersen's "The Wild Swans."

2 "The Fate of the Children of Lir," which exists in a manuscript from the Early Modern Period, is one of three stories that are known in Irish tradition as "The Three Sorrowful Tales of Erin." The other two are "The Tragic Story of the Children of Tuireann" (chapter 9) and the story of Deirdre (chapter 19). A translation is O'Duffy and Looney, *Oidhe Chloinne Lir: The Fate of the Children of Lir*. The story has been retold in Young, *Celtic Wonder Tales*, 145–60; in Gregory, *Gods and Fighting Men*, Part I, Book 5, 140–58; and in Yeats, *Irish Fairy and Folk Tales*, 1–9.

3 Ní Dhonnchadha, "Bardic Order, In Ireland," 174–6.

4 O'Neill, *The Irish Hand*, xviii.

5 Two important manuscripts of the Irish stories are the *Book of the Dun Cow*, written at the beginning of the twelfth century, and the *Book of Leinster*, a compilation of stories written about fifty years later at a monastery at Terryglass, Tipperary. Translations of the early Irish stories are Koch and Carey, *The Celtic Heroic Age*; Gantz, *Early Irish Myths and Sagas*; and Cross and Slover, *Ancient Irish Tales*.

6 Welsh narrative material is mainly in two manuscripts, the *White Book of Rhydderch* (c. 1350) and the *Red Book of Hergest* (c. 1400). Eleven traditional stories from these were translated and combined in one book, known today as the *Mabinogion*. Recommended translations are by Gwyn Jones and Thomas Jones, and by Sioned Davies. Two manuscripts containing early Welsh poetry are the *Black Book of Carmarthen* (c. 1250), translated by Meirion Pennar, and the *Book of Taliesin* (c. 1334), translated by Marged Haycock.

7 Lewis, "Bardic Order, In Wales," 176–83.

8 The Icelandic *Völsunga Saga*, written in the thirteenth century, connects the various Scandinavian heroic tales of the Völsungs from the sagas, the Eddas, and oral tradition into one long narrative, and in this version the hero Sigurd's ancestors are traced back to the god Odin. A translation is by Byock, *Saga of the Volsungs: The Norse Epic of Sigurd the Dragon Slayer.* William Morris told the story in *Volsunga Saga: The Story of the Volsungs and Niblungs.* Tolkien composed his own version of the legend in two poems, "The New Lay of the Völsungs" and "The New Lay of Gudrún," published posthumously in Tolkien and Tolkien, *The Legend of Sigurd and Gudrún.*

9 For examples of skaldic poetry see Hollander, *The Skalds.*

10 Abram, *Myths of the Pagan North*, 11.

11 Ibid., 181.

12 Recent translations of the *Poetic Edda* are by C. Larrington and A. Orchard. Older translations by L.M. Hollander and H.A. Bellows keep all of the Norse names and kennings and the original half-lines of the poems, and although old are still reliable. A single manuscript of the *Poetic Edda* survived, the *Codex Regius*, consisting of 45 leaves; a section of 8 leaves was lost. In 1663, an Icelandic bishop and collector sent this manuscript along with many others to the Danish king. Fortunately, this single copy of the *Poetic Edda* survived the Copenhagen fire.

13 Recent translations of Snorri Sturluson's *Prose Edda* are by J. Byock and A. Faulkes. Snorri Sturluson also wrote *Heimskringla: History of the Kings of Norway*, the first part of which, the *Ynglinga Saga*, includes stories of Norse mythology.

14 The original of *The Nibelungenlied* was composed by an unknown poet in Middle High German verse for court performance in Austria.

CHAPTER TWO

1 There are several stories with fairies in this manuscript. The tales of Bran and of Midir and Étaín are both incomplete, whereas the story of Connla exists as a complete story. The complicated tale of the wasting sickness of the hero Cúchulainn would have been a contender for the oldest tale with a fairy, but the *Cín Dromma Snechta* is evidence of the earlier existence of the Connla story.

2 There is ongoing debate about the date of the lost book. Although scholars consider the eighth century as likely, the ninth century has also been suggested, according to Koch, *Celtic Culture*, 437–8.

3 Jacobs, *Celtic Fairy Tales*, 1–4. I updated some of Jacobs' language, for example, changing "thou" to "you." A translation of the *Dun Cow* text is in Cross and Slover, *Ancient Irish Tales*, 488–90. Jacobs' text is a slightly shortened version of a translation.

4 Murphy, *The Annals of Clonmacnoise*, 58 and 59.

5 These words are accompanied in the original with the fairy telling Conn that it will not be long before the Law will be brought by "a righteous one," referring to St Patrick.

CHAPTER THREE

1 Digital images of the pages of Irish manuscripts, including the *Book of the Dun Cow* (*Lebor na hUidre*), are available on the website Irish Script on Screen, a project of the School of Celtic Studies at the Dublin Institute for Advanced Studies. www.isos.dias.ie

2 Cahill, *How the Irish Saved Civilization*, 166.

3 O'Neill, *The Irish Hand*, is an excellent source for details about manuscript preparation.

4 Cahill, 168.

5 Slavin, *The Ancient Books of Ireland*, 9.

6 "The Wooing of Étaín" (*Tochmarc Étaín*), "The Adventure of Connla," and "The Voyage of Bran" (*Imram Brain*) are all mentioned in the contents list of *Cín Dromma Snechta*, the lost monastic book referred to in chapter 2, indicating that these stories were known and had been written down in the eighth or ninth century. See chapter 2 n2.

7 Sjoestedt, *Gods and Heroes of the Celts*, 13.

8 Henderson, *Fled Bricrend: The Feast of Bricriu*, xxiv.

9 Nagy, *Conversing with Angels and Ancients*.

10 MacKillop, "Ciarán, Saint," in *A Dictionary of Celtic Mythology*, 88.

11 O'Clery and O'Donovon, *Annala Rioghachta Eireann: Annals of the Kingdom of Ireland, By the Four Masters*, vol. 2, 983.

12 Ó Néill, "The Impact of the Norman Invasion on Irish Literature," 177.

13 O'Rorke, *The History of Sligo*.

CHAPTER FOUR

1 Zipes, *The Irresistible Fairy Tale*, 3.

2 Zipes, "Fairy Tales and Folk Tales," in *The Oxford Encyclopedia of Children's Literature*, vol. 2, 45–54.

3 Tatar, *The Hard Facts of the Grimms' Fairy Tales*, 35.

4 Silver, *Strange and Secret Peoples*, 18.

5 Cott, *Beyond the Looking Glass*, xlv.

6 Ibid., xlvi.

7 Calvino, "Cybernetics and Ghosts," 18.

CHAPTER FIVE

1 Tolkien's "On Fairy Stories" was published in *Tree and Leaf*, 3–81. It is also included in *The Tolkien Reader*, 33–99, and in Tolkien and Tolkien, *The Monsters and the Critics, and Other Essays*, 109–61.

2 Sikes, *British Goblins*, 67–9.

3 Briggs, *The Fairies in Tradition and Literature*, 87–8.

4 Sjoestedt, *Gods and Heroes of the Celts*, 24.

5 Large fragments of the *Book of Invasions* exist in the *Book of Leinster* and the *Book of Ballymote*, which were written down in the twelfth and fourteenth centuries, respectively, from older books. A compilation of parts of this story from fifteen separate manuscripts is contained in *Lebor Gabála Érenn: The Book of the Taking of Ireland*, edited and translated by R.A. Stewart Macalister. All of these manuscripts agree in general in substance; they are a mix of history, legend, and mythology. These stories predate any written history that exists, and the real history of pre-Celtic Ireland is unknown.

6 Cross and Slover, *Ancient Irish Tales*, 215–38.

7 Roe and Dooley, *Tales of the Elders of Ireland*, 120–1.

8 Ibid., xvi. Collected twelfth-century stories of the Fianna are in this text by Roe and Dooley.

9 Ó hÓgáin, *Fionn mac Cumhaill*, 3, 4. This author explains that an ancient form of this hero's name was "Find."

10 Ibid., 155.

11 Ó hÓgáin's *Fionn mac Cumhaill* outlines the imagery and the different versions of the story, beginning with an eleventh-century verse in which Oisín's mother was called Blái Derg.

12 Gregory, *Gods and Fighting Men*, Part II, Book 1, chapter 4, 174–8, and *Lady Gregory's Complete Irish Mythology*, 126–8.

13 Gregory, *Visions and Beliefs in the West of Ireland*, 9.

14 This brief tale, which has been retold often, first appeared in Fitzgerald, "Popular Tales of Ireland," 189–90.

15 Hartland, *English Fairy and Other Folk Tales*, 91–4.

16 Douglas, *Scottish Folk and Fairy Tales*, 134.

CHAPTER SIX

1 Sveinsson, *The Folk-Stories of Iceland*, 178.

2 Lang, *Brown Fairy Book*, 190–6.

3 Simpson, *Icelandic Folktales and Legends*, 49–54. The tale is similar to "The Elfin Lover" in Árnason, *Icelandic Legends*, vol. 1, 58–65.

4 The segments of the saga relating to the elfin woman and the half-elf Skuld are in Byock, *The Saga of King Hrolf Kraki*, 21–3 and 70–86, and in Jones, "King Hrolf and His Champions" in *Eirik the Red and Other Icelandic Sagas*, 246–8 and 307–18.

5 Árnason, *Icelandic Legends*, vol. 1, 23–4.

6 Bayerschmidt and Hollander, *Njál's Saga*, 89 and n363.

7 Hilda Ellis Davidson links the elves with a cult of the dead in *The Road to Hel*.

8 Jolly, *Popular Religion in Late Saxon England: Elf Charms in Context*.

9 Ibid., 2.

10 Sections of the *Poetic Edda* that link together gods and elves are the poems "The Prophecy of the Seeress" (*Völuspá*) stanza 48, "The Sayings of Hár" (*Hávamál*) stanzas 159 and 160, "The Lay of Grímnir" (*Grímnismál*) stanza 4, "The Lay of Skírnir" (*Skírnismál*) stanzas 7, 17, and 18, "The Flyting of Loki" (*Lokasenna*) stanzas 2, 13, and 30, and "The Lay of Thrym" (*Thrymskvida*) two references in stanza 7.

11 Larrington, *The Poetic Edda*, 52 (stanza 4).

12 Ibid., 85 (stanza 2).

13 Ibid., 37 (stanza 159).

14 Snorri Sturluson (trans. Faulkes), *Edda*, 64.

CHAPTER SEVEN

1 Sveinsson notes that there are very few dwarfs in Icelandic folk literature in *The Folk-Stories of Iceland*, 160.

2 Larrington, *The Poetic Edda*, 3.

3 Two older translations of "*Völuspá*," by Bellows and Hollander, keep the Old Norse names in the dwarf list, stanzas 11–16, but provide translations of some names in footnotes. Recent translations by Larrington and Orchard translate out many of the names into English. I have kept the Old Norse names, but included translations of some of them.

4 This story is section 15 of the *Ynglinga Saga*, the first part of Snorri Sturluson's *Heimskringla*, online at the Online Medieval and Classical Library. www.omacl.org

5 Grimm and Taylor, *German Popular Stories and Fairy Tales*, 106–14.

6 "Snow White," also called "Snow-Drop," is from the Grimms' collections of fairy tales.

7 DuBois, *Nordic Religions in the Viking Age*, 159.

8 The first part of the tale about Freyja and the dwarfs is in "The Short Saga of Sorli" (*Sörla tháttr*) included within the "Saga of Olaf Tryggvason" in the Icelandic *Flatey-*

jarbók. The story in English is in Magnusson and Morris, *Three Northern Love Stories*, 203–7.

9 The story of Loki stealing the necklace and Heimdall winning it back was mentioned in the skaldic poem "*Húsdrápa*," which no longer exists, except for fragments. However, passages in the poem regarding this story are referred to in the "Poetic Diction" section of the *Prose Edda*, in Snorri Sturluson (trans. Faulkes), *Edda* (sections 8 and 16), 76.

10 An account of "*Húsdrápa*," which was commissioned by an Icelandic chieftain, Olaf Hoskuldsson, for the occasion of his daughter's wedding feast, is in *Laxdaela Saga*. The hall was crowded with guests when the skald recited his poem that described the scenes from well-known legends painted on the walls.

11 McKinnell, "The Context of *Völundarkvida*," 11–13.

CHAPTER EIGHT

1 A Swedish folk tale published in *Story Parade – A Magazine for Boys and Girls* in 1946. It is included in Werner, *Giant Golden Book of Elves and Fairies*, 10–18.

2 This story, collected by Herman Hofberg, is in Booss, *Scandinavian Folk and Fairy Tales*, 271–2.

3 These home and farm spirits do not appear in Icelandic folk stories (Sveinsson, *The Folk-Stories of Iceland*, 160).

4 The ármadr appears in "The Tale of Thorvald the Far-Travelled" (*Thorvalds tháttr vídförla*) and in *Kristni Saga* (Davidson, *The Lost Beliefs of Northern Europe*, 119).

5 Ibid., 117–18.

6 DuBois, *Nordic Religions in the Viking Age*, 51.

7 The saint's visions and teachings were recorded in Latin in *Liber Celestis*. This revelation is Book VI, "Revelationes," chapter 78. Sahlin, *Birgitta of Sweden and the Voice of Prohecy*, 129.

CHAPTER NINE

1 MacKillop, "Tír fo Thuinn," in *A Dictionary of Celtic Mythology*, 405.

2 "Although the core of the story may have been composed as early as the 11th century, as interpolations from the *Lebor Gabála* [*Book of Invasions*] imply, the earliest surviving text is 16th century" (MacKillop, *A Dictionary of Celtic Mythology*, 353). The story is in Cross and Slover, *Ancient Irish Tales*, 49-81, and retold in Joyce, *Old Celtic Romances*, 37–96.

3 Cross and Slover, 77–8.

4 The oldest native Irish historical records that have survived, purportedly compiled at Clonmacnoise by a learned abbot, Tigernach, who died in 1088. "They are considered to be the most trustworthy of the ancient Irish annals" (Slavin, *The Ancient Books of Ireland*, 183).

5 MacNiocaill, *The Annals of Tigernach*, Annal T622.3, 175.

6 Tortu, also known as Bile Tortan, was one of the sacred trees connected with the mythological pagan kings of Ireland (MacKillop, "Bile," in *A Dictionary of Celtic Mythology*, 41).

7 O'Reilly, "The Kerry Mermaid," 185–6, and Colum, *A Treasury of Irish Folklore*, 479–82.

8 Rhys, *Celtic Folklore*, 2–12.

9 Fee and Leeming, *Gods, Heroes and Kings*, 62.

10 This story of Diarmuid is in Gregory, *Gods and Fighting Men*, Part II, Book 6, chapter 3, 319–27, and *Lady Gregory's Complete Irish Mythology*, 218–23. It is also in Campbell, *Popular Tales of the West Highlands*, vol. 3, 421–38. These Gaelic tales of the Fianna were popular in Scotland.

11 The strange connection between supernatural beings and otherworld cattle in European legends, folk belief, and traditions is explored by Hilda Ellis Davidson in a paper "Otherworld Cattle" published in the periodical of archaeology, folklore, and mythology, *At the Edge*. Fairy cattle associated with water, as a theme in British and Irish narratives, is commented on by Briggs, in *The Fairies in Tradition and Literature*, 77–8.

12 See n8 above.

13 *The Silver Cow*, by Susan Cooper, captures the spirit of the Welsh stories of fairies or Tylwyth Teg who live in mountain lakes. The original folk tale is in Sikes, *British Goblins*, 36–7. Similar traditional Welsh stories are in John Rhys' *Celtic Folklore*, including the story of the mermaid who appeared with her cows walking on the surface of the water.

14 Sikes, *British Goblins*, 37.

15 Wilde, *Ancient Legends, Mystic Charms and Superstitions of Ireland*, vol. 2, 41–3.

16 Sources for the story of Lí Ban are Joyce, *Old Celtic Romances*, 97–105; the entry on Lí Ban in Ó hÓgáin, *Myth, Legend and Romance*, 271; and O'Grady, *Silva Gadelica*, vol. 2, Part XIII, 265–9.

17 O'Clery and O'Donovan, *Annala Rioghachta Eireann: Annals of the Kingdom of Ireland*, vol. 1, 201.

CHAPTER TEN

1 In "The Prophecy of the Seeress" (2–4), we learn from a seeress, who was raised by giants, that in the beginning before the world was created there was only a void out of which gods raised up the earth. The gods gave life to two trees, Ask and Embla (17–18). From "The Lay of Vafthrúdnir" (*Vafthrúdnismál*) (21), we hear from a poet descended from a primeval giant that the earth was created from the body of Ymir. From "The Lay of Grímnir" (41–2), we learn how the earth was shaped from the giant's blood and bones and Midgard was created for humans. In "*Gylfaginning*" (sections 4–13) of the *Prose Edda*, Snorri Sturluson adds more details to this creation story from unknown sources. The great abyss or void before creation was called Ginnunga gap, and it is interesting that in the eleventh century this was the name given to the sea between Greenland and Vinland, or America.

2 Lindow, *Norse Mythology*, 1.

3 Ibid., 2.

4 MacKillop, "*Fled Bricrenn*," in *A Dictionary of Celtic Mythology*, 237.

5 Koch and Carey, *The Celtic Heroic Age*, 102–3. This text is based on the translation by Henderson, *Fled Bricrend: The Feast of Bricriu*.

6 "The Battle of the Birds" is a Gaelic version of the tale in Douglas, *Scottish Folk and Fairy Tales*, 33–45. Originally it was in Campbell's *Popular Tales of the West Highlands*. An Irish version is "The Son of the King of Erin and the Giant of Loch Lein," and it was told by Welsh gypsies as "The Green Man of Norman's Land." The English version is "Nix Nought Nothing." There are also Norse, Swedish, and German versions of the tale. The following early Welsh story is retold in Lang, *Lilac Fairy Book*, 349–69.

7 Jones and Jones, *The Mabinogion*, 85–121.

8 Breeze, *Medieval Welsh Literature*, 80.

9 Ibid., 79.

10 Jones and Jones, 99.

11 The Eddic poem "The Short Seeress's Prophecy" (*Völuspá hin skamma*) presents some of these relationships with giant mothers and wives.

12 The poem "Haustlöng" was written by the skald Thjódólf of Hvin at the end of the ninth or beginning of the tenth century (Lindow, 16, 287).

13 A line in a poem by Bragi refers to Odin throwing the giant's eyes up into the sky to become stars. It also refers to Skadi as a ski-goddess (Snorri Sturluson, trans. Faulkes, *Edda*, section 23, 89). Bragi Boddason the Old was writing in the second half of the ninth century, according to Lindow, 15.

14 The story is in "Gylfaginning" (section 23) and "Skáldskaparmál" (sections 1 and 22)

of the *Prose Edda*, Snorri Sturluson (trans. Faulkes), *Edda*, 23–4, 59–61, 86–8. The myth is also referred to in several poems of the *Poetic Edda*: "The Lay of Grímnir" (11) and "The Short Seeress's Prophecy" (3).

15 "Hermod the Young," in Landstad, *Norske Folkeviser* (Norwegian Folk Songs), 28.

16 "The Night-Troll," in Simpson, *Icelandic Folktales and Legends*, 94–6.

17 Stanzas from "Haustlöng" (see n12), depicting the Hrungnir story, are included in "Skáldskaparmál" (section 17) of the *Prose Edda*. Snorri Sturluson (trans. Faulkes), *Edda*, 77–81.

18 Tolkien and Tolkien, *The Legend of Sigurd and Gudrún*, 17.

19 "The Lay of Hymir," stanzas 23–4, in Hollander, *The Poetic Edda*, 87. This translator keeps the pattern of alliteration in each line, as in the original Old Norse poetry. The Midgard serpent was born of Loki's intercourse with the giantess Angrboda. Garm was born of the same giantess, in a brood with the Fenrir wolf that will destroy gods in the end. Other translators use "wolf" or "Fenrir" instead of "Garm," so with this passage some accuracy may be lost in achieving the effect of the original alliteration and metre.

20 Abram, *Myths of the Pagan North*, 38–9.

21 Snorri Sturluson (trans. Faulkes), *Edda*, 74.

22 Abram, 187.

23 Snorri Sturluson (trans. Faulkes), 74.

24 See Davidson, *Pagan Scandinavia*, for the archaeological sites.

25 DuBois, *Nordic Religions in the Viking Age*, 74.

26 Ibid., 159.

CHAPTER ELEVEN

1 Bayerschmidt and Hollander, *Njál's Saga*, 153.

2 "The Second Lay of Helgi the Hunding-Slayer" (*Helgakvida Hundingsbana II*), stanzas 40–51.

3 Wynne, *The Sleeping Bard*, 1–4.

4 DuBois, *Nordic Religions in the Viking Age*, 46–7.

5 The University of Rochester Cinderella Bibliography includes a digital collection of the basic European Cinderella texts. d.lib.rochester.edu/cinderella

6 Bowman and Bianco, *Tales from a Finnish Tupa*, 187–98.

7 Lang, *Red Fairy Book*, 123–32.

8 Douglas, *Scottish Folk and Fairy Tales*, 45–58.

CHAPTER TWELVE

1 Tacitus, *Germania* (trans. Birley) 1.9.

2 Grimm, *Teutonic Mythology*, vol. 3, xxxv.

CHAPTER THIRTEEN

1 Croker, *Fairy Legends and Traditions of the South of Ireland*, 171–4.

2 Roberts, *Studies on Middle Welsh Literature*, 96.

3 Ibid.

4 Included in "The First Branch" of the *Mabinogion*, in Davies, *The Mabinogion*, 16–21.

5 An overview of the scholarship concerning the Taliesin material is in Ford, "Introduction," in *Ystoria Taliesin*, 1–10.

6 The account of Taliesin's birth is in the sixteenth century "Tale of Taliesin" (*Hanes Taliesin*). A translation is in Ford, *The Mabinogi and Other Medieval Welsh Tales*.

7 Creiddyledd's story is in the tale of Culhwch and Olwen in the *Mabinogion*, in Davies, 207.

8 There are two *Lives of Gildas*. The *Life* that includes this story and other early Arthurian episodes was written by the monk Caradoc of Llangarfan and can be dated to 1130–50.

9 A source for the ancient songs and ballads about Robin Hood is Ritson, *Robin Hood*, 2 vols. An Internet resource for early Robin Hood material is the University of Rochester's "Robin Hood Project," which includes a thorough bibliography of Robin Hood material (www.lib.rochester.edu/camelot/rh/rhhome.htm.). From this site the reader can access the text of many of the early ballads.

CHAPTER FOURTEEN

1 The popular story is from a ballad in Sir Walter Scott's *Minstrelsy of the Scottish Border*, vol. 2, 388–405. Scott composed his ballad based on printed versions of the poem that he had collected and on oral recitations he had written down.

2 Roe and Dooley, *Tales of the Elders of Ireland*, 116.

3 O'Grady, *Silva Gadelica*, vol. 2, 373–5.

4 Roe and Dooley, 51–4.

5 An incomplete version of this story, "The Intoxication of the Ulstermen" (*Mesca Ulad*), is in the *Book of the Dun Cow*. The story is in Cross and Slover, *Ancient Irish Tales*, 215–38, and in Gantz, *Early Irish Myths and Sagas*, 188–218.

6 Two parts of the Cúchulainn legend, the story of his birth and the words to Cúchulainn of a warrior woman, Scáthach, who trained him in fighting, are included in the

contents list of the lost book *Cín Dromma Snechta*, indicating that at least these parts of his story were known in the eighth or ninth centuries. See chapter 2 n2.

7 MacKillop, "Ulster Cycle," in *A Dictionary of Celtic Mythology*, 422.

8 There are several versions of the story of the birth of Cúchulainn, but in all of them Deichtine is his mother, and in the most familiar versions Lug is his father.

9 This episode, which is a fore-tale of "The Cattle Raid of Cooley," is in Cross and Slover, *Ancient Irish Tales*, 168–70.

10 Mael Muiri copied this story from a much earlier manuscript, the *Yellow Book of Slane*, which is now lost. The story is in Cross and Slover, 176–98, and in Gantz, 155–78.

11 "The Dream of Angus" survives only in a fifteenth-century manuscript in the British Museum. However, it was mentioned in the *Book of Leinster* (c. 1160), so the story was known at that time. The text is in Shaw, *The Dream of Óengus, Aislinge Óenguso*. This story was the inspiration for W.B. Yeats's poem "The Song of Wandering Aengus."

CHAPTER FIFTEEN

1 "Una the Elfwoman" is from the collection of Jón Arnason, *Icelandic Legends*, 80–4.

2 The story of Helge Thoreson is in several books on Teutonic legends, including Mackenzie, *Teutonic Myth and Legend*, 267–8.

3 Asbjørnsen, *Folk and Fairy Tales*, 149–50.

4 *The Saga of Grettir* or *Grettis Saga* is available in different translations, one by Eiríkr Magnusson and William Morris. A current translation, by Scudder, is in *The Complete Sagas of Icelanders*.

5 *Sir Gawain and the Green Knight* survives in a single manuscript along with three other poems, "Pearl," "Purity," and "Patience," assumed to be by the same author. I used the prose translation by Jessie Weston. J.R.R. Tolkien's edition of the text in Middle English includes ample notes to assist the reader.

6 Included in Christie, *Fairy Tales from Finland*, 29–54.

7 This story from Asbjørnsen and Moe's collection of Norse folk tales is included in Lang, *Blue Fairy Book*, 259–66.

8 Sveinsson, *The Folk-Stories of Iceland*, 294.

9 Sjoestedt, *Gods and Heroes of the Celts*, 40.

CHAPTER SIXTEEN

1 Zipes, *Breaking the Magic Spell*, 8–9.

2 Simpson, *Icelandic Folktales and Legends*, 14.

3 The story written with the original dialect is in Briggs and Tongue, *Folktales of England*, 16–26, and is from the collection of folklorist R.W. Thomson. The story is retold without dialect in Crossley-Holland, *The Magic Lands*, 68–79.

4 The wish-granting dwarf is in the Danish fairy tale "Maiden Bright-Eye," in Lang, *Pink Fairy Book*, 289–96.

5 Grimm, *Teutonic Mythology*, vol. 1, 138.

6 Grimm makes the connection of Wäinämöinen with "wish," in *Teutonic Mythology*, vol. 3, xxxi.

7 Lists of some of Odin's many names are in the *Prose Edda*, "Gylfaginning" (20), and in the *Poetic Edda*, "The Lay of Grímnir" (stanzas 46–50). Superstition about having power over someone by speaking his name is an old idea in folk belief, and is likely one reason for Odin having so many alternate names; he could be mentioned without being summoned. Gaining power over a magical person by naming him is the theme in tales such as "Tom Tit Tot" and "Rumpelstiltskin."

8 Grimm, vol. 1, 138.

9 Lindow, *Norse Mythology*, 151.

10 The story of the king known as Niall of the Nine Hostages is in Cross and Slover, *Ancient Irish Tales*, 508–13; in Koch and Carey, *The Celtic Heroic Age*, 203–8; and in Dillon, *The Cycles of the Kings*, 38–41.

CHAPTER SEVENTEEN

1 "The Three Fairies" is in Basile and Capena, *Giambattista Basile's the Tale of Tales, or, Entertainment for Little Ones*, 280–7.

2 This episode is in Roe and Dooley, *Tales of the Elders of Ireland*, 198.

3 "Find" and "Finn Emna," in MacKillop, *A Dictionary of Celtic Mythology*, 223 and 226.

4 "The Great Rout of Muirthemne" (*Brislech mór Maige Muirthemne*), the story known as "The Death of Cúchulainn," is from the *Book of Leinster*. Translations are in Koch and Carey, *The Celtic Heroic Age*, 134–143, and in Cross and Slover, *Ancient Irish Tales*, 333–40.

5 "The Story of Mjadveig, Daughter of Mani," an Icelandic tale in Sierra, *The Oryx Multicultural Folktale Series: Cinderella*, 81–7.

6 Green, *Celtic Art: Symbols and Imagery*, 123.

7 Davidson, *The Lost Beliefs of Northern Europe*, 120–1.

8 Cormac and Stokes, *Sanas Chormaic: Cormac's Glossary*, 23.

9 The story by Jacobs was published in 1890. An earlier source was an English chapbook written by a Shakespeare scholar, J.O. Halliwell-Phillipps. The folk tale was referred

to in a fantastical comedy, *The Old Wives' Tale* by George Peele, published in 1595. In the play, three men are lost in the woods and find shelter in the cottage of an old woman, where together they spend the whole night telling each other fairy tales, including a comic version of this tale.

10 A paper on the importance of the human head in pagan Celtic religion, including the severed head, deities with three heads, and images of these, is Ross, "The Human Head in Insular Pagan Celtic Religion."

11 "The Prophecy of the Seeress " (*Völuspá*) is considered to be one of the oldest poems in the *Poetic Edda*, and pre-Christian. See McKinnell, *Meeting the Other in Norse Myth and Legend*, 2.

12 Bellows, "*Voluspo,*" in *The Poetic Edda*, 9, stanzas 19, 20.

13 Lists of Welsh triads were collected in several manuscripts dating from the thirteenth to the fifteenth centuries: the *White Book of Rhydderch*, the *Red Book of Hergest*, the *Black Book of Carmarthon*, and the primary collection, the Peniarth MS16. The most comprehensive resource is Bromwich, *Trioedd Ynys Prydein: The Welsh Triads*.

CHAPTER EIGHTEEN

1 Originally from a Northumbrian ballad, the story is "The Laidly Worm of Spindleston Heugh," in Jacobs, *English Fairy Tales*, 183–7.

2 The enchantment of Bjorn is a small folklore-like episode from the chapter "The Story of Bothvar," in the saga "King Hrolf and His Champions," in Jones, *Eirik the Red and Other Icelandic Sagas*, 262–88. Another translation is Byock, *The Saga of King Hrolf Kraki*, 34–41.

3 The story is one of *The Four Branches of the Mabinogi*, originally written c. 1050–1120, according to Roberts, *Studies on Middle Welsh Literature*, 96.

4 Roe and Dooley, *Tales of the Elders of Ireland*, 74.

5 Ibid., 159.

6 "The Story of Tuan Son of Cairell" (*Scél Tuain meic Chairill*) is in Koch and Carey, *The Celtic Heroic Age*, 223–5.

7 Cahill, *How the Irish Saved Civilization*, 128.

8 This episode is in Byock, "Sigmund and Sinfjotli Don the Skins," in *The Saga of the Volsungs*, chapter 8, 44–7.

9 Glosecki, *Shamanism and Old English Poetry*, 188.

10 Glosecki, "Shamanism," in Lindahl et al., *Medieval Folklore*, 379.

11 Jacobs, *European Folk and Fairy Tales*, 98–104.

12 McKinnell, "The Context of *Volundarkvida*," 11–13.

13 The poem exists only in the *Codex Regius* manuscript of the *Poetic Edda*.

14 Bellows, *The Poetic Edda*, 255–7. I used the Bellows translation, although it is an older one (1936), because it indicates that many lines have been lost. His extensive translation notes explain the difficulties with the text. Where some translators have combined lines of fragmentary stanzas into one stanza, this translator shows the lines with their imperfections.

CHAPTER NINETEEN

1 Hatto, *The Nibelungenlied*, chapter 25, 190–8.

2 Tacitus, *Germania* (trans. Birley) 1.10.

3 This poem was found in only one manuscript, the *Codex Wormianus* of Snorri Sturluson's *Prose Edda*. However, now it is included in most translations of the *Poetic Edda*.

4 Sierra, *The Oryx Multicultural Folktale Series: Cinderella*, 81–7.

5 Simpson, *Icelandic Folktales and Legends*, 70–2.

6 Gantz, *Early Irish Myths and Sagas*, 256.

7 MacGiolla Léith, *The Violent Death of the Children of Uisneach*, 9.

8 Gantz, 256–67, and Cross and Slover, *Ancient Irish Tales*, 239–47.

9 Gantz, 258.

10 Ibid., 266.

11 The *Tháttr of Nornagest* is part of the "Saga of Olaf Tryggvason," included in the very large manuscript, *Flateyjarbók*, and it is not found in any other early sources. Another story of Olaf from the same saga is "Helge in the Glittering Plains" (chapter 15). Nornagest's story is in Chadwick, *Stories and Ballads of the Far Past*, 14–37. It is also told in "The Ballad of Nornagest," a poem in the Faroese language first published in Denmark in the nineteenth century.

12 "Sleeping Beauty" is an old story that is known in a variety of forms. The oldest is an episode in the fourteenth-century romance "Perceforest." Today, the Grimm brothers' "Brier Rose" (*Dornröschen*) is the most familiar version. The title "Sleeping Beauty" derived from translations of Perrault's version of the tale, first published in France in 1696 as "La Belle au Bois Dormant."

13 D'Aulaire and D'Aulaire, *D'Aulaires' Norse Gods and Giants*, 80.

14 Sjoestedt, *Gods and Heroes of the Celts*, 87.

15 Ibid., 88.

16 In Gantz, 60–106; and Cross and Slover, 93–126.

CHAPTER TWENTY

1 Bowman and Bianco, *Tales from a Finnish Tupa*, 34–41.

2 Tacitus, *Histories* (trans. Moore), 4.61 and 65.

3 *The Saga of Erik the Red* relates events that led up to Erik the Red being banished to Greenland, where he was the first settler. It also gives an account of his son, Leif Ericson's journey, around the year 1000, to the region of North America referred to as Vinland.

4 From Viking times Freyja was pictured riding in a chariot drawn by her sacred cats.

5 Jones, *Eirik the Red and Other Icelandic Sagas*, 134.

6 Ní Bhrolcháin, in *An Introduction to Early Irish Literature*, 53, bases the early dating of the story to three short texts that contain "the germ of the plot," the poem "Medb Makes Bad Contracts" (*Conailli Medb Míchuru*), "The Words of Scáthach" (*Verba Scáthaige*), and the Mórrígan's prophecy.

7 Although the story is in the *Book of the Dun Cow*, the version in the *Book of Leinster* is the more standard one. A translation is Carson, *The Táin*.

8 Medb's encounter with Fedelm is in Carson, section II, 12–15.

9 Ní Bhrolcháin, 138.

10 Translations of the Myrddin poems are in Goodrich, *The Romance of Merlin*. The source for four of them is the *Black Book of Carmarthen*, one of the earliest surviving manuscripts written in Welsh, compiled by a single scribe c. 1250. It is a large book of poetry, including prophetic verse in the voice of Myrddin and poems with references to Arthurian legend. The Myrddin poems in the *Black Book of Carmarthen* are considered to be at least as old as 1100, which predate sources for the more familiar legendary figure of Merlin as wizard and counsellor to King Arthur. A translation is Pennar, *The Black Book of Carmarthen*.

CHAPTER TWENTY-ONE

1 "The Ogress in the Stone Boat," in Boucher, *Mead Moondaughter and Other Icelandic Folk Tales*, 93.

2 Lang, *Blue Fairy Book*, 137.

3 From the stories "The Wooing of Seppo Ilmarinen," 73–80, and "Severi and Vappu," 96–104, in Bowman and Bianco, *Tales from a Finnish Tupa*.

4 Karen Louise Jolly discusses the implications of healing charms in use in late Saxon England in *Popular Religion in Late Saxon England: Elf Charms in Context*.

5 Niles, *Homo Narrans*, 27.

6 Virtanen and DuBois, *Finnish Folklore*, 180.

7 Accounts of wind spells in knotted cords are in Page, "Lapland Sorcerers," 226–31. The folk tale is "The Voyage in a Lapp Sled," from Hofberg, *Swedish Fairy Tales*, 218.

8 "Skáldskaparmál" (17) of the *Prose Edda*, in Snorri Sturluson (trans. Faulkes), *Edda*, 77–81.

9 The term "rune" also refers to the system of letters, comprised of lines carved in wood and stone, in use as the system of writing in Scandinavia prior to the third century. There is conflicting opinion about whether or not some letters of this alphabet were ever used with a magical intent. In any case, within the literature, carved runes were sometimes seen to possess mysterious power.

10 The lines in the *Poetic Edda* describing Odin acquiring the runes is known as the "Rune Poem," "The Sayings of Hár" (*Hávamál*), stanzas 138–45.

11 The *Saga of the Völsungs*, section 21; Byock's translation, 67–71.

12 Chanting from the top of a hill with a thorn from the whitethorn in one's hand may have been, in the literature, a druid-like activity for magic. See Ní Bhrolcháin, *An Introduction to Early Irish Literature*, 11.

13 "The Book of Invasions," in Koch and Carey, *The Celtic Heroic Age*, 267.

14 "Bricriu's Feast," in Koch and Carey, 99.

15 The long wound-healing spell is in Canto 9, in Lönnrot (trans. Bosley), *The Kalevala*, 88–104.

16 Hearn, "Note on the Influence of Finnish Poetry in English Literature," in *Books and Habits*, 231.

17 The match of singing spells is Canto 3, in Lönnrot (trans. Bosley), 22–35.

18 The baby's birth and the disappearance of Väinämöinen are Canto 50, "The Newborn King," in Lönnrot (trans. Bosley), 649–66.

CHAPTER TWENTY-TWO

1 Introduction and translation of "Kat Godeu" is in Haycock, *Legendary Poems from the Book of Taliesin*, 167–86.

2 Selection from Pliny's *Natural History* 16.24, translated in Koch and Carey, *The Celtic Heroic Age*, 32.

3 In *Annals* 14.30, Tacitus described the destruction of one of the last great sanctuaries of British druidism, the sacred grove at Mona, on the island of Anglesey, North Wales, translated in Koch and Carey, 34.

4 Eliade, *Patterns in Comparative Religion*, 265–330.

5 Davidson, *The Lost Beliefs of Northern Europe*, 68.

6 Snorri Sturluson (trans. Byock), *The Prose Edda*, 24.

7 The story of Trefuilngid Tre-eochair is from the *Yellow Book of Lecan*. Translation is in Best, "The Settling of the Manor of Tara."

8 The specially designated trees known as Ross, Mugna, Datha, Tortu, and Banba are described in Stokes, "The Prose Tales in the Rennes Dindshenchas," 419, 420, 431, 445. This is a text of the lore of Irish places gathered from early manuscripts, including the *Book of the Dun Cow*. Irish sacred trees were known by the term "bile"; see "Bile," in MacKillop, *A Dictionary of Celtic Mythology*, 41.

9 A comprehensive description of meanings and literary associations of many trees are in MacKillop, *A Dictionary of Celtic Mythology*.

10 This story is in Cross and Slover, *Ancient Irish Tales*, 503–7; in Koch and Carey, 184–7; and in Stokes and Windisch, "The Irish Ordeals, Cormac's Adventure in the Land of Promise."

11 From "Lippo and Tapio," in Bowman and Bianco, *Tales from a Finnish Tupa*, 65–72.

CHAPTER TWENTY-THREE

1 Boucher, *Mead Moondaughter and Other Icelandic Folk Tales*, 71–87.

2 Although fragments exist in the *Book of the Dun Cow*, the primary source for the story of Máel Dúin is the *Yellow Book of Lecan*. The early date for the story is proposed in MacKillop, *A Dictionary of Celtic Mythology*, 271. In *The Voyage of Mael Duin's Curragh*, Patricia Aakhus retells the story and gives it a fictional narrative framework in which a poet-druid relates the story to Mael Muiri, so he can write it in his manuscript.

3 The fragment of "The Voyage of Bran" in the *Book of the Dun Cow* is from the very end of the story. The other manuscripts in which the story is preserved with almost identical texts were likely all taken from one original source. Kuno Meyer, using preserved and readable parts from all the manuscripts, was able to create the full story, in *The Voyage of Bran Son of Febal to the Land of the Living*. The story is also in Cross and Slover, *Ancient Irish Tales*, 588–95. MacKillop, in *A Dictionary of Celtic Mythology*, 270, suggests that this narrative dates from the seventh or eighth century.

4 The main sources for the Norse mythological universe and its history are "The Prophecy of the Seeress" (*Völuspá*) in the *Poetic Edda* and "The Deluding of Gylfi" (*Gylfaginning*) in the *Prose Edda*.

5 Stories of dragons and dragon slaying are from a story tradition originating in the

mythologies of the Near East. Although dragons often appear in stories from the Far East, these are not stories that make heroes out of dragon slayers.

6 These birds are in a story of the birth of Cúchulainn, in Gantz, *Early Irish Myths and Sagas*, 130–3, and in Cross and Slover, 134–6.

7 The story was published by T. Crofton Croker in 1827, written just as it was told to him by a woman at a holy well. It is in Yeats, *Irish Fairy and Folk Tales*, 294–5.

CHAPTER TWENTY-FOUR

1 Keightley, *The Fairy Mythology*, 130–9.

Selected Bibliography

Aakhus, Patricia. *The Voyage of Mael Duin's Curragh*. Brownsville, Oregon: Story Line Press, 1990.

Aarne, Antti A. *The Types of the Folktale: A Classification and Bibliography*. Helsinki: Suomalainen Tiedeakatemia, 1961.

Abram, Christopher. *Myths of the Pagan North: The Gods of the Norsemen*. London: Continuum, 2011.

Acker, Paul, and Carolyne Larrington, eds. *The Poetic Edda: Essays on Old Norse Mythology*. New York: Routledge, 2002.

Aldhouse-Green, Miranda J. *Dictionary of Celtic Myth and Legend*. London: Thames and Hudson, 1997.

Aldhouse-Green, Miranda J., and Stephen Aldhouse-Green. *The Quest for the Shaman: Shape-shifters, Sorcerers, and Spirit-Healers of Ancient Europe*. London: Thames and Hudson, 2005.

Andersen, Hans Christian. *The Complete Stories*. Translated by Jean Hersholt. London: British Library, 2005.

Anderson, Graham. *Fairytale in the Ancient World*. London: Routledge, 2000.

Anderson, J.J., ed. *Sir Gawain and the Green Knight, Pearl, Cleanness, Patience*. London: Dent, 2005.

Árnason, Jón. *Icelandic Legends*. Translated by George E.J. Powell and Eiríkur Magnússon. London: Richard Bentley, 1864.

Asbjørnsen, Peter C., and H.L. Bræstad. *Folk and Fairy Tales*. New York: A.C. Armstrong and Son, 1883.

Asbjørnsen, Peter C., H.L. Bræstad, Erik T. Werenskiold, Theodor Kittelsen, Otto Sinding, and David Nutt. *Fairy Tales from the Far North*. London: David Nutt, 1897.

Aulnoy, Anne Macdonell, Elizabeth Lee, and DeWitt C. Peters. *The Fairy Tales of Madame D'Aulnoy*. London: Lawrence and Bullen, 1892.

Basile, Giambattista. *Giambattista Basile's the Tale of Tales, or, Entertainment for Little Ones.* Translated by Nancy L. Canepa. Detroit: Wayne State University Press, 2007.

Bayerschmidt, Carl F., and Lee M. Hollander, translators. *Njál's Saga.* Ware, Hertfordshire: Wordsworth, 1998.

Bellows, Henry Adams, translator. *The Poetic Edda.* Princeton: Princeton University Press, 1936.

Best, R.I. "The Settling of the Manor of Tara." *Ériu* 4 (1910), 121–72.

Best, R.I., and Osborn Bergin, eds. *Lebor na Huidre: Book of the Dun Cow.* Dublin: Hodges, Figgis & Co. for the Royal Irish Academy, 1929.

Bhreathnach, Edel. "Learning and Literature in Early Medieval Clonmacnoise." *Clonmacnoise Studies* 2 (1998), 97–104.

Blecher, Lone T., and George Blecher. *Swedish Folktales and Legends.* New York: Pantheon, 1993.

Booss, Claire, ed. *Scandinavian Folk and Fairy Tales: Tales from Norway, Sweden, Denmark, Finland, Iceland.* New York: Avenel Books, 1984.

Bottrell, William. *Traditions and Hearthside Stories of West Cornwall.* Penzance: Beare and Son, 1873.

Boucher, Alan. *Mead Moondaughter and Other Icelandic Folk Tales.* London: Hart-Davis, 1967.

Bowman, James Cloyd, and Margery Bianco. *Tales from a Finnish Tupa.* Translated by Aili Kolehmainen. Minneapolis: University of Minnesota Press, 2009.

Breeze, Andrew. *Medieval Welsh Literature.* Dublin: Four Courts Press, 1997.

Briggs, Katharine. *British Folk-Tales and Legends: A Sampler.* Boulder, CO: Paladin, 1977.

– *An Encyclopedia of Fairies: Hobgoblins, Brownies, Bogies, and Other Supernatural Creatures.* New York: Pantheon, 1976.

– *The Fairies in Tradition and Literature.* London: Routledge and Kegan Paul, 1967.

– *The Vanishing People: A Study of Traditional Fairy Beliefs.* London: B.T. Batsford, 1978.

Briggs, Katharine, and Ruth L. Tongue, eds. *Folktales of England.* London: Routledge and Kegan Paul, 1969.

Bringsværd, Tor Åge. *Phantoms and Fairies: From Norwegian Folklore.* Oslo: J.G. Tanum Forlag, 1970.

Bromwich, Rachel. *Trioedd Ynys Prydein: The Welsh Triads.* Cardiff: University of Wales Press, 1978.

Buchan, David. "Folk Literature," in *The Encyclopedia of Literature and Criticism,* 976–990. Detroit: Gale Research, 1991.

Selected Bibliography

Byock, Jesse L., translator. *The Saga of the Volsungs: The Norse Epic of Sigurd the Dragon Slayer*. London: Penguin, 1999.

– translator. *The Saga of King Hrolf Kraki*. London: Penguin, 1998.

Cahill, Thomas. *How the Irish Saved Civilization*. New York: Random House, 1996.

Calder, George, translator. *Auraicept na nEces: The Scholars' Primer*. Dublin: Four Courts Press, 1995.

Calvino, Italo. "Cybernetics and Ghosts," in *The Uses of Literature: Essays*, 3–27. San Diego: Harcourt Brace Jovanovich, 1986.

Campbell, J.F. *Popular Tales of the West Highlands*. Paisley: A. Gardner, 1890.

Caradoc, Monk of Ruys. *Two Lives of Gildas*. Translated by Hugh Williams. Felinfach: Llanerch Enterprises, 1990.

Carson, Ciaran. *The Táin: A New Translation of the Táin Bó Cúailnge*. London: Penguin, 2008.

Chadwick, Nora K., translator. *Stories and Ballads of the Far Past*. Cambridge: Cambridge University Press, 1921.

Child, Francis James. *The English and Scottish Popular Ballads*. New York: Cooper Square Publishers, 1965.

Christiansen, Reidar Thoralf, ed. *Folktales of Norway*. Chicago: University of Chicago Press, 1964.

– *Studies in Irish and Scandinavian Folktales*. Copenhagen: Published for Coimisiún Béaloideasa Éireann by Rosenkilde and Bagger, 1959.

Christie, Ella R. *Fairy Tales from Finland*. London: T. Fisher Unwin, 1896.

Colum, Padraic, ed. *A Treasury of Irish Folklore*. New York: Wings Books, 1992.

Cooper, Susan. *The Silver Cow: A Welsh Tale*. New York: Atheneum, 1983.

Cormac, John O'Donovan, and Whitley Stokes. *Sanas Chormaic: Cormac's Glossary*. Calcutta: Printed by O.T. Cutter for the Irish Archaeological and Celtic Society, 1868.

Cott, Jonathan, ed. *Beyond the Looking Glass: Extraordinary Works of Fantasy and Fairy Tale*. New York: Stonehill, 1973.

Crane, Lucy, translator. *Household Stories from the Collection of the Bros. Grimm*. London: Macmillan, 1882.

Croker, Crofton. *Fairy Legends and Traditions of the South of Ireland*. London: William Tegg, 1859.

Cross, Tom P., and Clark H. Slover. *Ancient Irish Tales*. New York: Barnes and Noble, 1996.

Crossley-Holland, Kevin. *British Folk Tales: New Versions*. London: Orchard, 1987.

– *The Faber Book of Northern Folk-Tales*. London: Faber and Faber, 1980.

– *The Magic Lands: Folk Tales of Britain and Ireland.* London: Orion Children's Books, 2006.

– *The Penguin Book of Norse Myths.* London: Penguin, 1980.

Curtin, Jeremiah. *Tales of the Fairies and of the Ghost World: Collected from Oral Tradition in South-West Munster.* Dublin: Talbot Press, 1974.

Dasent, George Webbe. *Popular Tales from the Norse.* New York: D. Appleton, 1859.

– *East o' the Sun and West o' the Moon: Fifty-nine Norwegian Folk Tales from the Collection of Peter Christen Asbjørnsen and Jørgen Moe.* New York: Dover, 1970.

D'Aulaire, Ingri, and Edgar P. D'Aulaire. *D'Aulaires' Norse Gods and Giants.* Garden City, NY: Doubleday, 1967.

Davidson, Hilda Ellis. " Dreams in Old Norse and Old Irish Literature," in *Northern Lights: Following Folklore in North-Western Europe; Aistí in Adhnó Do Bho Almqvist – Essays in Honour of Bo Almqvist*, 34–46. Dublin: University College Dublin Press, 2001.

– *Gods and Myths of Northern Europe.* London: Penguin, 1990.

– *The Lost Beliefs of Northern Europe.* London: Routledge, 1993.

– *Myths and Symbols in Pagan Europe: Early Scandinavian and Celtic Religions.* Manchester: Manchester University Press, 1988.

– "Otherworld Cattle." *At the Edge* 1 (March), 1996.

– *Pagan Scandinavia.* London: Thames and Hudson, 1967.

– *The Road to Hel: A Study of the Conception of the Dead in Old Norse Literature.* New York: Greenwood, 1968.

– *Roles of the Northern Goddess.* London: Routledge, 1998.

Davidson, Hilda Ellis, and Anna Chaudhri. *A Companion to the Fairy Tale.* Cambridge: D.S. Brewer, 2003.

Davies, Sioned, translator. *The Mabinogion.* Oxford: Oxford University Press, 2007.

Deane, Tony, and Tony Shaw. *Folklore of Cornwall.* Stroud: Tempus, 2003.

Dillon, Myles. *The Cycles of the Kings.* London: G. Cumberlege, 1946.

– *Early Irish Literature.* Chicago: University of Chicago Press, 1948.

Dolan, Brigid. *Important Manuscripts in the Royal Irish Academy: Notes and Bibliography.* Dublin: Royal Irish Academy, 1993.

Douglas, Barbara. *Favourite French Fairy Tales.* London: Harrap, 1966.

Douglas, George. *Scottish Folk and Fairy Tales.* Bath: Lomond, 2005.

Dronke, Ursula. *Myth and Fiction in Early Norse Lands.* Aldershot, UK: Variorum, 1996.

DuBois, Thomas A. *Nordic Religions in the Viking Age.* Philadelphia: University of Pennsylvania Press, 1999.

Edwards, Cyril W. *The Nibelungenlied: The Lay of the Nibelungs*. Oxford: Oxford University Press, 2010.

Eliade, Mircea. *Patterns in Comparative Religion*. Cleveland: World Publishing, 1963.

Eliade, Mircea, and Charles J. Adams et al. *The Encyclopedia of Religion*. New York: Macmillan, 1987.

Faulkes, Anthony. "Pagan Sympathy: Attitudes to Heathendom in the Prologue to *Snorra Edda*." Viking Society for Northern Research Website (www.vsnrweb-publications. org.uk).

Fee, Christopher R., and David A. Leeming. *Gods, Heroes and Kings: The Battle for Mythic Britain*. Oxford, New York: Oxford University Press, 2004.

Fitzgerald, David. "Popular Tales of Ireland." *Revue Celtique* 4 (1879–80), 171–200.

Ford, Patrick K. "Introduction," *Ystoria Taliesin*, 1–64. Cardiff: University of Wales Press, 1992.

– *The Mabinogi and Other Medieval Welsh Tales*. Berkeley: University of California Press, 2008.

Fraser, Antonia. *Robin Hood*. London: Orion Children's Books, 1993.

Gantz, Jeffrey. *Early Irish Myths and Sagas*. Harmondsworth: Penguin, 1981.

Glosecki, Stephen O. *Myth in Early Northwest Europe*. Tempe, Ariz.: Arizona Center for Medieval and Renaissance Studies, 2007.

– *Shamanism and Old English Poetry*. New York: Garland, 1989.

Goethe, Johann Wolfgang von. *Selected Poetry*. Translated by David Luke. London: Penguin, 2005

Goodrich, Peter. *The Romance of Merlin: An Anthology*. New York: Garland, 1990.

Green, Miranda. *Celtic Art: Symbols and Imagery*. New York: Sterling, 1997.

– *Gods of the Celts*. Gloucester: Barnes and Noble, 1986.

– *The World of the Druids*. New York: Thames and Hudson, 1997.

Gregory, Lady Augusta. *Gods and Fighting Men*. London: J. Murray, 1904.

– *Cuchulain of Muirthemne, The Story of the Men of the Red Branch of Ulster*. London: J. Murray, 1902.

– *Lady Gregory's Complete Irish Mythology*. New York: Smithmark, 1996.

– *Visions and Beliefs in the West of Ireland*. Toronto: Macmillan, 1976.

Grimm, Jacob. *Teutonic Mythology*, vols 1–4. Translated by James Steven Stallybrass. London: George Bell and Sons, London, 1883 and 1888; republished New York: Dover, 1966.

Grimm, Jacob, and Wilhelm Grimm. *Grimm's Fairy Tales: Stories and Tales of Elves, Goblins and Fairies*. New York: Harper and Bros., 1917.

Grimm, Jacob, and Edgar Taylor. *German Popular Stories and Fairy Tales.* London: H.G. Bohn, 1856.

Gwynn, Edward J. *The Metrical Dindsenchas.* Dublin: Published at the [Royal Irish] Academy House, 1903.

Haase, Donald. *The Greenwood Encyclopedia of Folktales and Fairy Tales.* Westport, CT: Greenwood, 2008.

Hall, Alaric. *Elves in Anglo-Saxon England: Matters of Belief, Health, Gender and Identity.* Woodbridge, UK: Boydell Press, 2007.

Hartland, Edwin Sidney. *English Fairy and Other Folk Tales.* London: Walter Scott, 1906.

Hatto, A.T., translator. *The Nibelungenlied.* London: Penguin, 1969.

Haycock, Marged. *Legendary Poems from the Book of Taliesin.* Aberystwyth: CMCS Publications, 2007.

Hayman, Richard. *Trees: Woodlands and Western Civilization.* London: Hambledon and London, 2003.

Heaney, Seamus, translator, and John D. Niles. *Beowulf: An Illustrated Edition.* New York: W.W. Norton, 2008.

Hearn, Lafcadio. "Note on the Influence of Finnish Poetry in English Literature," in *Books and Habits: From the Lectures of Lafcadio Hearn,* 228–60. London: William Heinemann, 1922.

Henderson, George, translator. *Fled Bricrend: The Feast of Bricriu.* London: Published for the Irish Texts Society, by D. Nutt, 1899.

Hofberg, Herman. *Swedish Fairy Tales,* translated by W.H. Myers. Chicago: Belford-Clarke, 1890.

Hollander, Lee M., translator. *The Poetic Edda.* 1962. Austin: University of Texas Press, 2nd ed. 2000.

– *The Skalds: A Selection of Their Poems.* Princeton: Princeton University Press for the American-Scandinavian Foundation, 1947.

Hreinsson, Vidar, ed. *The Complete Sagas of Icelanders.* Reykjavik: Leifur Eiriksson Pub., 1997.

Hyde, Douglas. *A Literary History of Ireland from Earliest Times to the Present Day.* London: Benn, 1980.

Jacobs, Joseph. *Celtic Fairy Tales.* London: David Nutt, 1892.

– *English Fairy Tales.* London: David Nutt, 1890.

– *European Folk and Fairy Tales.* New York: G.P. Putnam's Sons, 1916.

– *More Celtic Fairy Tales.* London: David Nutt, 1894.

– *More English Fairy Tales.* London: David Nutt, 1894.

Jarman, A.O.H. "The Merlin Legend and the Welsh Tradition of Prophecy," in *The Arthur of the Welsh: The Arthurian Legend in Medieval Welsh Literature*, 117–46. Cardiff: University of Wales Press, 1991.

Jarvie, Gordon. *Scottish Folk and Fairy Tales from Burns to Buchan*. London: Penguin, 2008.

Johnson, W. Branch. *Folktales of Brittany*. London: Methuen, 1927.

Jolly, Karen Louise. *Popular Religion in Late Saxon England: Elf Charms in Context*. Chapel Hill: University of North Carolina Press, 1996.

Jones, Gwyn, translator. *Eirik the Red and Other Icelandic Sagas*. Oxford: Oxford University Press, 1980.

– and Thomas Jones, translators. *The Mabinogion*. New York: Alfred A. Knopf, 2000.

Joyce, P.W. *Old Celtic Romances*. Dublin: The Educational Co. of Ireland, 1920.

Keightley, Thomas. *The Fairy Mythology*. London: George Bell and Sons, 1892; reprinted as *The World Guide to Gnomes, Fairies, Elves and Other Little People*. New York: Avenel Books, 1978.

Kennedy, Patrick. *The Fireside Stories of Ireland*. Norwood, PA: Norwood Editions, 1975.

Kirk, G.S. "On Defining Myths," in *Sacred Narrative, Readings in the Theory of Myth*, 53–71. Berkeley: University of California Press, 1984.

Koch, John T. *Celtic Culture: A Historical Encyclopedia*. Santa Barbara, CA: ABC-CLIO, 2006.

Koch, John T., and John Carey, eds. *The Celtic Heroic Age: Literary Sources for Ancient Celtic Europe and Early Ireland and Wales*. Aberystwyth: Celtic Studies Publications, 2009.

Kristjánsson, Jónas. *Icelandic Manuscripts: Sagas, History and Art*. Reykjavik: Icelandic Literary Society, 1993.

Kvideland, Reimund, and Henning K. Sehmsdorf, eds. *Scandinavian Folk Belief and Legend*. Minneapolis: University of Minnesota Press, 1988.

Landstad, M.B. *Norske Folkeviser* (Norwegian Folk Songs). Christiania: Christian Tonsberg, 1853.

Lang, Andrew. *Blue Fairy Book*. Philadelphia: David McKay, 1921.

– *Brown Fairy Book*. New York: Dover, 1965.

– *Lilac Fairy Book*. London: Longmans, Green, and Co., 1910.

– *Pink Fairy Book*. New York: Longmans, Green, 1904.

– *Red Fairy Book*. London: Longmans, Green, 1891.

Larrington, Carolyne, translator. *The Poetic Edda*. Oxford: Oxford University Press, 2008.

Lewis, Ceri W. "Bardic Order, In Wales," in *Celtic Culture: A Historical Encyclopedia*, vol. 1, 176–83. Santa Barbara, CA: ABC-CLIO, 2006.

Lindahl, Carl, John McNamara, and John Lindow, eds. *Medieval Folklore: A Guide to Myths, Legends, Tales, Beliefs, and Customs*. Oxford: Oxford University Press, 2002.

Lindow, John. *Norse Mythology: A Guide to the Gods, Heroes, Rituals, and Beliefs*. Oxford: Oxford University Press, 2002.

– *Swedish Legends and Folktales*. Berkeley: University of California Press, 1978.

– "Thættir and Oral Performance," in *Oral Tradition in the Middle Ages*, 179–86. Binghamton, NY: Medieval and Renaissance Texts and Studies, 1995.

Lönnrot, Elias. *The Kalevala: An Epic Poem after Oral Tradition*. Translated with an introduction and notes by Keith Bosley. Oxford: Oxford University Press, 1999.

Lönnrot, Elias. *Kalevala, the Land of Heroes*. Translated by W.R. Kirby. London: Dent, [1961–62].

Macalister, R.A. Stewart, translator. *Lebor Gabála Érenn: The Book of the Taking of Ireland*. Dublin: Published for the Irish Texts Society by the Educational Co. of Ireland, Part IV, 1941; Part V, 1956.

MacCana, Proinsias. "Note on the Motif of the Wading Giant in Irish and Welsh," in *Northern Lights: Following Folklore in North-Western Europe; Aistí in Adhnó Do Bho Almqvist = Essays in Honour of Bo Almqvist*, 141–7. Dublin: University College Dublin Press, 2001.

Mac Giolla Léith, Caoimhín. *Oidheadh Chloinne hUisneach: The Violent Death of the Children of Uisneach*. London: Irish Texts Society, 1993.

Mackenzie, Donald A. *Teutonic Myth and Legend*. London: Gresham, 1912.

MacKillop, James. *A Dictionary of Celtic Mythology*. Oxford: Oxford University Press, 2004.

MacNiocaill, G., translator. *The Annals of Tigernach*. Online at Celt: The Corpus of Electronic Texts. www.ucc.ie/celt

Magnusson, Eiríkr, and William Morris. *The Story of Grettir the Strong*. London: Longmans, Green, 1901.

– *Three Northern Love Stories and Other Tales*. New York: Longmans, Green, 1901.

Malory, Thomas, and John Matthews. *Le Morte d'Arthur*. London: Cassell, 2000.

Marwick, Ernest W. *The Folklore of Orkney and Shetland*. London: B.T. Batsford, 1975.

McCone, Kim. *Pagan Past and Christian Present in Early Irish Literature*. Maynooth: An Sagart, 1990.

McKinnell, John. "The Context of Volundarkvida." *Saga-Book* 23 (1990), 1–27.

– *Meeting the Other in Norse Myth and Legend*. Woodbridge, UK: D.S. Brewer, 2005.

McKinnell, John, Rudolf Simek, and Klaus Düwel. *Runes, Magic and Religion: A Sourcebook*. Wien: Fassbaender, 2004.

Meyer, Kuno. *The Voyage of Bran Son of Febal to the Land of the Living: An Old Irish Saga Now First Edited, with Translation, Notes, and Glossary*. London: David Nutt in the Strand, 1895.

Moore, A.W. *The Folk-Lore of the Isle of Man*. [Yorkshire, Eng.]: S.R. Publishers, 1971.

Morris, William. *Volsunga Saga: The Story of the Volsungs and Niblungs*. New York: Collier, 1971.

Motz, Lotte. *The Wise One of the Mountain: Form, Function, and Significance of the Subterranean Smith: A Study in Folklore*. Göppingen: Kümmerle, 1983.

Murphy, Denis. *The Annals of Clonmacnoise, Being Annals of Ireland from the Earliest Period to A.D. 1408*. Dublin: Printed at the University Press for the Royal Society of Antiquaries of Ireland, 1896.

Nagy, Joseph Falaky. *Conversing with Angels and Ancients: Literary Myths of Medieval Ireland*. Ithaca: Cornell University Press, 1997.

– "Orality in Medieval Irish Narrative: An Overview." *Oral Tradition* 1/2 (1986), 272–301.

Ní Bhrolcháin, Muireann. *An Introduction to Early Irish Literature*. Dublin: Four Courts Press, 2011.

Ní Dhonnchadha, Máirín. "Bardic Order, In Ireland," in *Celtic Culture: a Historical Encyclopedia*, vol. 1, 174–6. Santa Barbara, CA: ABC-CLIO, 2006.

Niles, John D. *Homo Narrans: The Poetics and Anthropology of Oral Literature*. Philadelphia: University of Pennsylvania Press, 1999.

– "Pagan Survivals and Popular Beliefs," in *The Cambridge Companion to Old English Literature*, 126–41. Cambridge: Cambridge University Press, 1991.

Ó Cathasaigh, Thomás. "Semantics of Sid." *Éigse* 17 (1977–78), 137–55.

O'Clery, Michael, Cucogry O'Clery, Ferfeasa O'Mulconry, Cucogry O'Duigenan, Conary O'Clery, and John O'Donovan. *Annala Rioghachta Eireann: Annals of the Kingdom of Ireland, By the Four Masters*. Dublin: Hodges, Smith, 1856.

O'Curry, E., translator. "*Oidhe Chloinne Lir.*" *The Atlantis* 4 (1863), 114–55.

O'Donoghue, Heather. *Old Norse-Icelandic Literature: A Short Introduction*. Oxford: Blackwell, 2004.

O'Duffy, R.J., and B. O'Looney. *Oidhe Chloinne Lir: The Fate of the Children of Lir*. Dublin: Gill and Son, for the Society for the Preservation of the Irish Language, 1883.

O'Grady, Standish H. *Silva Gadelica (I–XXXI): A Collection of Tales in Irish with Extracts Illustrating Persons and Places*, vol. 2. London: Williams and Norgate, 1892.

Ó hÓgáin, Dáithá. *Fionn mac Cumhaill: Images of the Gaelic Hero.* Dublin: Gill and Macmillan, 1988.

– *Myth, Legend and Romance: An Encyclopaedia of the Irish Folk Tradition.* London: Ryan, 1990.

Olenius, Elsa. *Great Swedish Fairy Tales.* [New York]: Delacorte Press/S. Lawrence, 1973.

Ó Néill, Pádraig. "The Impact of the Norman Invasion on Irish Literature." *Anglo-Norman Studies* 20 (1997), 171–86.

O'Neill, Timothy. *The Irish Hand: Scribes and Their Manuscripts from the Earliest Times to the Seventeenth Century, with an Exemplar of Irish Scripts.* Mountrath, Ireland: Dolmen Press, 1984.

Orchard, Andy, translator. *The Elder Edda: A Book of Viking Lore.* London: Penguin, 2011.

O'Reilly, Michael. "The Kerry Mermaid." *The Gael* (June 1903), 185–6.

O'Rorke, Terence. *The History of Sligo: Town and County.* Dublin: J. Duffy, 1890.

Ó Súilleabháin, Seán. *A Handbook of Irish Folklore.* Detroit: Singing Tree Press, 1970.

Owen, Elias. *Welsh Folk-Lore: A Collection of the Folk-Tales and Legends of North Wales.* Norwood, PA: Norwood Editions, 1973.

Page, R.I. "Lapland Sorcerers." *Saga-Book of the Viking Society* 16 (1962–65), 215–32.

Pennar, Meirion. *The Black Book of Carmarthen.* Lampeter: Llanerch Enterprises, 1989.

Pentikäinen, Juha. *Kalevala Mythology.* Translated by Ritva Poom. Bloomington: Indiana University Press, 1999.

Perrault, Charles, and Ann Lawrence. *Tales from Perrault.* Oxford; Toronto: Oxford University Press, 1988.

Philip, Neil. *The Penguin Book of English Folktales.* London: Penguin, 1992.

Pliny the Elder. *Natural History, a Selection.* Translated with an introduction and notes by John F. Healy. London: Penguin, 1991.

Porteous, Alexander. *Forest Folklore, Mythology, and Romance.* Detroit: Singing Tree Press, 1968.

Pourrat, Henri. *French Folktales from the Collection of Henri Pourrat.* Selected by Carl Gustaf Bjurström. Translated by Royall Tyler. New York: Pantheon, 1989.

Pyle, Howard. *The Merry Adventures of Robin Hood.* New York: Dover, 1968.

Rees, Alwyn, and Brinley Rees. *Celtic Heritage: Ancient Tradition in Ireland and Wales.* London: Thames and Hudson, 1973.

Rhys, Ernest. *Fairy Gold: A Book of Old English Fairy Tales.* Mineola, NY: Dover, 2008.

Rhys, John. *Celtic Folklore: Welsh and Manx.* Oxford: Clarendon, 1901.

Ritson, Joseph. *Robin Hood: A Collection of all the Ancient Poems, Songs, and Ballads.* East Ardsley, Eng.: E.P. Publishing, 1972.

Roberts, Brynley. "From Traditional Tale to Literary Story: Middle Welsh Prose Narratives," in *The Craft of Fiction: Essays in Medieval Poetics*, 211–30. Rochester, Mich.: Solaria Press, 1984.

– *Studies on Middle Welsh Literature*. Lewiston, NY: E. Mellen, 1992.

Roe, Harry, and Ann Dooley, translators. *Tales of the Elders of Ireland (Acallam Na Senórach)*. Oxford: Oxford University Press, 2008.

Ross, Anne. "The Human Head in Insular Pagan Celtic Religion," in *Proceedings of the Society of Antiquaries of Scotland*, 1957–58.

– *The Pagan Celts*. London: B.T. Batsford, 1986.

Ross, Margaret C. *The Cambridge Introduction to the Old Norse-Icelandic Saga*. Cambridge: Cambridge University Press, 2010.

– "From Iceland to Norway: Essential Rites of Passage for an Early Icelandic Skald." *alvíssmál* 9 (1999), 55–72.

Sahlin, Claire L. *Birgitta of Sweden and the Voice of Prohecy*. Woodbridge [England]: Boydell, 2001.

Schacker, Jennifer. *National Dreams: The Remaking of Fairy Tales in Nineteenth-Century England*. Philadelphia: University of Pennsylvania Press, 2003.

Scott, Sir Walter. *Minstrelsy of the Scottish Border*. Edinburgh: W. Blackwood, 1902.

Scudder, Bernard, translator. *The Saga of Grettir the Strong*. London: Penguin, 2005.

– *Egil's Saga*. London: Penguin, 2004.

Shaw, Francis, ed. *The Dream of Óengus, Aislinge Óenguso: An Old Irish Text*. Dublin: Browne and Nolan, 1977.

Sierra, Judy. *The Oryx Multicultural Folktale Series: Cinderella*. Phoenix, Ariz.: Orxy Press, 1992.

Sigurdur, Nordal. *Völuspá*. Durham: Durham and St Andrews Medieval Texts, 1978.

Sikes, Wirt. *British Goblins: Welsh Folk-lore, Fairy Mythology, Legends and Traditions*. London: Sampson Low, Marston, Searle, and Rivington, 1880.

Silver, Carole G. *Strange and Secret Peoples: Fairies and Victorian Consciousness*. New York: Oxford University Press, 1999.

Simek, Rudolf. *Dictionary of Northern Mythology*. Cambridge; Rochester, NY: D.S. Brewer, 1993.

Simpson, Jacqueline. *Icelandic Folktales and Legends*. Stroud: Tempus, 2009.

Sjoestedt, Marie-Louise. *Gods and Heroes of the Celts*. Translated by Myles Dillon. Berkeley: Turtle Island Foundation, 1982.

Slavin, Michael. *The Ancient Books of Ireland*. Montreal and Kingston: McGill-Queen's University Press, 2005.

Snorri Sturluson. *Edda*. Translated and edited by Anthony Faulkes. London: Dent, 1995.

Snorri Sturluson. *The Prose Edda: Norse Mythology*. Translated and edited by Jesse L. Byock. London: Penguin Books, 2005.

Snorri Sturluson. *Heimskringla: History of the Kings of Norway*. Translated with notes and introduction by Lee M. Hollander. Austin: Published for the American-Scandinavian Foundation by the University of Texas Press, 1964.

Stokes, Whitley. "The Prose Tales in the Rennes Dindshenchas." *Revue Celtique* 15 (1894), 418–84.

Stokes, Whitley, and E. Windisch. "The Irish Ordeals, Cormac's Adventure in the Land of Promise and the Decision as to Cormac's Sword." *Irische Texte*, series 3 (1), 183–229. Leipzig: Hirzel, 1891.

Straparola, Giovanni Francesco. *The Pleasant Nights*. Edited with an introduction by Donald Beecher. Translated by W.G. Waters. Toronto: University of Toronto Press, 2012.

Sveinsson, Einar Ólafur. *The Folk-Stories of Iceland*. Translated by Bendedikt Benedikz. Revised by Einar G. Pétursson. Edited by Anthony Faulkes. London: Viking Society for Northern Research, University College London, 2003.

Synge, John Millington. *Deirdre of the Sorrows: A Play*. Shannon: Irish University Press, 1971.

Tacitus, Cornelius. *Agricola and Germany*. Translated by Anthony Birley. Oxford: Oxford University Press, 1999.

Tacitus, Cornelius. *The Histories*. Translated by Clifford H. Moore. Cambridge, MA: Harvard University Press, 1962.

Tatar, Maria. *The Annotated Classic Fairy Tales*. New York: W.W. Norton, 2002.

– *The Classic Fairy Tales: Texts, Criticism*. New York: W.W. Norton, 1999.

– *The Hard Facts of the Grimms' Fairy Tales*. Princeton, NJ: Princeton University Press, 2003.

Tatar, Maria, translator and editor. *The Grimm Reader: The Classic Tales of the Brothers Grimm*. New York: W.W. Norton, 2010.

Thomas, W. Jenkyn. *The Welsh Fairy Book*. London: Abela Publishing, 2010.

Thompson, Stith. *The Folktale*. New York: AMS Press, 1979.

Thorpe, Benjamin. *Yule-tide Stories; A Collection of Scandinavian and North German Popular Tales and Traditions, from the Swedish, Danish, and German*. New York: AMS Press, 1968.

Tolkien, J.R.R. *The Tolkien Reader*. New York: Ballantine, 1989.

– *Tree and Leaf*. London: HarperCollins, 2001.

Selected Bibliography

Tolkien, J.R.R, and E.V. Gordon, eds. *Sir Gawain and the Green Knight.* Oxford: Clarendon Press, 1936.

Tolkien, J.R.R, and Christopher Tolkien. *The Legend of Sigurd and Gudrún.* London: HarperCollins, 2010.

– *The Monsters and the Critics, and Other Essays.* London: HarperCollins, 2006.

Turville-Petre, Gabriel. *Myth and Religion of the North: the Religion of Ancient Scandinavia.* London: Weidenfeld and Nicolson, 1964.

– *Origins of Icelandic Literature.* Oxford: Clarendon Press, 1953.

Virtanen, Leea, and Thomas A. DuBois. *Finnish Folklore.* Helsinki: Finnish Literature Society, 2000.

Warner, Marina. *From the Beast to the Blonde: On Fairy Tales and Their Tellers.* New York: Farrar, Straus and Giroux, 1995.

Werner, Jane. *The Giant Golden Book of Elves and Fairies.* New York: Golden Books, 2008.

Weston, Jessie. *Sir Gawain and the Green Knight.* Mineola, NY: Dover, 2003.

Wilde, Lady Francesca. *Ancient Legends, Mystic Charms and Superstitions of Ireland.* London: Ward and Downey, 1887.

Williams, Noel. "The Semantics of the Word *Fairy*: Making Meaning Out of Thin Air," in *The Good People: New Fairyland Essays*, 457–78. New York: Garland, 1991.

Wynne, Ellis. *The Sleeping Bard, Or, Visions of the World, Death, and Hell.* London: John Murray, 1860.

Yeats, William Butler. *Fairy and Folk Tales of Ireland.* With a foreword by Kathleen Raine. Gerrards Cross: C. Smythe, 1977.

– ed. *Fairy and Folk Tales of the Irish Peasantry.* New York: Dover; London: Constable, 1991.

– ed. *Irish Fairy and Folk Tales.* New York: Dorset Press, 1986.

– "Preface," in *Gods and Fighting Men*, 1904; republished in *Lady Gregory's Complete Irish Mythology* (New York: Smithmark, 1994, 1–9).

Young, Ella. *Celtic Wonder Tales.* Dublin: Maunsel, 1910.

– *The Wonder Smith and His Son.* Edinburgh: Floris, 1992.

Zimmerman, Georges Denis. *The Irish Storyteller.* Dublin: Four Courts Press, 2001.

Ziolkowski, Jan M. *Fairy Tales from Before Fairy Tales: The Medieval Latin Past of Wonderful Lies.* Ann Arbor: University of Michigan Press, 2007.

Zipes, Jack. *Breaking the Magic Spell: Radical Theories of Folk and Fairy Tales.* Lexington: University Press of Kentucky, 2002.

– translator. *The Complete Fairy Tales of the Brothers Grimm.* New York: Random House, 2003.

Selected Bibliography

- *Fairy Tale as Myth/Myth as Fairy Tale*. Lexington: University Press of Kentucky, 1994.
- "Fairy Tales and Folk Tales," in *The Oxford Encyclopedia of Children's Literature*, vol. 2, 45–54. Oxford: Oxford University Press, 2006.
- *The Great Fairy Tale Tradition: From Straparola and Basile to the Brothers Grimm: Texts, Criticism*. New York: W.W. Norton, 2001.
- *The Irresistible Fairy Tale: The Cultural and Social History of a Genre*. Princeton: Princeton University Press, 2012.
- *The Oxford Companion to Fairy Tales: The Western Fairy Tale Tradition from Perrault to Pratchett*. New York: Oxford University Press, 2000.
- *When Dreams Came True: Classical Fairy Tales and Their Tradition*. New York: Routledge, 2007.

USEFUL BIBLIOGRAPHICAL SITES ONLINE

Celt: The Corpus of Electronic Texts, produced by University College Cork, Ireland. www.ucc.ie/celt

Irish Script on Screen, Dublin Institute for Advanced Studies. www.isos.dias.ie

University of Florida, Baldwin Library of Historical Children's Literature Digital Collection. www.ufdc.ufl.edu/juv

University of Rochester Cinderella Bibliography. http://d.lib.rochester.edu/cinderella

Viking Society for Northern Research Website. www.vsnrweb-publications.org.uk

Index

Index